hton
n
urt

Texas GO Math!

Grade 5

Assessment Guide

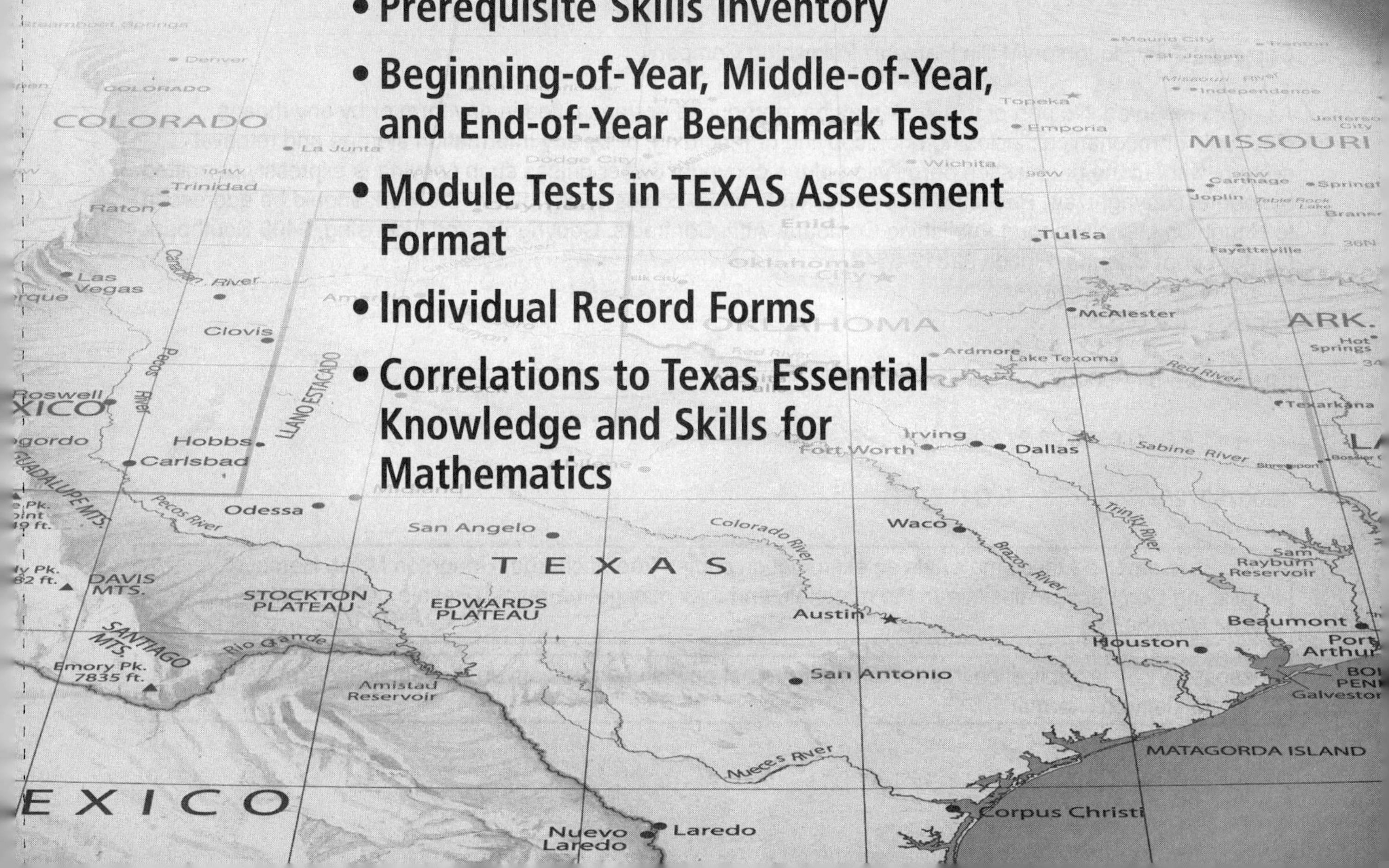

- Prerequisite Skills Inventory
- Beginning-of-Year, Middle-of-Year, and End-of-Year Benchmark Tests
- Module Tests in TEXAS Assessment Format
- Individual Record Forms
- Correlations to Texas Essential Knowledge and Skills for Mathematics

Printed in the U.S.A.

ISBN 978-0-544-06037-1

8 9 10 0982 22 21 20

4500789728 B C D E F G

Contents

Tests and Record Forms

Unit 5

Unit 6 (Module 17)

Overview of *Texas GO Math!* Assessment

How Assessment Can Help Individualize Instruction

The *Assessment Guide* contains several types of assessment for use throughout the school year. The following pages will explain how these assessments can help teachers evaluate students' understanding of the Texas Essential Knowledge and Skills (TEKS). This *Assessment Guide* also contains Individual Record Forms (IRF) to help guide teachers' instructional choices to improve students' performance. The record forms may be used to monitor students' progress toward their mastery of the Texas Essential Knowledge and Skills for this grade.

Diagnostic Assessment

Prerequisite Skills Inventory in the *Assessment Guide* should be given at the beginning of the school year or when a new student arrives. This short answer test assesses students' understanding of prerequisite skills. Test results provide information about the review or intervention that students may need in order to be successful in learning the mathematics related to the TEKS for the grade level. The IRF for the Prerequisite Skills Inventory provides suggestions for intervention based on the student's performance.

Beginning-of-Year Test in the *Assessment Guide* should be given early in the year to determine which skills for the current grade students may already understand. The items on this test are in STAAR format, with multiple-choice and griddable items. This benchmark test will facilitate customization of instructional content to optimize the time spent teaching specific objectives. The IRF for the Beginning-of-Year Test provides suggestions for intervention based on the student's performance.

Show What You Know in the *Student Edition* is provided for each unit. It assesses prior knowledge from previous grades as well as content taught earlier in the current grade. Teachers can customize instructional content using the suggested intervention options. The assessment should be scheduled at the beginning of each unit to determine if students have the prerequisite for the skills unit.

Formative Assessment

Are You Ready? items appear in the *Assessment Guide*. These are quick checks to determine if students have the prerequisite skills they need for a particular lesson in the *Texas GO Math! Student Edition*. They may be reproduced for each student or shown to the class on a document camera. If several students have trouble with the Are You Ready? items, teachers may wish to review concepts before teaching the next lesson.

Middle-of-Year Test in the *Assessment Guide* assesses the same TEKS as the Beginning-of-Year Test, allowing students' progress to be tracked and providing opportunity for instructional adjustments, when required. The items on this test are in STAAR format with multiple-choice and griddable items.

Summative Assessment

Module and Unit Assessments in the *Texas GO Math! Student Edition* indicate whether additional instruction or practice is necessary for students to master the concepts and skills taught in the module or unit. These tests include constructed-response, multiple-choice, and griddable items.

Module and Unit Tests in the *Assessment Guide* evaluate students' mastery of concepts and skills taught in the module or unit. There is a test for each module. When only one module comprises a unit, the unit test assesses the content in just that module. When there are multiple modules in a unit, there are designated module tests and a comprehensive unit test. The items on this test are in STAAR format with multiple-choice and griddable items.

End-of-Year Test in the *Assessment Guide* assesses the same TEKS as the Beginning- and Middle-of-Year Tests. The items on this test are in STAAR format, with multiple-choice and griddable items. It is the final benchmark test for the grade level. When student performance on the End-of-Year Test is compared to performance on Beginning- and Middle-of-Year Tests, teachers are able to document student growth.

Using Correlations to TEKS

The final section of the *Assessment Guide* contains correlations to the TEKS. To identify which items in the *Assessment Guide* test a particular TEKS, locate that TEKS in the chart. The column to the right will list the test and specific items that assess the TEKS. Correlations to TEKS are also provided in the Individual Record Form for each test.

Assessment Technology

Online Assessment System offers flexibility to individualize assessment for each child. Teachers can assign entire tests from the *Assessment Guide* or build customized tests from a bank of items. For customized tests, specific TEKS can be selected to test.

Multiple-choice and fill-in-the-blank items are automatically scored by the Online Assessment System. This provides immediate feedback. Tests may also be printed and administered as paper-and-pencil tests.

The same intervention resources are available in the Online Assessment System as in the *Assessment Guide*. So, whether students take tests online or printed from the Online Assessment System, teachers have access to materials to help students succeed in *Texas GO Math!*

Data-Driven Decision Making

Texas GO Math! allows for quick and accurate data-driven decision making so teachers will have more instructional time to meet students' needs. There are several intervention and review resources available with *Texas GO Math!* Every lesson in the *Student Edition* has a corresponding lesson in the *Texas GO Math! Response to Intervention Tier 1 Lessons* online resource. There are also *Tier 2 Skills* and *Tier 3 Examples* available for students who need further instruction or practice. For online intervention lessons, students may complete lessons in *Soar to Success Math*. These resources provide the foundation for individual prescriptions for students who need extra support.

Using Individual Record Forms

The *Assessment Guide* includes Individual Record Forms (IRF) for all tests. On these forms, each test item is correlated to the TEKS it assesses. There are intervention resources correlated to each item as well. A common error explains why a student may have missed the item. These forms can be used to:

- Follow progress throughout the year.
- Identify strengths and weaknesses.
- Make assignments based on the intervention options provided.

How to Complete a Grid

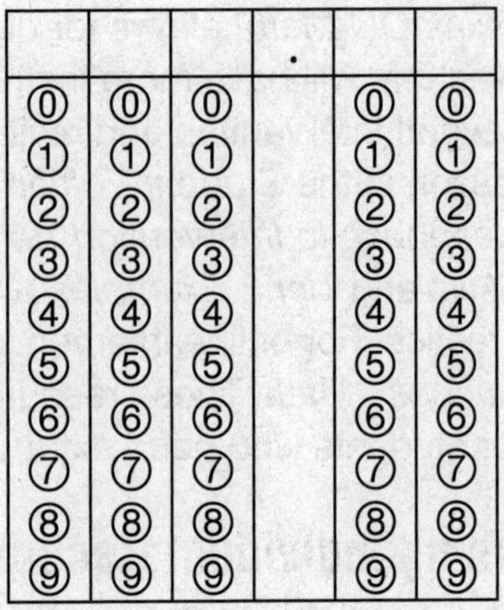

You will answer some of the problems on the tests for your *Texas GO Math!* book by filling in a grid. This page will explain how to fill in the grid.

You will use a grid like the one at the right to record your answers after you solve problems. The boxes at the top are the answer boxes. The circles with numbers inside them are the answer bubbles.

The directions on the test will say:

> Record your answer and fill in the bubbles on the grid. Be sure to use the correct place value.

Step 1
Read the problem and solve it.

> Sandy's book has 102 pages. Emma's book has 231 pages. How many more pages are in Emma's book than Sandy's book?

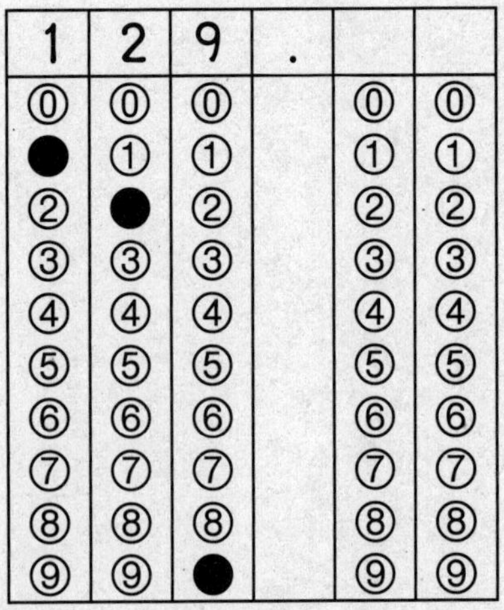

Step 2
Emma's book has 129 more pages than Sandy's book. Record your answer in the answer boxes. So, write 129.

Step 3
Fill in the bubbles on the grid. To show 129, fill in ① in the hundreds place, ② in the tens place, and ⑨ in the ones place.

Remember to check the place value of the digits. For example, a one-digit answer must be recorded in the ones place. You may record 0 in the tens and hundreds places or leave them blank.

Student's Name ______________________ Date ____________

Answer Sheet for __________ Test

1. Ⓐ Ⓑ Ⓒ Ⓓ
2. Ⓐ Ⓑ Ⓒ Ⓓ
3. Ⓐ Ⓑ Ⓒ Ⓓ
4. Ⓐ Ⓑ Ⓒ Ⓓ
5. Ⓐ Ⓑ Ⓒ Ⓓ
6. Ⓐ Ⓑ Ⓒ Ⓓ
7. Ⓐ Ⓑ Ⓒ Ⓓ
8. Ⓐ Ⓑ Ⓒ Ⓓ
9. Ⓐ Ⓑ Ⓒ Ⓓ
10. Ⓐ Ⓑ Ⓒ Ⓓ
11. Ⓐ Ⓑ Ⓒ Ⓓ
12. Ⓐ Ⓑ Ⓒ Ⓓ
13. Ⓐ Ⓑ Ⓒ Ⓓ
14. Ⓐ Ⓑ Ⓒ Ⓓ
15. Ⓐ Ⓑ Ⓒ Ⓓ
16. Ⓐ Ⓑ Ⓒ Ⓓ
17. Ⓐ Ⓑ Ⓒ Ⓓ
18. Ⓐ Ⓑ Ⓒ Ⓓ
19. Ⓐ Ⓑ Ⓒ Ⓓ
20. Ⓐ Ⓑ Ⓒ Ⓓ
21. Ⓐ Ⓑ Ⓒ Ⓓ
22. Ⓐ Ⓑ Ⓒ Ⓓ
23. Ⓐ Ⓑ Ⓒ Ⓓ
24. Ⓐ Ⓑ Ⓒ Ⓓ
25. Ⓐ Ⓑ Ⓒ Ⓓ
26. Ⓐ Ⓑ Ⓒ Ⓓ
27. Ⓐ Ⓑ Ⓒ Ⓓ
28. Ⓐ Ⓑ Ⓒ Ⓓ
29. Ⓐ Ⓑ Ⓒ Ⓓ
30. Ⓐ Ⓑ Ⓒ Ⓓ
31. Ⓐ Ⓑ Ⓒ Ⓓ
32. Ⓐ Ⓑ Ⓒ Ⓓ
33. Ⓐ Ⓑ Ⓒ Ⓓ
34. Ⓐ Ⓑ Ⓒ Ⓓ
35. Ⓐ Ⓑ Ⓒ Ⓓ
36. Ⓐ Ⓑ Ⓒ Ⓓ
37. Ⓐ Ⓑ Ⓒ Ⓓ
38. Ⓐ Ⓑ Ⓒ Ⓓ
39. Ⓐ Ⓑ Ⓒ Ⓓ
40. Ⓐ Ⓑ Ⓒ Ⓓ
41. Ⓐ Ⓑ Ⓒ Ⓓ
42. Ⓐ Ⓑ Ⓒ Ⓓ
43. Ⓐ Ⓑ Ⓒ Ⓓ
44. Ⓐ Ⓑ Ⓒ Ⓓ
45. Ⓐ Ⓑ Ⓒ Ⓓ
46. Ⓐ Ⓑ Ⓒ Ⓓ
47. Ⓐ Ⓑ Ⓒ Ⓓ
48. Ⓐ Ⓑ Ⓒ Ⓓ
49. Ⓐ Ⓑ Ⓒ Ⓓ
50. Ⓐ Ⓑ Ⓒ Ⓓ

Student's Name ______________________________ Date ________________

Grids for __________ Test

Number ______

			.		
⓪	⓪	⓪		⓪	⓪
①	①	①		①	①
②	②	②		②	②
③	③	③		③	③
④	④	④		④	④
⑤	⑤	⑤		⑤	⑤
⑥	⑥	⑥		⑥	⑥
⑦	⑦	⑦		⑦	⑦
⑧	⑧	⑧		⑧	⑧
⑨	⑨	⑨		⑨	⑨

Number ______

			.		
⓪	⓪	⓪		⓪	⓪
①	①	①		①	①
②	②	②		②	②
③	③	③		③	③
④	④	④		④	④
⑤	⑤	⑤		⑤	⑤
⑥	⑥	⑥		⑥	⑥
⑦	⑦	⑦		⑦	⑦
⑧	⑧	⑧		⑧	⑧
⑨	⑨	⑨		⑨	⑨

Number ______

			.		
⓪	⓪	⓪		⓪	⓪
①	①	①		①	①
②	②	②		②	②
③	③	③		③	③
④	④	④		④	④
⑤	⑤	⑤		⑤	⑤
⑥	⑥	⑥		⑥	⑥
⑦	⑦	⑦		⑦	⑦
⑧	⑧	⑧		⑧	⑧
⑨	⑨	⑨		⑨	⑨

Number ______

			.		
⓪	⓪	⓪		⓪	⓪
①	①	①		①	①
②	②	②		②	②
③	③	③		③	③
④	④	④		④	④
⑤	⑤	⑤		⑤	⑤
⑥	⑥	⑥		⑥	⑥
⑦	⑦	⑦		⑦	⑦
⑧	⑧	⑧		⑧	⑧
⑨	⑨	⑨		⑨	⑨

Number ______

			.		
⓪	⓪	⓪		⓪	⓪
①	①	①		①	①
②	②	②		②	②
③	③	③		③	③
④	④	④		④	④
⑤	⑤	⑤		⑤	⑤
⑥	⑥	⑥		⑥	⑥
⑦	⑦	⑦		⑦	⑦
⑧	⑧	⑧		⑧	⑧
⑨	⑨	⑨		⑨	⑨

Number ______

			.		
⓪	⓪	⓪		⓪	⓪
①	①	①		①	①
②	②	②		②	②
③	③	③		③	③
④	④	④		④	④
⑤	⑤	⑤		⑤	⑤
⑥	⑥	⑥		⑥	⑥
⑦	⑦	⑦		⑦	⑦
⑧	⑧	⑧		⑧	⑧
⑨	⑨	⑨		⑨	⑨

Name ______________________

Are You Ready?
Lesson 1.1

1. Add.

12 + 8 + 3 = ___

Ⓐ 23

Ⓑ 11

Ⓒ 20

Ⓓ 15

2. Multiply.

23 × 5 = ___

Ⓐ 100

Ⓑ 15

Ⓒ 115

Ⓓ 85

Name ______________________

Are You Ready?
Lesson 1.2

1. In the number 3,528, what digit is in the hundreds place?

Ⓐ 3

Ⓑ 5

Ⓒ 2

Ⓓ 8

2. What is the standard form of two and three tenths?

Ⓐ 0.23

Ⓑ 2.03

Ⓒ 2.3

Ⓓ 23

Name ______________________________

Are You Ready?
Lesson 1.3

1. What is the relationship between 0.3 and 0.03?

Ⓐ 0.03 is 10 times as much as 0.3

Ⓑ 0.3 is $\frac{1}{10}$ of 0.03

Ⓒ 0.3 is equal to 0.03

Ⓓ 0.3 is 10 times as much as 0.03

2. What number is 10 times as much as 2.357?

Ⓐ 23.57

Ⓑ 235.7

Ⓒ 0.2357

Ⓓ 2.357

Name ______________________________

Are You Ready?
Lesson 1.4

1. In which number does the digit 6 have the greatest value?

Ⓐ 1.236

Ⓑ 5.634

Ⓒ 3.06

Ⓓ 4.16

2. In 135.782, which digit is in the hundredths place?

Ⓐ 8

Ⓑ 5

Ⓒ 7

Ⓓ 1

Name ______________________________

Are You Ready?
Lesson 1.5

1. What number shows 3,589 rounded to the nearest hundred?

Ⓐ 3,600

Ⓑ 3,590

Ⓒ 4,000

Ⓓ 3,500

2. In 2.675, which digit is in the tenths place?

Ⓐ 2

Ⓑ 6

Ⓒ 7

Ⓓ 5

Name ______________________________

Are You Ready?
Lesson 1.6

1. What number shows 5.67 rounded to the nearest tenth?

Ⓐ 5.00

Ⓑ 5.7

Ⓒ 6

Ⓓ 5.6

2. Melissa had $10 to buy lunch. She spent $2.50 for a drink. How much money does she have left?

Ⓐ $8

Ⓑ $8.50

Ⓒ $7

Ⓓ $7.50

Name ___________________________

Are You Ready?
Lesson 1.7

1. Kyoko has $6.35 in her pocket. She buys some yarn for $2.15. Which of the following is a good estimate for the amount of money she has left?

Ⓐ $4

Ⓑ $3

Ⓒ $8

Ⓓ $5

2. Add.

350 + 167 = ____

Ⓐ 417

Ⓑ 507

Ⓒ 410

Ⓓ 517

Name ___________________________

Are You Ready?
Lesson 1.8

1. Add.

425 + 107 + 325 = ____

Ⓐ 757

Ⓑ 857

Ⓒ 532

Ⓓ 750

2. Subtract.

25.2 − 10.1 = ____

Ⓐ 10.1

Ⓑ 25.1

Ⓒ 35.3

Ⓓ 15.1

Name ____________________

Are You Ready?
Lesson 2.1

1. What is the value of the underlined digit?

3<u>4</u>,276

Ⓐ 4
Ⓑ 40,000
Ⓒ 4,000
Ⓓ 1,000

2. Regroup.

____ tens 17 ones = 5 tens 7 ones

Ⓐ 5
Ⓑ 4
Ⓒ 6
Ⓓ 15

Name ____________________

Are You Ready?
Lesson 2.2

1. Regroup.

27 hundreds 13 tens = 2 thousands ____ hundreds 3 tens

Ⓐ 7
Ⓑ 17
Ⓒ 8
Ⓓ 18

2. Multiply.

$347 \times 8 =$ ____

Ⓐ 2,776
Ⓑ 2,426
Ⓒ 2,726
Ⓓ 2,476

Name ____________________

Are You Ready?
Lesson 2.3

1. Multiply.

5,718 × 9 = ____

Ⓐ 45,392

Ⓑ 51,392

Ⓒ 51,442

Ⓓ 51,462

2. Divide.

624 ÷ 6 = ____

Ⓐ 14

Ⓑ 140

Ⓒ 104

Ⓓ 114

Name ____________________

Are You Ready?
Lesson 2.4

1. Find the unknown factor.

10 × ____ = 890

Ⓐ 89

Ⓑ 890

Ⓒ 8,990

Ⓓ 1,890

2. Divide.

406 ÷ 4 = ____

Ⓐ 102

Ⓑ 101

Ⓒ 101 R2

Ⓓ 112

Name ____________________

Are You Ready?
Lesson 2.5

1. Estimate the quotient.

4,279 ÷ 8 = ____

Ⓐ 600

Ⓑ 50

Ⓒ 500

Ⓓ 60

2. Ania read 576 pages in 6 days. If she read about the same amount of pages each day, about how many pages did Ania read each day?

Ⓐ 90

Ⓑ 60

Ⓒ 115

Ⓓ 100

Name ____________________

Are You Ready?
Lesson 2.6

1. Find the unknown factor.

50 × ____ = 1,250

Ⓐ 125

Ⓑ 25

Ⓒ 250

Ⓓ 210

2. Divide.

7,316 ÷ 8 = ____

Ⓐ 914 R5

Ⓑ 914 R4

Ⓒ 915

Ⓓ 902

Name ______________________________

Are You Ready?
Lesson 2.7

1. Natalia bought a package of 1,285 beads. She is making friendship pins with the beads. Each friendship pin uses 7 beads. How many friendship pins can Natalia make with the package of beads?

Ⓐ 180
Ⓑ 184
Ⓒ 183
Ⓓ 185

---

2. Find the product.

583 × 26 = ____

Ⓐ 15,158
Ⓑ 4,664
Ⓒ 15,156
Ⓓ 13,654

Name ______________________________

Are You Ready?
Lesson 2.8

1. Marco hit 3 times as many home runs during the season as Han. Together they hit 24 home runs. How many home runs did Marco hit during the season?

Ⓐ 8
Ⓑ 18
Ⓒ 72
Ⓓ 6

---

2. Divide.

7,248 ÷ 3 = ____

Ⓐ 2,086
Ⓑ 2,416
Ⓒ 2,415
Ⓓ 2,082

Name ______________________

Are You Ready?
Lesson 3.1

1. What is the next number in the pattern below?

71, 710, 7,100, 71,000...

Ⓐ 71,100

Ⓑ 7,100,000

Ⓒ 710,000

Ⓓ 71,010

2. Latoya packs 26 books in each box. How many books does she pack if she fills 100 boxes?

Ⓐ 260

Ⓑ 26

Ⓒ 2,600

Ⓓ 26,000

Name ______________________

Are You Ready?
Lesson 3.2

1. Find the product.

78×8

Ⓐ 120

Ⓑ 626

Ⓒ 624

Ⓓ 780

2. If a year has 365 days, how many days are in 3 years?

Ⓐ 995

Ⓑ 1,095

Ⓒ 985

Ⓓ 1,085

Name ______________________________

Are You Ready?
Lesson 3.3

1. What is the unknown number?

$126 \times 6 = (100 \times 6) + (\_\_\_\_ \times 6) + (6 \times 6)$

Ⓐ 126

Ⓑ 20

Ⓒ 6

Ⓓ 100

2. Which shows an example of the Distributive Property?

Ⓐ $86 + 34 = 34 + 86$

Ⓑ $86 \times 1 = 86$

Ⓒ $86 \times (6 \times 10) = (86 \times 6) \times 10$

Ⓓ $86 \times 34 = (86 \times 30) + (86 \times 4)$

Name ______________________________

Are You Ready?
Lesson 3.4

1. A theater has 25 rows. Each row has 34 seats. How many seats does the theater have?

Ⓐ 750

Ⓑ 900

Ⓒ 850

Ⓓ 238

2. Multiply.

$15 \times 0.1 = \_\_\_\_$

Ⓐ 15

Ⓑ 10

Ⓒ 1.5

Ⓓ 0.15

Name ______________________________

Are You Ready?
Lesson 3.5

1. Multiply.

$3.1 \times 8 =$ ____

Ⓐ 24

Ⓑ 24.1

Ⓒ 24.8

Ⓓ 2.48

2. If the average monthly rainfall in Springfield is 0.8 inch, about how much rain would it get in 6 months?

Ⓐ 4.8 inches

Ⓑ 48 inches

Ⓒ 0.48 inch

Ⓓ 4.2 inches

Name ______________________________

Are You Ready?
Lesson 3.6

1. $3.5 = 3$ and ____ tenths.

Ⓐ 5

Ⓑ 50

Ⓒ 0.5

Ⓓ 0.50

2. Yuki sells 18 cups of lemonade in an hour. If she charges $0.40 per cup, how much money will she earn?

Ⓐ $7.20

Ⓑ $72.00

Ⓒ $4.20

Ⓓ $80.00

Name ____

Are You Ready?
Lesson 3.7

1. Which is the best estimate for the product of 3.5 and 6?

Ⓐ 2.4

Ⓑ 40

Ⓒ 24

Ⓓ 0.24

2. Find the product.

$3.12 × 7

Ⓐ $21.00

Ⓑ $21.74

Ⓒ $218.4

Ⓓ $21.84

Name ____

Are You Ready?
Lesson 3.8

1. Find the product.

0.5 × 0.5

Ⓐ 0.25

Ⓑ 25.00

Ⓒ 2.50

Ⓓ 0.025

2. A city park covers 0.8 acre. Three tenths of the park is used for a rose garden. How large is the rose garden?

Ⓐ 24 acres

Ⓑ 2.4 acres

Ⓒ 80 acres

Ⓓ 0.24 acre

Name ______________________________

Are You Ready?
Lesson 4.1

1. What is the unknown number?

81,000 ÷ ______ = 81

Ⓐ 1

Ⓑ 10

Ⓒ 1,000

Ⓓ 100

2. Miu has 2,550 stamps. If she places 10 stamps per page in her album, how many pages does she need to display all the stamps?

Ⓐ 25,500

Ⓑ 25.5

Ⓒ 255

Ⓓ 2,550

Name ______________________________

Are You Ready?
Lesson 4.2

1. What equation does the model show?

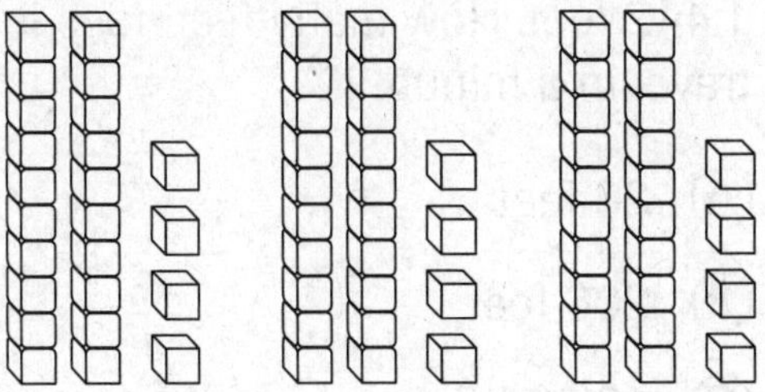

Ⓐ 3 × 72 = 216

Ⓑ 72 ÷ 3 = 24

Ⓒ 72 ÷ 20 = 3.6

Ⓓ 24 + 24 = 48

2. A library stores 488 books on 8 shelves. If each shelf has the same number of books, how many books are on each shelf?

Ⓐ 61

Ⓑ 71

Ⓒ 60

Ⓓ 46

Name ______________________

Are You Ready?
Lesson 4.3

1. Nora buys a novel that has 393 pages. About how many pages should she read each day if she wants to finish the novel in 5 days?

Ⓐ 60

Ⓑ 50

Ⓒ 80

Ⓓ 40

2. Which is the best estimate for the quotient?

198 ÷ 7

Ⓐ 15

Ⓑ 50

Ⓒ 10

Ⓓ 30

Name ______________________

Are You Ready?
Lesson 4.4

1. Which of the following is the same as 4 tenths and 2 hundredths?

Ⓐ 42 hundreds

Ⓑ 42 thousandths

Ⓒ 42 hundredths

Ⓓ 42 tens

2. An elevator takes 7 minutes to travel 1,442 feet. How many feet does it travel in a minute?

Ⓐ 26 feet

Ⓑ 206 feet

Ⓒ 10,094 feet

Ⓓ 200 feet

1. Divide.

2.8 ÷ 7 = _____

Ⓐ 0.04

Ⓑ 4

Ⓒ 40

Ⓓ 0.4

2. A stairwell has 1,365 stairs. There are 21 stairs per floor. How many floors does the stairwell connect?

Ⓐ 70

Ⓑ 60

Ⓒ 55

Ⓓ 65

Name ____________________

Are You Ready?
Lesson 5.1

1. Find the sum.

$\frac{2}{8} + \frac{3}{8}$

Ⓐ $\frac{5}{16}$

Ⓑ $\frac{1}{8}$

Ⓒ $\frac{5}{8}$

Ⓓ $\frac{10}{11}$

2. Which fraction is in simplest form?

Ⓐ $\frac{5}{10}$

Ⓑ $\frac{4}{5}$

Ⓒ $\frac{6}{10}$

Ⓓ $\frac{8}{12}$

Name ____________________

Are You Ready?
Lesson 5.2

1. Find the difference.

$\frac{9}{10} - \frac{2}{10}$

Ⓐ $\frac{1}{8}$

Ⓑ $\frac{7}{10}$

Ⓒ $\frac{11}{10}$

Ⓓ $\frac{7}{0}$

2. Which fraction is in simplest form?

Ⓐ $\frac{4}{10}$

Ⓑ $\frac{3}{12}$

Ⓒ $\frac{2}{3}$

Ⓓ $\frac{6}{8}$

Name ____________________

Are You Ready?
Lesson 5.3

1. Which letter represents the point located at $\frac{6}{10}$?

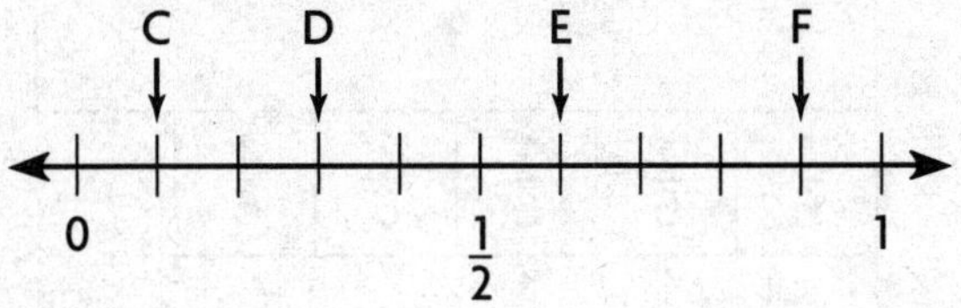

Ⓐ C

Ⓑ D

Ⓒ E

Ⓓ F

2. Which fraction is closest to 1?

Ⓐ $\frac{2}{5}$

Ⓑ $\frac{1}{2}$

Ⓒ $\frac{7}{10}$

Ⓓ $\frac{2}{3}$

Name ____________________

Are You Ready?
Lesson 5.4

1. What number is next in the pattern?

2, 4, 6, 8, ____

Ⓐ 15

Ⓑ 12

Ⓒ 18

Ⓓ 10

2. Which fraction is equivalent to $\frac{2}{3}$?

Ⓐ $\frac{1}{3}$

Ⓑ $\frac{4}{9}$

Ⓒ $\frac{6}{12}$

Ⓓ $\frac{8}{12}$

Name ______________________________

Are You Ready?
Lesson 5.5

1. Use the fractions strips to find the sum.

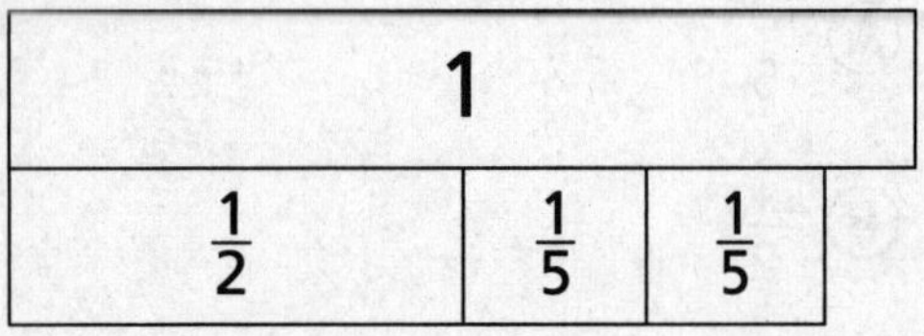

Ⓐ $\frac{3}{12}$

Ⓑ $\frac{9}{10}$

Ⓒ $\frac{3}{7}$

Ⓓ $\frac{1}{12}$

2. Use the fractions strips to find the difference.

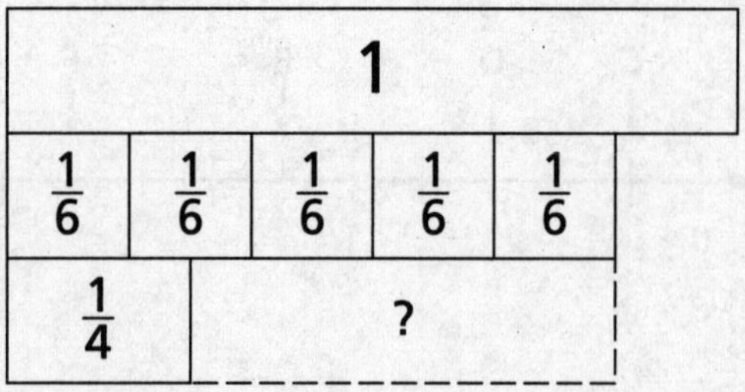

Ⓐ $\frac{1}{2}$

Ⓑ $\frac{6}{10}$

Ⓒ $\frac{4}{2}$

Ⓓ $\frac{7}{12}$

Name ______________________________

Are You Ready?
Lesson 5.6

1. Which fractions use the least common denominator and are equivalent to $\frac{2}{5}$ and $\frac{1}{3}$?

Ⓐ $\frac{6}{15}$ and $\frac{5}{15}$

Ⓑ $\frac{20}{30}$ and $\frac{10}{30}$

Ⓒ $\frac{10}{15}$ and $\frac{5}{15}$

Ⓓ $\frac{12}{30}$ and $\frac{10}{30}$

2. Find the sum.

$\frac{3}{8} + \frac{1}{4}$

Ⓐ $\frac{4}{12}$

Ⓑ $\frac{4}{8}$

Ⓒ $\frac{3}{32}$

Ⓓ $\frac{5}{8}$

Name ______________________________

Are You Ready?
Lesson 5.7

1. Eighteen of twenty-four soccer players were at practice on Tuesday. In simplest form, what fraction of the soccer players were at practice on Tuesday?

Ⓐ $\frac{6}{8}$

Ⓑ $\frac{3}{4}$

Ⓒ $\frac{12}{9}$

Ⓓ $\frac{9}{12}$

2. Rename the mixed number.

$2\frac{7}{8}$

Ⓐ $\frac{42}{8}$

Ⓑ $\frac{80}{8}$

Ⓒ $2\frac{10}{16}$

Ⓓ $\frac{23}{8}$

Name ______________________________

Are You Ready?
Lesson 5.8

1. Find the sum. Write your answer in simplest form.

$\frac{3}{4} + \frac{1}{2} + \frac{1}{4}$

Ⓐ $\frac{5}{10}$

Ⓑ $1\frac{2}{4}$

Ⓒ $1\frac{1}{2}$

Ⓓ $\frac{6}{4}$

2. Which property or properties does the problem below use?

$2 + (3 + 4) = (2 + 3) + 4$

Ⓐ Associative Property

Ⓑ Commutative Property

Ⓒ Distributive Property

Ⓓ Identity Property of Addition

Name ____________________

Are You Ready?
Lesson 6.1

1. What fraction names the shaded part?

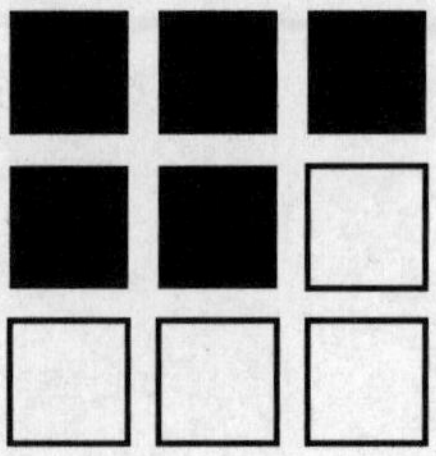

Ⓐ $\frac{4}{9}$

Ⓑ $\frac{5}{9}$

Ⓒ $\frac{4}{5}$

Ⓓ $\frac{5}{4}$

2. A sporting goods store received a shipment of socks. There were 24 pairs of blue socks in each box. The store received a total of 6 boxes in the shipment. How many pairs of blue socks did the store receive?

Ⓐ 5

Ⓑ 6

Ⓒ 144

Ⓓ 15

Name ____________________

Are You Ready?
Lesson 6.2

1. Find the sum.

$\frac{3}{5} + \frac{3}{5} + \frac{3}{5}$

Ⓐ $\frac{9}{15}$

Ⓑ $\frac{3}{15}$

Ⓒ $\frac{5}{9}$

Ⓓ $\frac{9}{5}$

2. Jameson fills 7 of the 15 pages of his autograph book. What fraction of his autograph book is filled?

Ⓐ $\frac{15}{7}$

Ⓑ $\frac{7}{15}$

Ⓒ $2\frac{1}{5}$

Ⓓ $1\frac{5}{7}$

Name ______________________________

Are You Ready?
Lesson 6.3

1. Claire rides her bike 15 miles each day for 3 days. How far will Claire ride in that time?

Ⓐ 5 miles

Ⓑ 18 miles

Ⓒ 45 miles

Ⓓ 35 miles

2. Simplify the fraction.

$\frac{15}{8}$

Ⓐ $\frac{8}{15}$

Ⓑ $2\frac{1}{8}$

Ⓒ $1\frac{7}{8}$

Ⓓ $1\frac{5}{8}$

Name ______________________________

Are You Ready?
Lesson 6.4

1. Fill in the blanks.

Since 3 × _____ = 24, then
24 ÷ _____ = 3.

Ⓐ 8

Ⓑ 6

Ⓒ 72

Ⓓ 21

2. How many fourths are in 2?

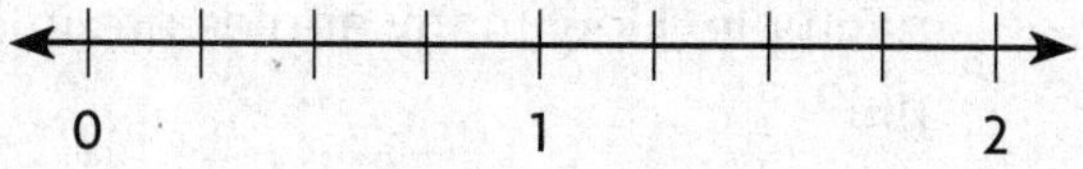

Ⓐ 8

Ⓑ 6

Ⓒ 9

Ⓓ 7

Name ______________________________

Are You Ready?
Lesson 6.5

1. Find the product.

$6 \times \frac{1}{5}$

Ⓐ $\frac{6}{30}$

Ⓑ 30

Ⓒ $\frac{7}{5}$

Ⓓ $1\frac{1}{5}$

2. Which can you use to check the quotient?

$4 \div \frac{1}{3} = \_\_\_\_$

Ⓐ $4 + \frac{1}{3} = \_\_\_\_$

Ⓑ $\_\_\_\_ \times \frac{1}{3} = 4$

Ⓒ $\frac{1}{3} \div 4 = \_\_\_\_$

Ⓓ $\frac{11}{3} - 4 = \_\_\_\_$

Name ______________________________

Are You Ready?
Lesson 6.6

1. Suni has 30 apples to make 5 pies. She uses the same number of apples in each pie. How many apples are in each pie?

Ⓐ 6

Ⓑ 150

Ⓒ 25

Ⓓ 35

2. Phillipe filled each of 7 plant containers with $\frac{3}{4}$ cup of soil. How much soil did Phillipe use in all?

Ⓐ $7\frac{3}{4}$ cups

Ⓑ $\frac{28}{3}$ cups

Ⓒ $6\frac{1}{4}$ cups

Ⓓ $5\frac{1}{4}$ cups

Name ______________________

Are You Ready?
Lesson 7.1

1. What is the quotient?

   24 ÷ 8

   Ⓐ 16
   Ⓑ 3
   Ⓒ 4
   Ⓓ 2

2. The number of students in the cafeteria is an even number. Which number is an even number?

   Ⓐ 55
   Ⓑ 9
   Ⓒ 21
   Ⓓ 40

Name ______________________

Are You Ready?
Lesson 7.2

1. Dan made 36 muffins. Which number is a factor of 36?

   Ⓐ 5
   Ⓑ 6
   Ⓒ 11
   Ⓓ 8

2. What is the product?

   3 × 9

   Ⓐ 24
   Ⓑ 18
   Ⓒ 27
   Ⓓ 30

Name ______________________

Are You Ready?
Lesson 7.3

1. Which operation do the words describe?

Greg has $17. He spends $9 on school supplies.

Ⓐ addition
Ⓑ subtraction
Ⓒ multiplication
Ⓓ division

---

2. Emma writes 6 × 3 to represent words. What could the words be?

Ⓐ Ed has 6 swimming medals. He wins 3 more medals.
Ⓑ Marty shares 6 stickers among 3 friends.
Ⓒ There are 3 chairs at each of 6 tables.
Ⓓ Linda has 6 snow globes. She sells 3 snow globes.

Name ______________________

Are You Ready?
Lesson 7.4

1. What is the product?

4 × 2 × 3

Ⓐ 11
Ⓑ 8
Ⓒ 24
Ⓓ 16

2. What is the sum?

6 + 2 + 4

Ⓐ 14
Ⓑ 8
Ⓒ 48
Ⓓ 12

1. Which operation do you perform first to simplify the numerical expression?

$12 - (2 + 3) \times 6$

Ⓐ addition

Ⓑ subtraction

Ⓒ multiplication

Ⓓ division

---

2. What is the value of the numerical expression?

$42 \div (6 + 1) - 5$

Ⓐ 3

Ⓑ 21

Ⓒ 7

Ⓓ 1

Name ______________________

Are You Ready?
Lesson 8.1

1. What is the value of the expression?

$20 - 5 \times 3$

Ⓐ 15
Ⓑ 35
Ⓒ 45
Ⓓ 5

2. Which operation do you perform first to simplify the expression?

$7 + 9 - 8 \div 2 \times 3$

Ⓐ addition
Ⓑ subtraction
Ⓒ multiplication
Ⓓ division

Name ______________________

Are You Ready?
Lesson 8.2

1. What is the missing addend?

$23 + \_\_\_\_ = 38$

Ⓐ 51
Ⓑ 61
Ⓒ 15
Ⓓ 5

2. There are 49 passengers on a train. At the first stop, 7 passengers get off. How many passengers are on the train after the first stop?

Ⓐ 7
Ⓑ 56
Ⓒ 32
Ⓓ 42

Name ______________________________

Are You Ready?
Lesson 8.3

1. What is the missing factor?

$\_\_\_\_ \times 12 = 60$

Ⓐ 48

Ⓑ 2

Ⓒ 5

Ⓓ 6

2. There are 32 movie posters on the wall of a poster store. The posters are in 8 equal rows. How many posters are in each row?

Ⓐ 4

Ⓑ 40

Ⓒ 5

Ⓓ 24

Name ______________________________

Are You Ready?
Lesson 8.4

1. Pedro sends 7 text messages to each of 4 friends. He receives a total of 16 text messages back from his friends. How many more text messages does Pedro send than receive?

Ⓐ 27

Ⓑ 28

Ⓒ 12

Ⓓ 5

2. A grocer opens a box of 48 cans of soup. She stacks 12 cans in a display at the end of the aisle. She puts an equal number of the remaining cans on each of 4 shelves. How many cans of soup are on each shelf?

Ⓐ 32

Ⓑ 12

Ⓒ 36

Ⓓ 9

Name ______________________________

Are You Ready?
Lesson 9.1

1. What is the unknown number?

$12 \times 13 =$ ______

Ⓐ 144

Ⓑ 156

Ⓒ 120

Ⓓ 130

2. Which of the following has four sides that are of equal length?

Ⓐ rectangle

Ⓑ triangle

Ⓒ trapezoid

Ⓓ square

Name ______________________________

Are You Ready?
Lesson 9.2

1. What is the product?

$8 \times 7 \times 9 =$ ______

Ⓐ 56

Ⓑ 504

Ⓒ 63

Ⓓ 560

2. Rami has a rectangular garden plot that is 6 feet long and 4 feet wide. How large is Rami's garden plot?

Ⓐ 20 feet

Ⓑ 24 feet

Ⓒ 24 square feet

Ⓓ 20 square feet

Name ______________________

Are You Ready?
Lesson 9.3

1. Myra's courtyard is shaped like a square. The length of the courtyard is 5 feet. How large is the courtyard?

Ⓐ 625 sq feet

Ⓑ 25 sq feet

Ⓒ 20 feet

Ⓓ 625 feet

2. Which of the following shapes forms the base of a cube?

Ⓐ circle

Ⓑ hexagon

Ⓒ rhombus

Ⓓ square

Name ______________________

Are You Ready?
Lesson 9.4

1. Which of the following shows the formula for the perimeter of a rectangle?

Ⓐ $P = l \times w$

Ⓑ $P = l \div w$

Ⓒ $P = l + w$

Ⓓ $P = 2l + 2w$

2. What is the ■?

$2 \times (3 + 4) =$ ■

Ⓐ 6

Ⓑ 14

Ⓒ 8

Ⓓ 10

Name ______________________

Are You Ready?
Lesson 10.1

1. What is the next number in the pattern below?

1, 3, 5, 7, 9, ____

Ⓐ 10

Ⓑ 11

Ⓒ 12

Ⓓ 13

2. Ramon makes a design using red and green tiles. He uses 3 red tiles for every green tile. How many red tiles does he need if he uses 3 green tiles?

Ⓐ 3

Ⓑ 9

Ⓒ 6

Ⓓ 12

Name ______________________

Are You Ready?
Lesson 10.2

1. Marguerite uses the pattern below to record the number of stamps she collects each week. Which of the following statements describes the pattern?

8, 10, 12, 14, 16, …

Ⓐ Marguerite loses two stamps each week.

Ⓑ Marguerite multiplies the number of stamps by 2.

Ⓒ Marguerite's collection always has an odd number of stamps.

Ⓓ Marguerite adds two new stamps each week.

2. Rafael records the number of flowers in his garden. Which of the following could be used to describe the pattern he sees?

4, 8, 16, 32…

Ⓐ Add 4.

Ⓑ Multiply by 4.

Ⓒ Multiply by 2.

Ⓓ Add 2.

Name ____________________

Are You Ready?
Lesson 10.3

1. The rule for the pattern is *add* 2. Which of the following matches the pattern rule?

Ⓐ 2, 4, 2, 4, ...

Ⓑ 2, 4, 8, 16, ...

Ⓒ 8, 6, 4, 2, ...

Ⓓ 2, 4, 6, 8, ...

2. The table shows the relationship between the number of pots made and the time it takes to make the pots. Which number pair could be used in the table?

Hours	1	2	3	4
Number of Pots	3	6	9	12

Ⓐ (1, 15)

Ⓑ (15, 3)

Ⓒ (5, 15)

Ⓓ (3, 15)

Name ____________________

Are You Ready?
Lesson 10.4

1. The rule for the pattern is *multiply by 5.* Which of the following matches the pattern rule?

Ⓐ 5, 15, 25, 35, ...

Ⓑ 5, 10, 15, 20, ...

Ⓒ 5, 25, 125, 625, ...

Ⓓ 50, 55, 60, 65, ...

2. Find ■ to complete the pattern in the table.

x	1	2	3	4
y	4	5	6	■

Ⓐ 8

Ⓑ 7

Ⓒ 9

Ⓓ 4

Name ____

Are You Ready?
Lesson 11.1

1. How many vertices does the figure have?

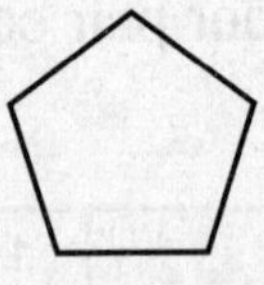

Ⓐ 6

Ⓑ 10

Ⓒ 5

Ⓓ 0

2. Beena draws a rectangle. Which of the following could be Beena's drawing?

Ⓐ 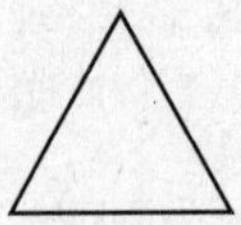

Ⓑ 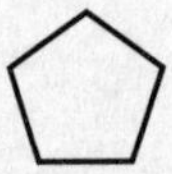

Ⓒ 

Ⓓ 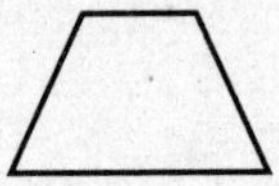

Name ____

Are You Ready?
Lesson 11.2

1. Which of the following describes the angle shown below?

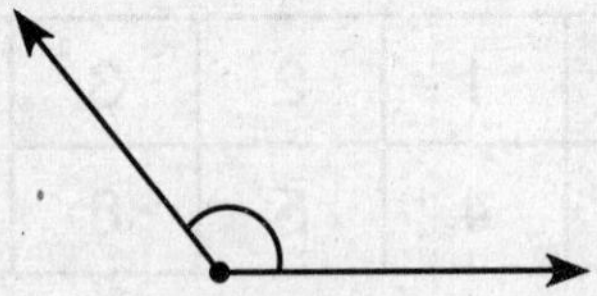

Ⓐ obtuse angle

Ⓑ right angle

Ⓒ straight angle

Ⓓ acute angle

2. How many acute angles does this triangle have?

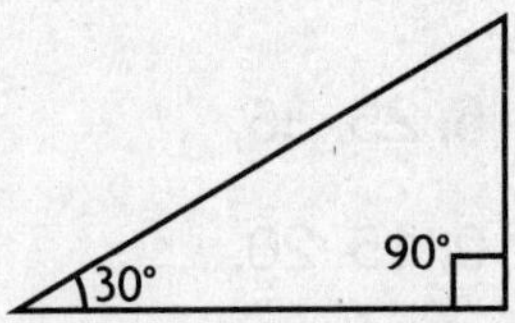

Ⓐ 3

Ⓑ 0

Ⓒ 2

Ⓓ 1

Name ______________________________

Are You Ready?
Lesson 11.3

1. Which of the following lists a pair of parallel sides?

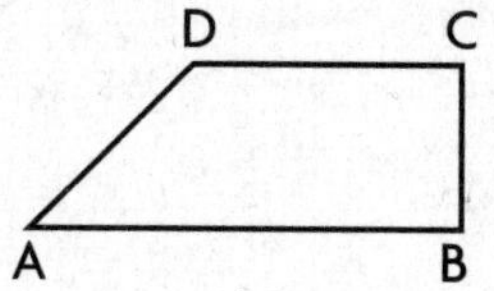

Ⓐ Sides AB and BC

Ⓑ Sides AD and BC

Ⓒ Sides AB and AD

Ⓓ Sides AB and CD

2. Which of the following lines create a right angle when they intersect?

Ⓐ parallel lines

Ⓑ perpendicular lines

Ⓒ congruent lines

Ⓓ similar lines

Name ______________________________

Are You Ready?
Lesson 11.4

1. Marina paints two squares that are congruent. Which of the following statements describing the shapes is NOT true?

Ⓐ The squares are the same size.

Ⓑ The squares are rectangles.

Ⓒ The squares are trapezoids.

Ⓓ The squares are the same shape.

2. How many congruent sides does an equilateral triangle have?

Ⓐ 1

Ⓑ 3

Ⓒ 2

Ⓓ 0

Name ______________________________

Are You Ready?
Lesson 12.1

1. Which figure DOES NOT have congruent sides?

Ⓐ square

Ⓑ equilateral triangle

Ⓒ regular pentagon

Ⓓ trapezoid

2. Yvonne cuts a square piece of fabric with sides that measure 1 foot. What is the area of the piece of fabric?

Ⓐ 1 square foot

Ⓑ 4 square feet

Ⓒ 4 feet

Ⓓ 2 feet

Name ______________________________

Are You Ready?
Lesson 12.2

1. How many faces does a rectangular prism have?

Ⓐ 4

Ⓑ 1

Ⓒ 3

Ⓓ 6

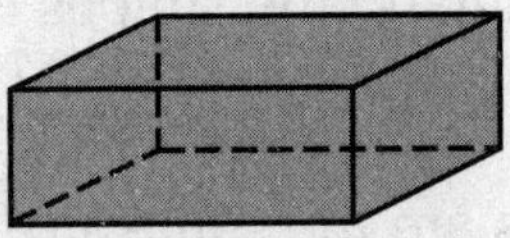

2. What is the product?

$6 \times 8 \times 4 =$ ______

Ⓐ 48

Ⓑ 192

Ⓒ 32

Ⓓ 168

Name ______________________________

Are You Ready?
Lesson 12.3

1. Stella has a rectangular garden plot. The length of the plot is 5 meters and the width is 8 meters. What is the area of the garden plot?

Ⓐ 40 square meters

Ⓑ 13 square meters

Ⓒ 26 square meters

Ⓓ 26 meters

2. Which of the following expressions can you use to find the area of the rectangle?

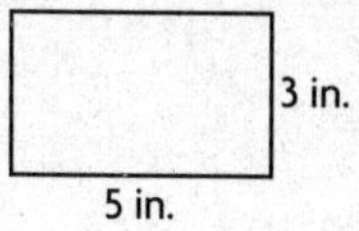

Ⓐ $5 + 3 + 5 + 3$

Ⓑ $(2 \times 5) + (2 \times 3)$

Ⓒ $5 + 3$

Ⓓ 5×3

Name ______________________________

Are You Ready?
Lesson 12.4

1. Simplify the expression.

$(5 \times 7) \times 10$

Ⓐ 35

Ⓑ 350

Ⓒ 70

Ⓓ 45

2. What is the area of the figure?

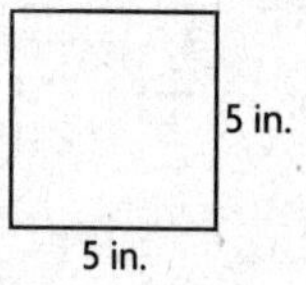

Ⓐ 25 square inches

Ⓑ 20 square inches

Ⓒ 5 square inches

Ⓓ 10 square inches

1. Which of the following is NOT a factor of 100?

Ⓐ 1

Ⓑ 10

Ⓒ 75

Ⓓ 50

---

2. Juan uses a box to store his collection of stickers. The box is a rectangular prism with a length of 8 inches. The width of the box is 6 inches and the height is 7 inches. What is the volume of the box?

Ⓐ 48 cubic inches

Ⓑ 42 cubic inches

Ⓒ 48 square inches

Ⓓ 336 cubic inches

Name ____________________

Are You Ready?
Lesson 13.1

1. Jin asks the vet to tell her how heavy her dog is. What does the vet measure?

   Ⓐ length
   Ⓑ capacity
   Ⓒ weight
   Ⓓ height

2. Alan wants to know how much lemonade a pitcher can hold. What does Alan measure?

   Ⓐ length
   Ⓑ capacity
   Ⓒ weight
   Ⓓ height

Name ____________________

Are You Ready?
Lesson 13.2

1. Ryan measures the length of his classroom. Which customary unit would you use to measure the length of a classroom?

   Ⓐ pound
   Ⓑ mile
   Ⓒ yard
   Ⓓ cup

2. What is the quotient?

   $84 \div 12$

   Ⓐ 72
   Ⓑ 7
   Ⓒ 9
   Ⓓ 96

Name ______________________________________

Are You Ready?
Lesson 13.3

1. What is the quotient?

36 ÷ 4

Ⓐ 8

Ⓑ 32

Ⓒ 7

Ⓓ 9

---

2. Beth measures the capacity of her cat's water bowl. Which customary unit would you use to measure the capacity of a cat's water bowl?

Ⓐ foot

Ⓑ gallon

Ⓒ pound

Ⓓ cup

Name ______________________________________

Are You Ready?
Lesson 13.4

1. A watermelon is weighed at a farmers' market. Which customary unit is best to use when weighing a watermelon?

Ⓐ ounce

Ⓑ cup

Ⓒ pound

Ⓓ inch

2. What is the product?

5 × 16

Ⓐ 50

Ⓑ 80

Ⓒ 21

Ⓓ 90

Name ______________________________

Are You Ready?
Lesson 13.5

1. Sarah is working on a crossword puzzle that has 18 words going across and 24 words going down. She filled in 36 words. How many words does Sarah need to find to complete the puzzle?

Ⓐ 14

Ⓑ 6

Ⓒ 32

Ⓓ 16

---

2. Students in grade 5 are having their picture taken. They are standing in 4 rows of 12 students and 5 rows of 9 students. How many students are in the picture?

Ⓐ 48

Ⓑ 45

Ⓒ 93

Ⓓ 83

Name ______________________________

Are You Ready?
Lesson 13.6

1. A scientist measures the length of an ant. Which metric unit would you use to measure the length of an ant?

Ⓐ liter

Ⓑ gram

Ⓒ kilometer

Ⓓ millimeter

2. What is the product?

4.7×100

Ⓐ 47

Ⓑ 470

Ⓒ 0.47

Ⓓ 4,700

Name ____________________

1. Use the table to solve the problem.

pt	1	2	3	4	5
gal	$\frac{1}{8}$	$\frac{1}{4}$	$\frac{3}{8}$	$\frac{1}{2}$	$\frac{5}{8}$

Jared has $\frac{1}{2}$ gallon of paint left after painting his clubhouse. How many pints of paint are left?

Ⓐ 2 pints
Ⓑ 1 pint
Ⓒ 4 pints
Ⓓ 5 pints

2. Use the table to solve the problem.

m	1	2	3	4	5
cm	100	200	300	400	500

A track for a turtle race is 3 meters long. What is the length of the track in centimeters?

Ⓐ 100 centimeters
Ⓑ $\frac{1}{300}$ centimeter
Ⓒ 3 centimeters
Ⓓ 300 centimeters

Name ____________________

Are You Ready?
Lesson 14.1

1. The pattern rule is *multiply input by 7.* What is the output if the input is 8?

Ⓐ 8

Ⓑ 7

Ⓒ 56

Ⓓ 15

---

2. Ryan lives at 121 Mulberry Street. The house numbers on Ryan's side of the street are consecutive odd numbers. If Ricardo lives three houses down from Ryan, which of the following could be his house number?

Ⓐ 124

Ⓑ 127

Ⓒ 123

Ⓓ 131

Name ____________________

Are You Ready?
Lesson 14.2

1. Which of the following is the horizontal number line in a coordinate grid?

Ⓐ *y*-axis

Ⓑ *y*-coordinate

Ⓒ *x*-coordinate

Ⓓ *x*-axis

---

2. Hilda reads the following directions for plotting a point on the coordinate grid: Move 4 units to the right from the origin and then move 2 units up. What is the ordered pair Hilda is trying to plot?

Ⓐ (2, 4)

Ⓑ (0, 4)

Ⓒ (4, 2)

Ⓓ (0, 2)

Name ____________________

Are You Ready?
Lesson 14.3

1. The rule for the pattern is *multiply input by 2.*

Input	5	6	7	8
Output	10	12	14	■

Find the unknown output.

Ⓐ 8

Ⓑ 2

Ⓒ 16

Ⓓ 4

2. The table shows the relationship between the number of tricycles and the total number of wheels. Find ■.

Tricycles	1	2	3	4	5
Number of Wheels	3	6	9	12	■

Ⓐ 3

Ⓑ 6

Ⓒ 15

Ⓓ 5

Name ____________________

Are You Ready?
Lesson 14.4

1. The rule for the pattern is *multiply input by 5.* If the input is 7, which ordered pair shows the relationship between the input and output?

Ⓐ (5, 7)

Ⓑ (7, 5)

Ⓒ (5, 35)

Ⓓ (7, 35)

2. Find ■ to complete the pattern in the table.

x	1	2	3	4
y	7	8	9	■

Ⓐ 12

Ⓑ 10

Ⓒ 6

Ⓓ 4

Name ______________________________

Are You Ready?
Lesson 15.1

Fran records the shapes of windows in her house.

1. How many windows are rectangles?

circle	rectangle	hexagon
rectangle	circle	rectangle
hexagon	rectangle	hexagon
circle	hexagon	rectangle

Ⓐ 12
Ⓑ 4
Ⓒ 5
Ⓓ 3

2. How many different shapes of windows are in Fran's house?

Ⓐ 4
Ⓑ 1
Ⓒ 2
Ⓓ 3

Name ______________________________

Are You Ready?
Lesson 15.2

Students voted for their favorite type of online store. The results are in the frequency table.

1. How many students voted for clothing stores?

Favorite Online Store	
Types of Stores	**Frequency**
Electronics	45
Sports	15
Clothing	34
Game	10

Ⓐ 45
Ⓑ 15
Ⓒ 34
Ⓓ 10

2. How many types of stores are in the frequency table?

Ⓐ 5
Ⓑ 4
Ⓒ 6
Ⓓ 45

Name ____________________

Are You Ready?
Lesson 15.3

1. The owner of an online T-shirt shop records the number of each color of T-shirt sold over the weekend. The greatest number of T-shirts sold is which color?

T-Shirts Sold				
Size	Blue	Red	White	Black
Number	18	26	24	20

Ⓐ blue

Ⓑ red

Ⓒ white

Ⓓ black

2. Which list shows numbers that are all multiples of 2?

Ⓐ 8, 12, 15, 27, 30

Ⓑ 16, 21, 36, 40, 48

Ⓒ 4, 8, 12, 16, 20

Ⓓ 1, 2

Name ____________________

Are You Ready?
Lesson 15.4

1. What is the scale of the graph?

Ⓐ 40

Ⓑ 10

Ⓒ 20

Ⓓ 0

2. Where does the bar for flower stickers end?

Ⓐ 20

Ⓑ 10

Ⓒ 15

Ⓓ 25

Name ______________________________

Are You Ready?
Lesson 16.1

1. Mark recorded the types of trees he saw on a nature walk. How many maple trees did he see?

Ⓐ 2

Ⓑ 4

Ⓒ 5

Ⓓ 3

Types of Trees				
oak	maple	pine	elm	maple
elm	oak	elm	oak	oak
oak	pine	maple	pine	maple

2. Which list shows the numbers in order from least to greatest?

Ⓐ 23.0, 23.25, 23.75, 23.5, 24.0

Ⓑ 23.0, 23.5, 23.25, 23.75, 24.0

Ⓒ 23.0, 23.25, 23.5, 23.75, 24.0

Ⓓ 24.0, 23.75, 23.5, 23.25, 23.0

Name ______________________________

Are You Ready?
Lesson 16.2

1. The dot plot shows the number of goals students scored. How many students scored 4 goals?

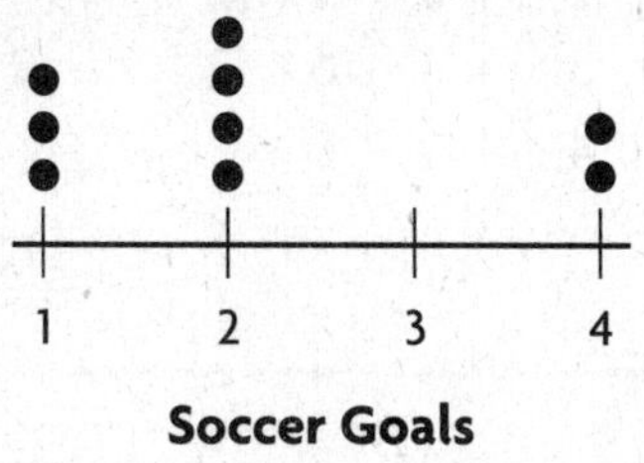

Ⓐ 3 Ⓒ 4

Ⓑ 0 Ⓓ 2

2. What number of goals did 3 students score?

Ⓐ 2

Ⓑ 4

Ⓒ 1

Ⓓ 3

Name ____________________

Are You Ready?
Lesson 16.3

1. Which list of numbers is in order from least to greatest?

Ⓐ 9, 8, 7, 6, 5

Ⓑ 2, 3, 5, 4, 6

Ⓒ 4, 5, 6, 7, 8

Ⓓ 6, 5, 4, 2, 3

2. In which place is the digit 7?

78

Ⓐ hundreds

Ⓑ thousands

Ⓒ ones

Ⓓ tens

Name ____________________

Are You Ready?
Lesson 16.4

1. Which number is on the stem-and-leaf plot?

Ⓐ 32

Ⓑ 41

Ⓒ 22

Ⓓ 31

Weight of Fish (oz)

Stem	Leaf
1	2 4 5 6 6 8
2	0 3 3
3	1 6 7 7 9
4	2 5

1 | 2 = 12.

2. Which statement about the stem-and-leaf plot is true?

Ⓐ The stem for 2 and leaf for 0 show the number 2.

Ⓑ The stem for 3 has 4 leaves.

Ⓒ The stem for 1 has the most leaves.

Ⓓ The key shows that 1 | 2 = 21.

Name ____________________

Are You Ready?
Lesson 16.5

1. Which ordered pair describes the location of Point *T*?

Ⓐ (5, 3)

Ⓑ (3, 3)

Ⓒ (3, 5)

Ⓓ (5, 5)

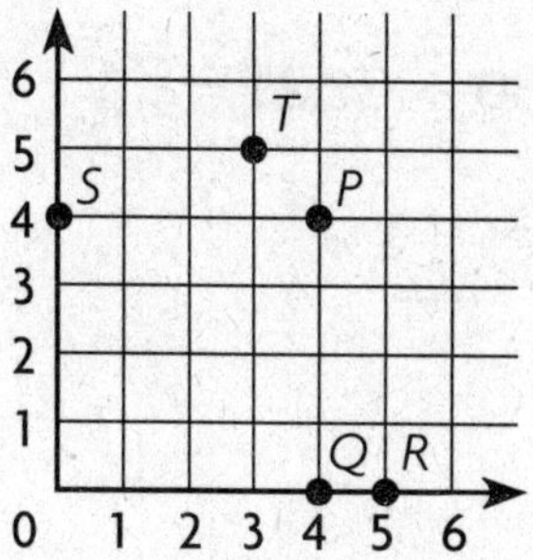

2. Which point is located at (4, 0)?

Ⓐ *P*

Ⓑ *Q*

Ⓒ *R*

Ⓓ *S*

Name ____________________

Are You Ready?
Lesson 16.6

1. What type of data display is this?

Ⓐ stem-and-leaf plot

Ⓑ bar graph

Ⓒ line plot

Ⓓ scatter plot

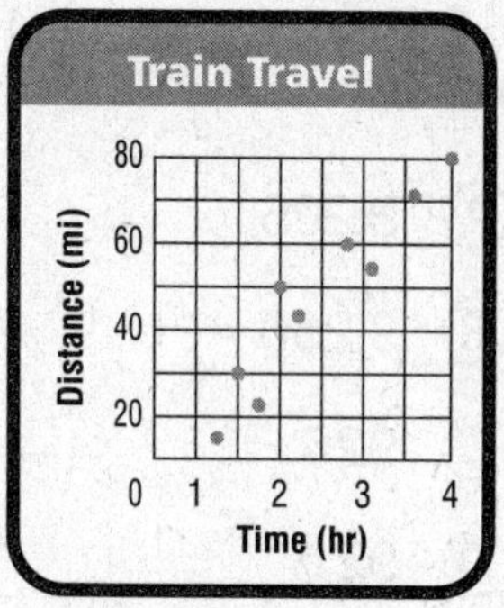

2. What does the data display show?

Ⓐ the relationship between speed and distance

Ⓑ the relationship between time and distance

Ⓒ the relationship between trains and time

Ⓓ the relationship between time and speed

Name ____________________

Are You Ready?
Lesson 17.1

1. Find the sum.

82.9 + 76.30 + 37.21 = ■

Ⓐ 195.60
Ⓑ 186.41
Ⓒ 195.41
Ⓓ 196.41

2. Find the difference.

848.08 − 94.56

Ⓐ 753.52
Ⓑ 853.52
Ⓒ 754.52
Ⓓ 752.52

Name ____________________

Are You Ready?
Lesson 17.2

1. What is 100 × 9.25?

Ⓐ 9,205
Ⓑ 9,250
Ⓒ 925
Ⓓ 92.5

2. How many thousands are in 63,000?

Ⓐ 630
Ⓑ 63
Ⓒ 6,300
Ⓓ 60

Name ______________________________

Are You Ready?
Lesson 17.3

1. What is 53 less than the sum of 79 and 24?

Ⓐ 103

Ⓑ 26

Ⓒ 50

Ⓓ 40

2. Find the difference.

$2,059.17 − $1,380.08 = ■

Ⓐ $779.09

Ⓑ $679.09

Ⓒ $670.09

Ⓓ $679.19

Name ______________________________

Are You Ready?
Lesson 17.4

1. Carmelita bought some office supplies. Her receipt shows that she spent $29.83, $18.99, and $33.10. How much did she spend?

Ⓐ $81.82

Ⓑ $81.92

Ⓒ $71.92

Ⓓ $80.92

2. Jake practiced piano for 30 minutes on each of 3 days and 45 minutes the fourth day. How many minutes did he practice in the 4 days?

Ⓐ 135 minutes

Ⓑ 90 minutes

Ⓒ 165 minutes

Ⓓ 210 minutes

Name ______________________________

Are You Ready?
Lesson 17.5

1. Julio had \$9.75 in his pocket. If he spends \$2.91, how much does he have left?

Ⓐ \$6.86

Ⓑ \$7.84

Ⓒ \$6.84

Ⓓ \$7.84

2. Sofia has \$24.66. Then she finds 3 quarters in the sofa. How much does she have now?

Ⓐ \$25.41

Ⓑ \$24.91

Ⓒ \$23.91

Ⓓ \$24.41

Name ______________________________

Are You Ready?
Lesson 17.6

1. What number plus 53 is equal to 102?

Ⓐ 59

Ⓑ 41

Ⓒ 51

Ⓓ 49

2. Which number makes the equation true?

(3 × \$18) + \$7 = ■

Ⓐ \$54

Ⓑ \$61

Ⓒ \$71

Ⓓ \$28

1. Which statement is true?

Ⓐ \$794 < \$749

Ⓑ \$794 > \$749

Ⓒ \$749 > \$794

Ⓓ \$497 < \$479

---

2. How many mini model cars will Dana have if he begins with 17, then doubles the number, and finally gives away 12 cars?

Ⓐ 34 cars

Ⓑ 22 cars

Ⓒ 32 cars

Ⓓ 5 cars

Name ____________________

Write the correct answer.

1. A river is 60 meters wide.

Metric Units of Length		
1 centimeter (cm)	=	10 millimeters (mm)
1 decimeter (dm)	=	10 centimeters
1 meter (m)	=	10 decimeters
1 meter (m)	=	100 centimeters
1 meter (m)	=	1,000 millimeters

What is the width of the river in centimeters?

____

2. Look at the figure.

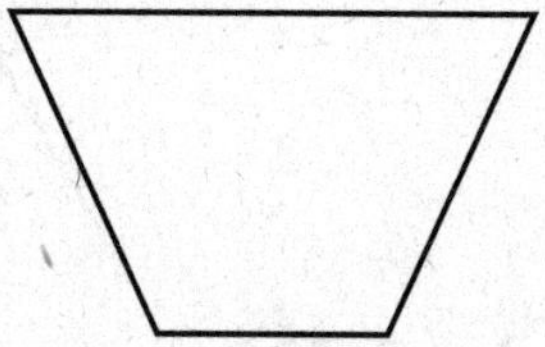

How many lines of symmetry does the figure have?

____

3. A state park is in the shape of a rectangle. The park is 11 miles long and 5 miles wide. What is the area of the park?

____

4. Use the number line.

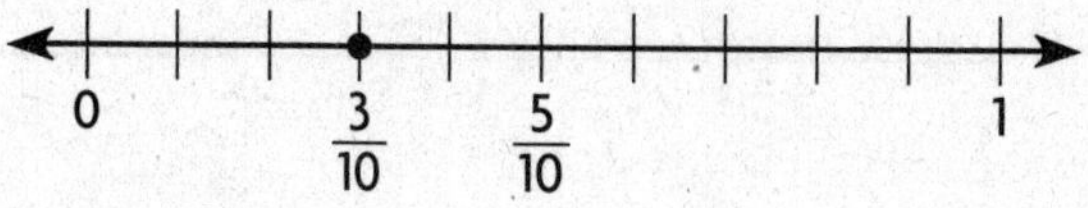

What decimal number represents the point shown on the number line?

____

5. Sharon completes a race in 53.2 seconds. Karri finishes the race 0.8 seconds before Sharon. How long does it take Karri to finish the race?

____

6. Ms. Browning drives a delivery truck. She drives 3,145 miles on her route each month. How many miles does she drive in 8 months?

____

GO ON

Name ______________________

7. Carlin buys 6 sports cards for $1.95 each and sells them for $4 each. What is her profit from the sports cards?

____

8. What fraction is represented by the sum of $\frac{1}{11} + \frac{1}{11} + \frac{1}{11} + \frac{1}{11} + \frac{1}{11}$?

____

9. Complete the statement by writing *more* or *less*.

A swimming pool holds ________ than 1 gallon of water.

10. Jack's dog eats $\frac{3}{8}$ pound of dry dog food and $\frac{2}{8}$ pound of canned dog food. How much dog food does his dog eat in all?

____

11. A university enrolls 37,932 students for the spring semester. What is this number rounded to the nearest ten thousand?

____

12. Kim adds $\frac{4}{10}$ and $\frac{5}{10}$ to find the sum $\frac{9}{10}$. What benchmark fractions could she add to determine whether her answer is reasonable?

____

13. Use the model.

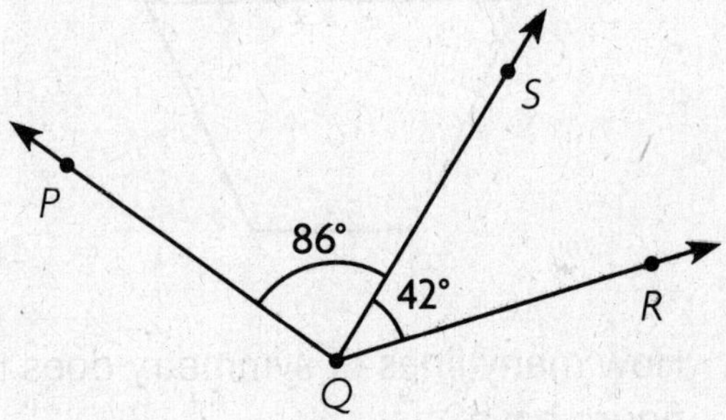

What is the measure of angle *PQR*?

____

GO ON

14. Jerry used a table to track his expenses for a month. Which expense in the table is a fixed expense?

Jerry's Expenses

Expense	Amount
Rent	$260
Gasoline	$95
Entertainment	$49
Electricity	$78

____

15. Gil scored 4,225 points in a video game. David scored 138 points more than Gil in the same game. They use a strip diagram to find how many points they scored in all.

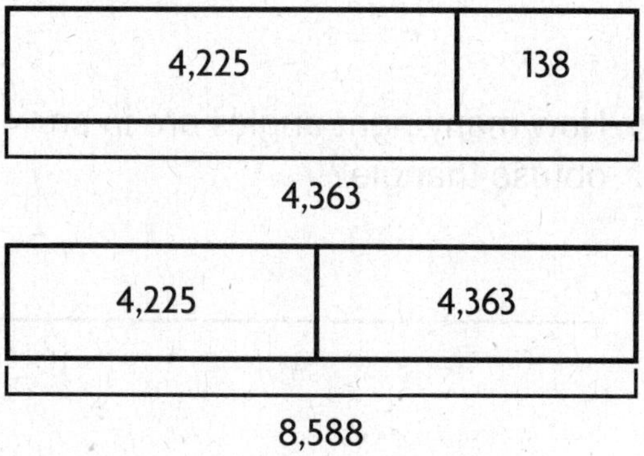

Which value in the strip diagram represents David's score?

____

16. Write <, =, or > to make the statement true.

67,023 ______ 64,978.

17. Tamara eats $\frac{1}{4}$ of a pizza. What fraction with a denominator of 12 is equivalent to $\frac{1}{4}$?

____

18. For an art project, 8 students used a total of 2,368 tiles. If each student used the same number of tiles, how many tiles did each student use?

____

19. A bead kit contains 1,578 small beads and 984 large beads. How many beads are in the kit?

____

20. Ms. Bell makes 19 costumes for a play. She uses 48 inches of ribbon to make each costume. What is a good estimate for the total number of inches of ribbon she will use?

____

GO ON

Name ______________________________

21. The population of Centerburg is 48,902. What is this number in expanded form?

____

22. Use the number line.

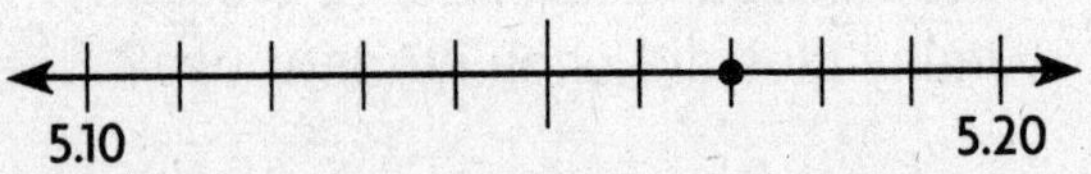

What decimal number represents the point shown on the number line?

____

23. A movie begins at 4:35 P.M. and lasts 1 hour 35 minutes. At what time does the movie end?

____

24. What is $\frac{15}{100}$ written as a decimal?

____

25. Look at the angle.

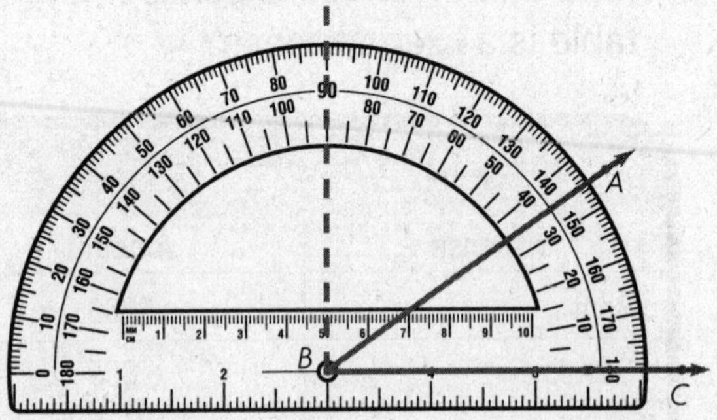

What is the approximate measure of the angle?

____

26. Write <, =, or > to make the statement true.

$\frac{1}{5}$ ______ $\frac{2}{4}$

27. How many right angles are in an obtuse triangle?

____

GO ON

Name ____

28. Workers at a truck factory make engines that each weigh 27 pounds. What is the weight of 100 of these engines?

____

29. Look at the models.

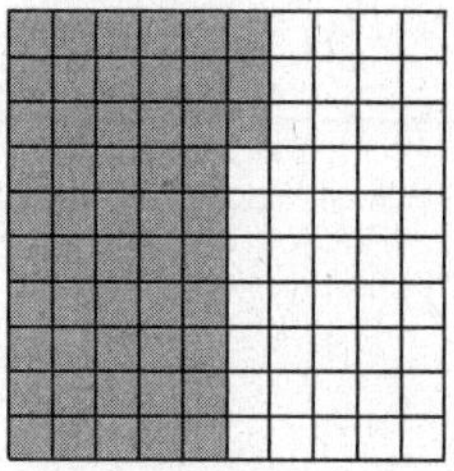

0.53

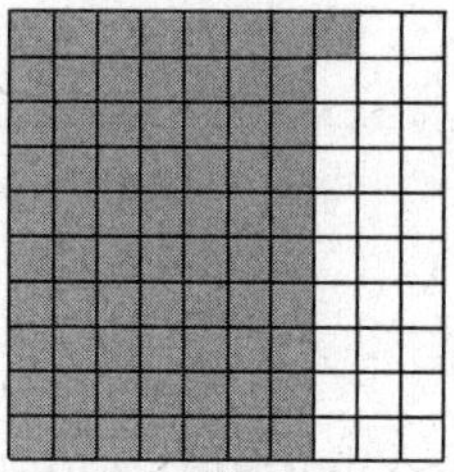

0.71

Write <, =, or > to make the statement true.

0.53 _____ 0.71

30. The table shows the weight, in pounds, of watermelons sold at the market.

Weights of Watermelons (pounds)

Weight	Frequency
$6\frac{1}{2}$	2
7	4
$7\frac{1}{2}$	5
8	1
$8\frac{1}{2}$	3
9	4

How many more watermelons weigh 8 pounds or more than weigh 7 pounds or less?

____

31. The input-output table shows the number of beetles, *b*, and the number of legs, *l*, on the beetles.

Input	***b***	1	2	4	8
Output	***l***	6			

If the output is $b \times 6$, how many legs are on 8 beetles?

____

32. There are 7,803 students in a school district. There are 9 schools in the district. Suppose the same number of students attend each school.

$9\overline{)7,803}$

How many students would attend each school?

____

33. Ellie has 8 pounds of berries. She uses $\frac{1}{10}$ of that amount in a recipe. What decimal is $\frac{1}{10}$ of 8?

____

GO ON

34. Use the number line.

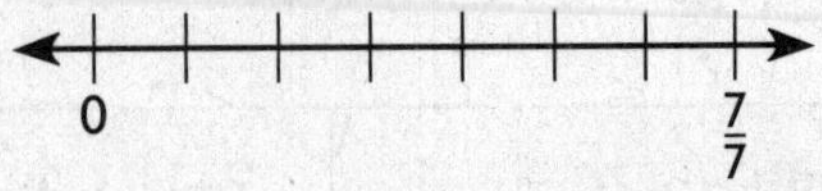

What fraction is represented by the sum of $\frac{2}{7} + \frac{3}{7} + \frac{1}{7}$?

____

35. Grace makes this area model to find the product 13×13.

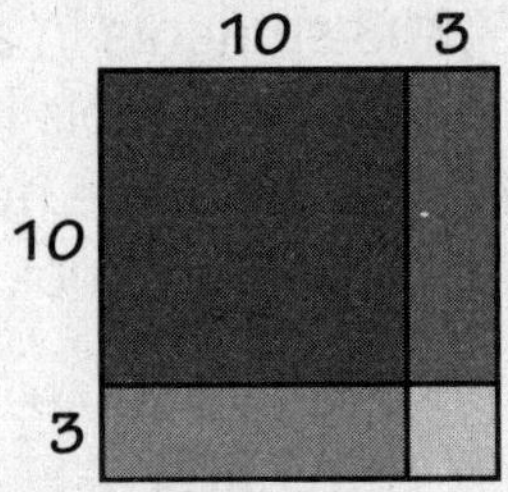

What is the product?

____

36. Tom draws a figure with 2 pairs of parallel sides, 4 sides of equal length, and 4 right angles. What is the best name for this figure?

____

37. Tickets to a play cost $10 for adults and $6 for children. How much will it cost for 9 adults and 8 children to buy tickets to the play?

____

38. Lora buys the picture frame represented by the rectangle.

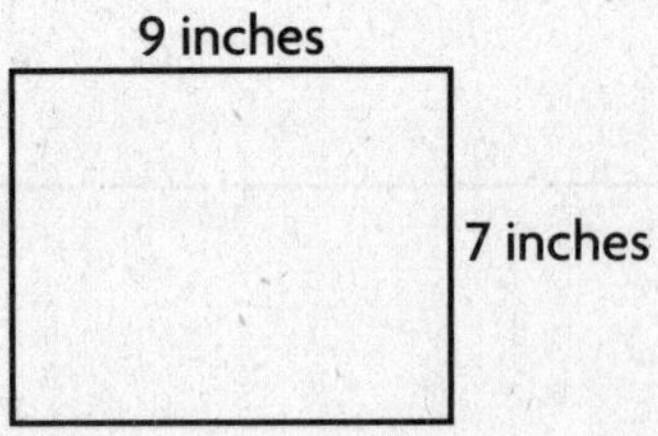

What is the perimeter of the frame?

____

39. Use the model.

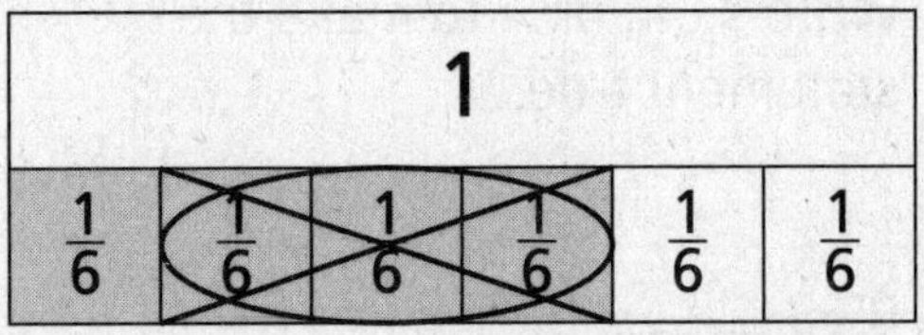

Alice has $\frac{4}{6}$ quart of juice. She and her friends drink $\frac{3}{6}$ quart. What fraction of a quart of juice is left?

____

40. Daniele wants to put 86 crayons into gift bags for her friends. If she puts 9 crayons into each bag, how many gift bags can she make, and how many crayons will she have left over?

____

STOP

Fill in the bubble for the correct answer.

1. To solve \$0.04 × 0.5 Trishala multiplies whole numbers. She writes 4 × 5 = 20. Which shows where Trishala should place the decimal point in the product?

Ⓐ \$20.00 Ⓒ \$2.00

Ⓑ \$0.02 Ⓓ \$0.20

2. Lia drew a model to help solve a problem. Which division expression does the model represent?

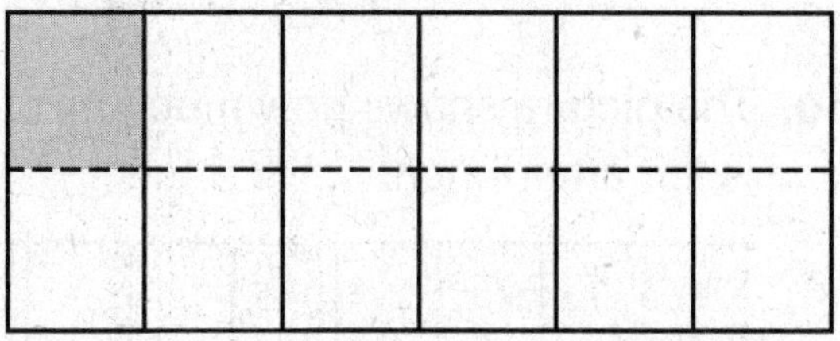

Ⓐ $\frac{1}{6} \div 2$ Ⓒ $3 \div \frac{1}{6}$

Ⓑ $\frac{2}{6} \div 3$ Ⓓ $\frac{1}{6} \div \frac{1}{2}$

3. Murray is 1.287 meters tall. What is 1.287 rounded to the nearest hundredth?

Ⓐ 1.3 Ⓒ 1.29

Ⓑ 1.2 Ⓓ 1.28

4. Lola plots a point on a coordinate grid to represent the ordered pair (7, 4). Which is true about the *x*-coordinate in the ordered pair?

Ⓐ It is 7 units up from the *x*-axis.

Ⓑ It is 7 units to the right of the *y*-axis.

Ⓒ It is 4 units to the right of the *y*-axis.

Ⓓ It is 4 units below the *x*-axis.

5. Dar made a table to classify different kinds of triangles.

		Triangle by Length of Sides	
		Scalene	**Isosceles**
Triangle by Angle Measure	**Acute**	?	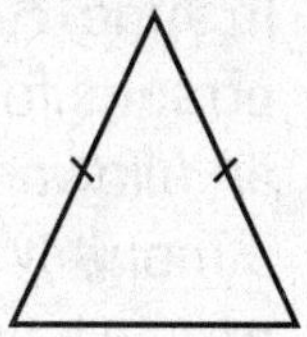
	Obtuse	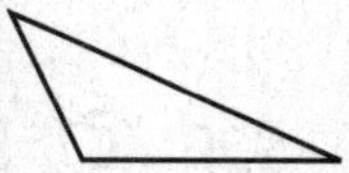	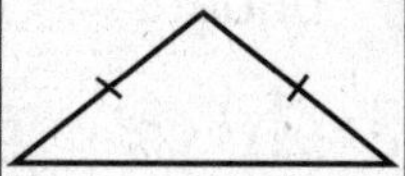

Which triangle completes the table?

Ⓐ 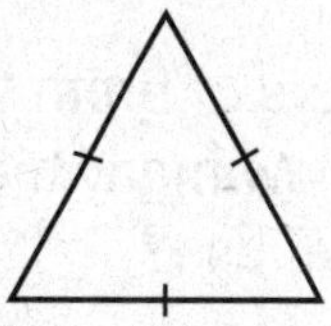

Ⓒ 

Ⓑ 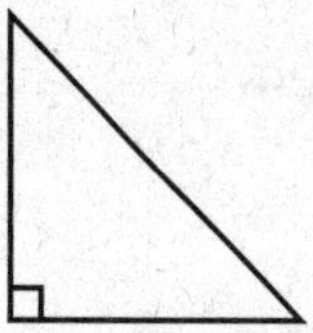

Ⓓ 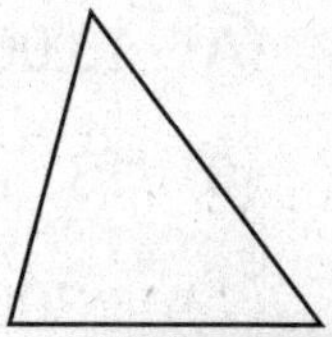

GO ON

6. The owner of a clothing store records the relationship between the outside temperature and the number of sweaters he sells. He wants to plot the information on a scatter plot.

Sweaters Sold						
Number of Sweaters	25	10	15	30	20	35
Temperature (°F)	32	50	45	30	40	25

Which ordered pair would **NOT** represent a point on a scatter plot of the data?

Ⓐ (30, 30) Ⓒ (15, 45)

Ⓑ (45, 30) Ⓓ (35, 25)

7. In June, Aaron earns \$15 running errands for a neighbor and receives an allowance totaling \$24. He makes a monthly budget and sees that his expenses are \$55. How much more does Aaron need to earn to balance his budget?

Ⓐ \$6 Ⓑ \$39 Ⓒ \$16 Ⓓ \$8

8. A chef uses 13 liters of broth to make a batch of soup. How many milliliters of broth does the chef use?

Ⓐ 13,000 milliliters

Ⓑ 130 milliliters

Ⓒ 1,300 milliliters

Ⓓ 1.3 milliliters

9. The table uses the rule $a = 3b$.

Input	***b***	4	5	6	7
Output	***a***	■	■	■	■

Which set of numbers correctly completes the output values in the table?

Ⓐ 7, 8, 9, 10

Ⓑ 40, 50, 60, 70

Ⓒ 12, 15, 18, 21

Ⓓ 1, 2, 3, 4

10. The picture shows how much meatloaf is left after lunch.

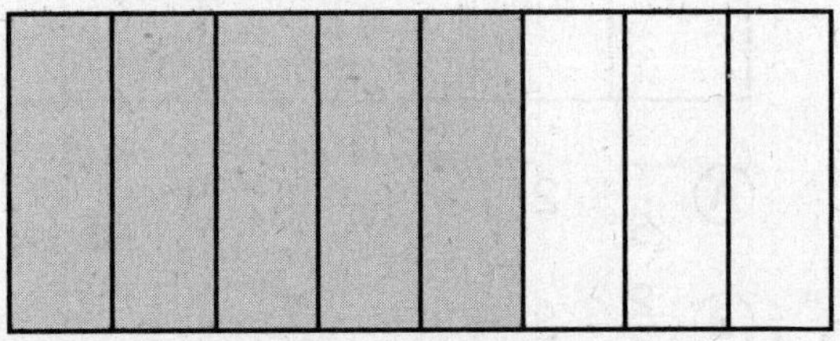

Jared eats $\frac{1}{4}$ of the whole meatloaf for dinner. Which subtraction sentence represents how much meatloaf is left after dinner?

Ⓐ $\frac{3}{8} - \frac{1}{4} = \frac{1}{8}$

Ⓑ $1 - \frac{3}{8} = \frac{5}{8}$

Ⓒ $\frac{5}{8} - \frac{1}{2} = \frac{1}{8}$

Ⓓ $\frac{5}{8} - \frac{1}{4} = \frac{3}{8}$

GO ON

11. A house sparrow has a mass of about 39.5 grams. What is the value of 5 in 39.5?

Ⓐ 5 hundredths

Ⓑ 5 tenths

Ⓒ 5 tens

Ⓓ 5 thousandths

12. The bar graph shows the amount of recycling items collected by students in different grades.

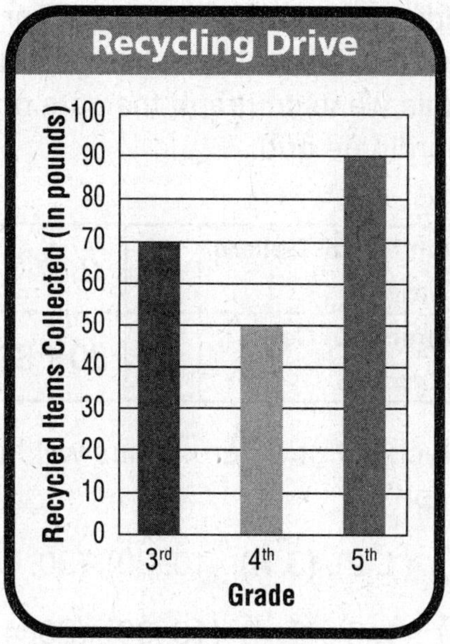

For every pound they collected, students earned $2. How much more money did the 5th grade students earn than the 4th grade students?

Ⓐ $40

Ⓑ $20

Ⓒ $100

Ⓓ $80

13. What is the area of the rectangle?

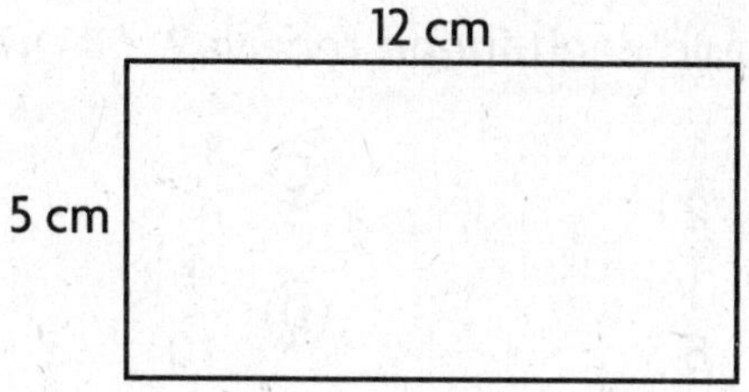

Ⓐ 17 square centimeters

Ⓑ 34 square centimeters

Ⓒ 60 square centimeters

Ⓓ 24 square centimeters

14. Tabitha built a rectangular prism with inch cubes. She used 8 inch cubes to make the bottom layer. If the prism was built with a total of 48 cubes, how many layers does the prism have?

Ⓐ 40

Ⓑ 12

Ⓒ 14

Ⓓ 6

15. Mr. Pareja had a starting balance of $826.94 in his checking account. How much money will he have left after he withdraws $49.57?

Ⓐ $777.37

Ⓑ $331.24

Ⓒ $876.51

Ⓓ $168.76

GO ON

Name ______________________________

16. Five friends want to share $\frac{1}{2}$ of a pie equally. What fraction of the whole pie should each friend receive?

Ⓐ $\frac{1}{2}$

Ⓑ $\frac{1}{8}$

Ⓒ $\frac{1}{4}$

Ⓓ $\frac{1}{10}$

17. Which correctly compares the decimals 2.18 and 2.108?

Ⓐ $2.108 > 2.18$

Ⓑ $2.18 = 2.108$

Ⓒ $2.18 < 2.108$

Ⓓ $2.108 < 2.18$

18. Jackie drew a model to help her multiply a whole number by a fraction. Which multiplication expression does her model represent?

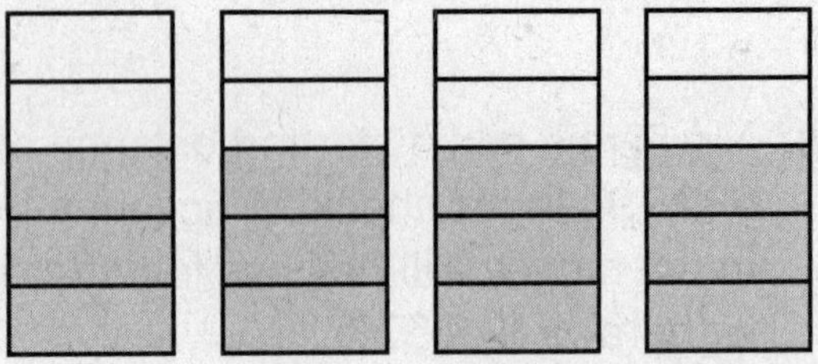

Ⓐ $3 \times \frac{2}{5}$

Ⓑ $4 \times \frac{3}{5}$

Ⓒ $5 \times \frac{1}{5}$

Ⓓ $4 \times \frac{2}{3}$

19. Lars buys 2 packages of 6 oranges each and 3 packages of 5 oranges each. He uses 18 oranges to make orange juice.

Which equation shows how to find *n*, the number of oranges Lars has left?

Ⓐ $2 \times 6 + 3 \times 5 - 18 = n$

Ⓑ $2 + 6 \times 3 + 5 + 18 = n$

Ⓒ $2 \times 6 + 3 \times 5 + 18 = n$

Ⓓ $2 \times 5 + 3 \times 6 - 18 = n$

20. Eddie has a savings account. For each dollar he earns, he saves 10 cents. Eddie wants to graph the data on a coordinate grid.

Number of Dollars Earned	1	2	3	4
Number of Cents Saved	10	20	30	40

Which set of ordered pairs will he graph?

Ⓐ (1, 2), (3, 4), (10, 20), (30, 40)

Ⓑ (1, 3), (2, 4), (10, 30), (20, 40)

Ⓒ (1, 10), (2, 20), (3, 30), (4, 40)

Ⓓ (10, 1), (20, 2), (30, 3), (40, 4)

GO ON

21. What is the value of the expression?

$7 \times [(18 + 5) - (4 \times 5)]$

Ⓐ 161

Ⓑ 21

Ⓒ 127

Ⓓ 42

22. Which is the best estimate of 3×687?

Ⓐ 2,100

Ⓑ 690

Ⓒ 2,800

Ⓓ 1,000

23. Which rule describes the pattern in the table?

Input	**x**	3	4	5	6
Output	**y**	9	10	11	12

Ⓐ $y = x + 6$

Ⓑ $y = 3x$

Ⓒ $x = y + 3$

Ⓓ $y = 6x$

24. Martha has a length of fabric measuring 12.36 meters long. She cuts the fabric into 12 equal pieces.

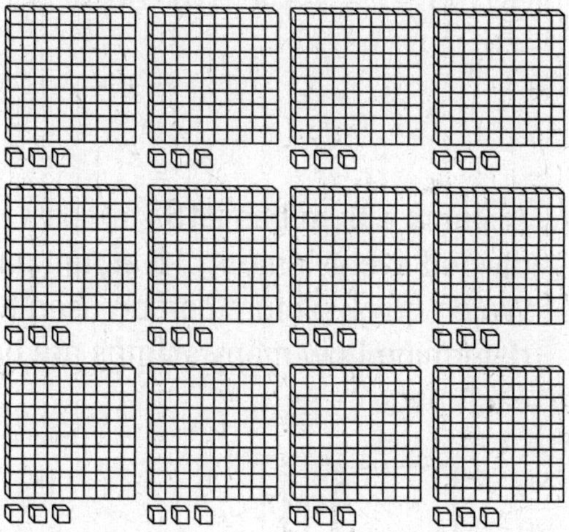

How long is each piece of fabric?

Ⓐ 1.3 meters

Ⓑ 12.1 meters

Ⓒ 1.36 meters

Ⓓ 1.03 meters

25. Bai has 6 small pizzas. She cuts each pizza into fourths. How many $\frac{1}{4}$-size pieces of pizza does she have?

Record your answer and fill in the bubbles on the grid. Be sure to use the correct place value.

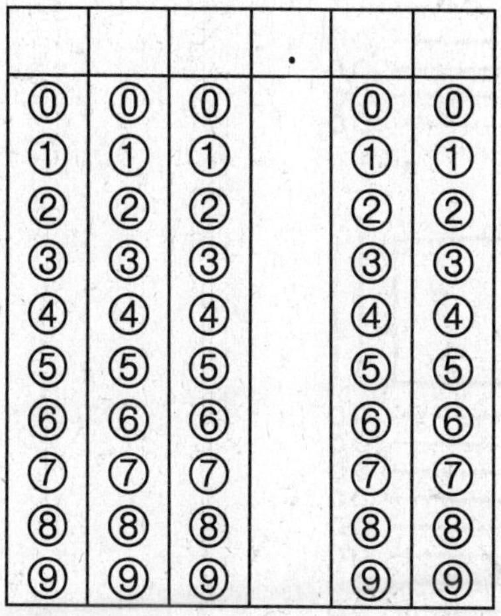

GO ON

26. Which is a prime number?

Ⓐ 33
Ⓑ 77
Ⓒ 23
Ⓓ 80

27. A stamp album has 216 stamps divided evenly among 18 album pages. Which quick picture can be used to determine how many stamps are on each page?

Ⓐ 

Ⓑ 

Ⓒ 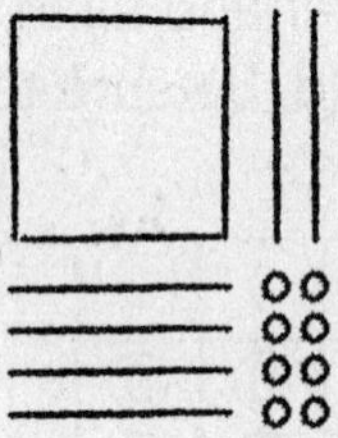

Ⓓ 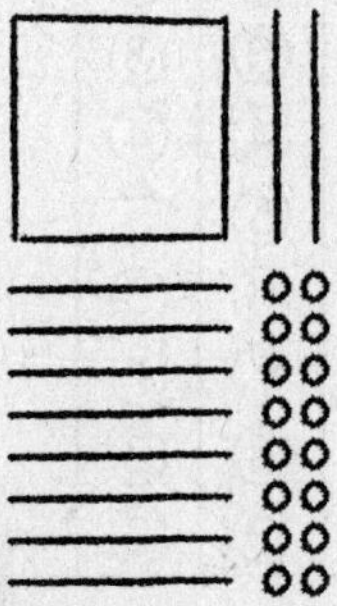

28. Mr. Evans' new shed has a value of $5,000. The property tax in his town is $12.50 for every $1,000 of property value. How much will Mr. Evans pay in property tax on his new shed?

Ⓐ $62.50
Ⓑ $5,062.50
Ⓒ $5,012.50
Ⓓ $625

29. Paola colored $\frac{1}{8}$ of a picture purple and $\frac{2}{3}$ of the picture red. She left the rest of the picture uncolored. How much of her picture did Paola color?

Ⓐ $\frac{4}{24}$
Ⓑ $\frac{3}{11}$
Ⓒ $\frac{3}{5}$
Ⓓ $\frac{19}{24}$

30. The Miller family's monthly income is $3,500. They budget $1,200 for rent, $825 for food, $400 for utilities, $375 for transportation, $300 for savings, $200 for education, and $250 for miscellaneous expenses. Which of the following should the Millers do to balance their budget?

Ⓐ Increase the amount for food by $50.
Ⓑ Decrease the amount for miscellaneous spending by $50.
Ⓒ Decrease savings by $30.
Ⓓ Increase the amount for food by $30.

GO ON

31. Lu-Anh plots a point to represent the ordered pair (4, 2). Which describes how to locate this point?

Ⓐ Move 4 units up from the origin and then 2 units to the right.

Ⓑ Move 2 units up from the origin and then 4 units to the right.

Ⓒ Move 4 units to the right of the origin and then 2 more units to the right.

Ⓓ Move 4 units to the right of the origin and then 2 units up.

32. Jerome drew a square.

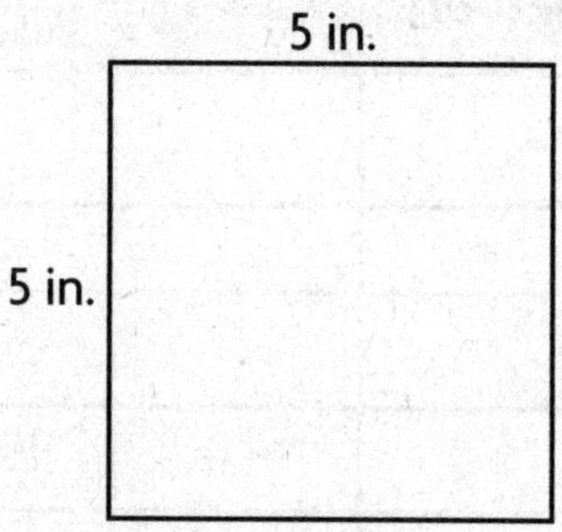

Which equation represents the perimeter of the square?

Ⓐ $P = 2 \times 5 + 5$

Ⓑ $P = 5 + 5 + 5 + 5$

Ⓒ $P = 2 \times 5$

Ⓓ $P = 5 \times 5$

33. Frida's thumb is 1.915 centimeters wide. What is the width of Frida's thumb rounded to the nearest tenth?

Ⓐ 1.9 centimeters

Ⓑ 1.91 centimeters

Ⓒ 2 centimeters

Ⓓ 1.92 centimeters

34. A baker used 37.51 ounces of yeast to make 10 loaves of bread. If he uses the same amount of yeast in each loaf of bread, how many ounces of yeast does he use in 1 loaf of bread?

Ⓐ 375.1 ounces

Ⓑ 3,751 ounces

Ⓒ 3.751 ounces

Ⓓ 0.375 ounce

35. There are 2,738 students that will travel by bus to a field trip. Each bus holds 74 students. How many buses are needed to transport all of the students?

Record your answer and fill in the bubbles on the grid. Be sure to use the correct place value.

			.		
⓪	⓪	⓪		⓪	⓪
①	①	①		①	①
②	②	②		②	②
③	③	③		③	③
④	④	④		④	④
⑤	⑤	⑤		⑤	⑤
⑥	⑥	⑥		⑥	⑥
⑦	⑦	⑦		⑦	⑦
⑧	⑧	⑧		⑧	⑧
⑨	⑨	⑨		⑨	⑨

GO ON

36. AnChi uses inch cubes to build a rectangular prism.

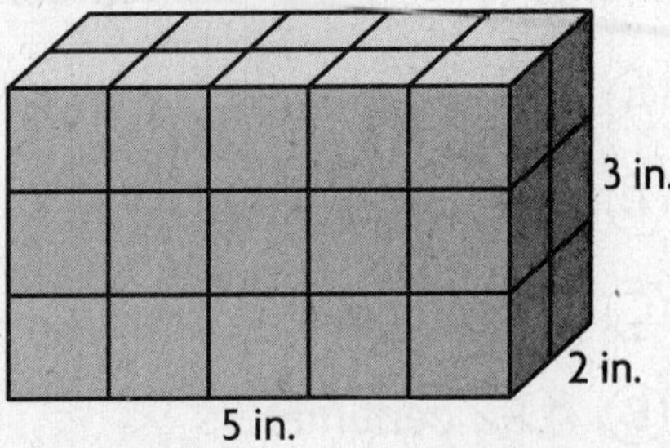

Which equation can AnChi use to find the volume of the rectangular prism?

Ⓐ $V = 5 \times 2 \times 3$

Ⓑ $V = 5 + 2 + 3$

Ⓒ $V = (2 \times 5) + (2 \times 3)$

Ⓓ $V = 5 \times 2$

37. Jennie buys 2 packages of 10 green ribbons and 3 packages of 14 yellow ribbons. She uses 23 of the ribbons to wrap presents. Which equation shows how to solve for r, the number of ribbons Jennie has left?

Ⓐ $2 \times 10 + 3 \times 14 - 23 = r$

Ⓑ $2 \times 10 + 14 - 23 = r$

Ⓒ $2 \times 10 + 3 \times 14 + 23 = r$

Ⓓ $2 + 10 \times 3 + 14 - 23 = r$

38. Which decimal is greater than 2.445?

Ⓐ 2.045

Ⓑ 2.405

Ⓒ 2.450

Ⓓ 2.440

39. Anya's gross monthly income is $1,500. She pays $200 in taxes each month. What is Anya's net monthly income if only these taxes are taken out of her check?

Ⓐ $1,700

Ⓑ $1,300

Ⓒ $3,000

Ⓓ $200

40. Larry made a chart to keep track of his money.

Larry's Financial Record: Month of February

Date	Description	Received ($)	Expenses ($)	Available Funds ($)
	Balance: end of January			0
1	allowance	25		25
4	snow shoveling	15		40
5	mittens		11.46	28.54
7	ice skating		6.50	22.04
7	babysitting	18.75		40.79

Which expression shows how much Larry has in available funds after he buys mittens?

Ⓐ $11.46 − $6.50

Ⓑ $28.54 − $22.04

Ⓒ $40 − $28.54

Ⓓ $40 − $11.46

GO ON

41. Ann uses $\frac{1}{4}$ cup of oil and $\frac{1}{3}$ cup of vinegar to make salad dressing.

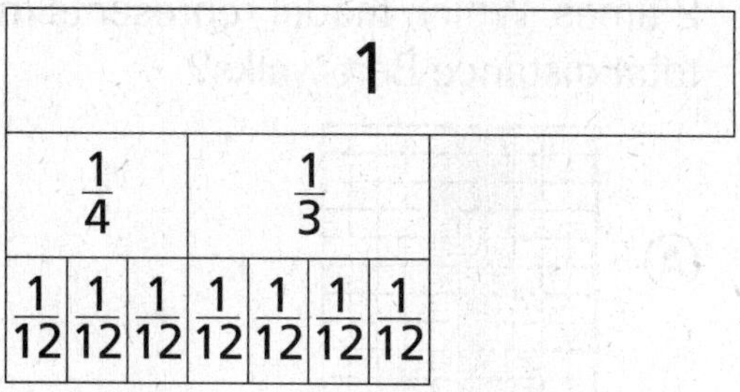

How many cups of salad dressing does she make?

Ⓐ $\frac{7}{12}$ cup
Ⓑ $\frac{5}{12}$ cup
Ⓒ $\frac{2}{7}$ cup
Ⓓ $\frac{2}{12}$ cup

42. A carpenter needs enough lumber to cut 24 one-foot lengths of wood. How many yards of wood does the carpenter need?

Ⓐ 4 yards
Ⓑ 2 yards
Ⓒ 8 yards
Ⓓ 6 yards

43. During a 4-hour period, it snowed 2.7 inches. If it snowed the same amount each hour, about how many inches did it snow each hour?

Ⓐ 0.3 inch
Ⓑ 0.7 inch
Ⓒ 10 inches
Ⓓ 0.2 inch

Use the data and dot plot for 44–45.

Colin measured the height of several plants.

In inches the heights are: 9, 9, 8.5, 8, 8.25, 8, 8.5, 9, 8.5, 9.

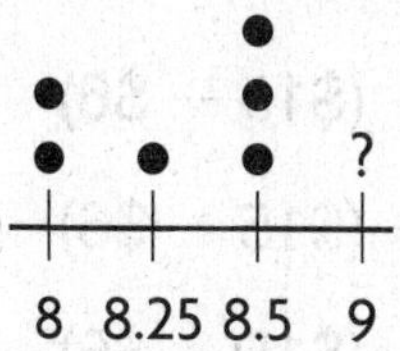

Height of Plants (in.)

44. Colin is making a dot plot of the data. How many dots should he mark above 9?

Record your answer and fill in the bubbles on the grid. Be sure to use the correct place value.

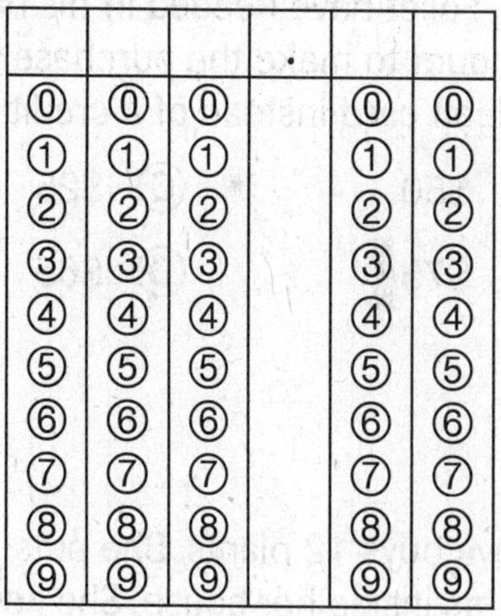

45. How many more plants have a height of 8.5 inches than have a height of 8 inches?

Ⓐ 1
Ⓑ 3
Ⓒ 10
Ⓓ 4

GO ON

46. Robbie had \$37 to spend at the amusement park. He spent \$15 on gifts and \$6 on snacks.

Which expression matches the words?

Ⓐ (\$37 + \$15) − \$6

Ⓑ \$37 − (\$15 − \$6)

Ⓒ \$37 + (\$15 − \$6)

Ⓓ \$37 − (\$15 + \$6)

47. Mr. Follet wanted to purchase a computer that costs \$475. He had \$400 in his bank account, so he used a credit card to pay for the computer. How much more money would Mr. Follet have needed in his bank account to make the purchase with a debit card instead of a credit card?

Ⓐ \$50   Ⓒ \$25

Ⓑ \$75   Ⓓ \$65

48. Treva buys 12 plants. She puts $\frac{2}{3}$ of the plants inside her house. She keeps the rest of the plants outside. How many plants does Treva put inside her house?

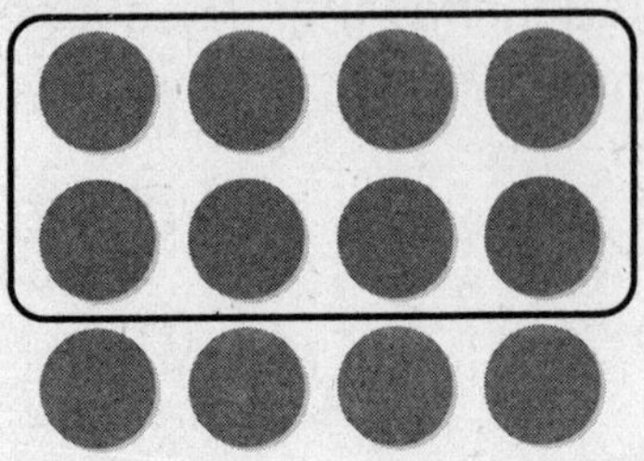

Ⓐ 4   Ⓑ 10   Ⓒ 8   Ⓓ 6

49. The distance around a pond is 0.28 mile on a walking path. Bert walks the complete distance on the path 2 times. Which model represents the total distance Bert walks?

Ⓐ 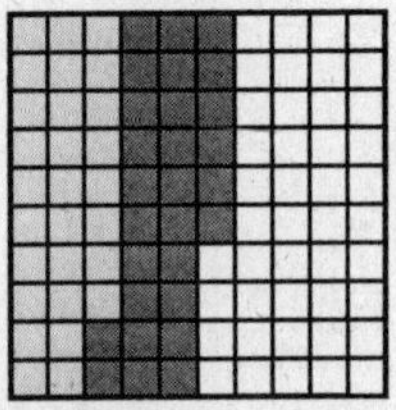

Ⓑ 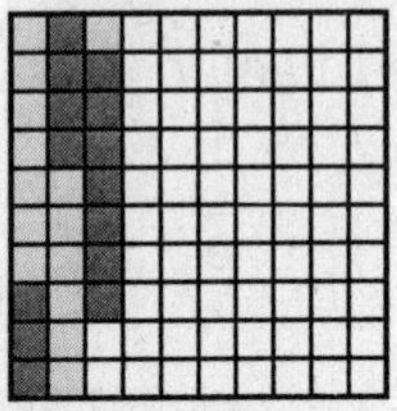

Ⓒ 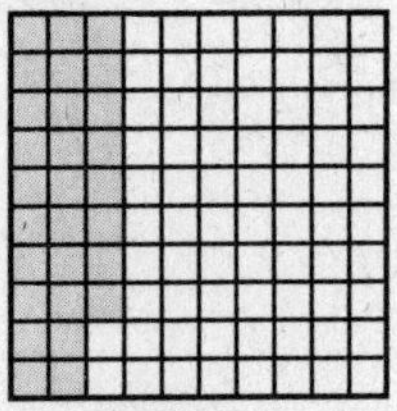

Ⓓ 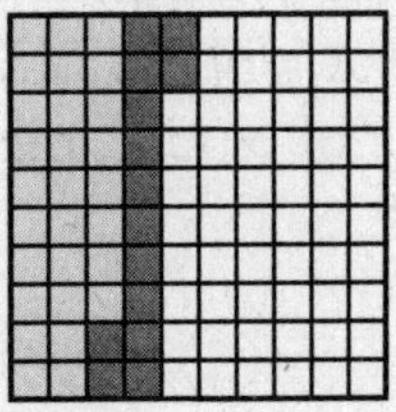

50. Each storage unit at a dairy farm holds 165 gallons of milk. How many gallons of milk can be held by 32 storage units?

Ⓐ 6,000 gallons   Ⓒ 5,280 gallons

Ⓑ 3,260 gallons   Ⓓ 4,170 gallons

STOP

Name ___________________________________

Fill in the bubble for the correct answer.

1. Mai multiplies $2.30 by 0.7. What is the place value of the decimal in the product?

Ⓐ Ones
Ⓑ Thousandths
Ⓒ Tenths
Ⓓ Hundredths

2. Which model represents the expression?

$$2 \div \frac{1}{4}$$

Ⓐ 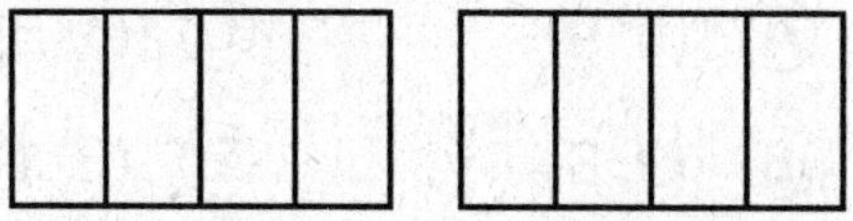

Ⓑ 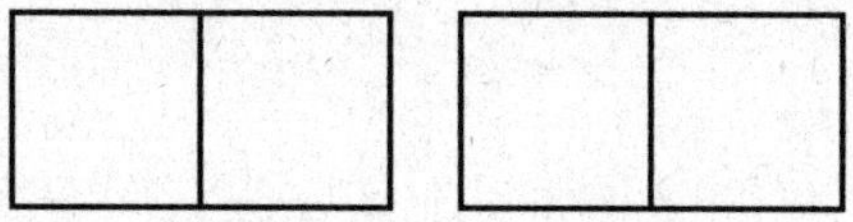

Ⓒ 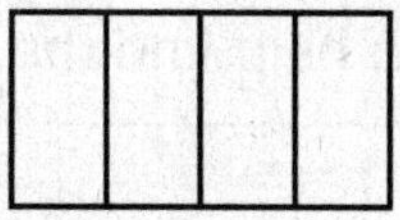

Ⓓ 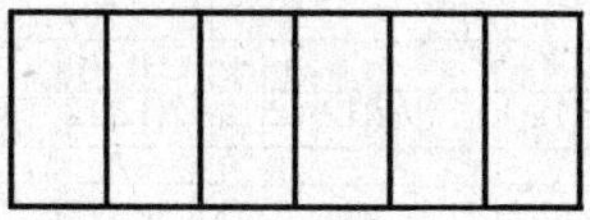

3. Donnel pours 8.712 liters of water into a fish tank. What is 8.712 rounded to the nearest tenth?

Ⓐ 8.8
Ⓑ 8.7
Ⓒ 8.72
Ⓓ 9

4. Ivan plots a point to represent the ordered pair (3, 8). Which is true about the *y*-coordinate in the ordered pair?

Ⓐ It is 8 units to the right of the *y*-axis.
Ⓑ It is 8 units up from the *x*-axis.
Ⓒ It is 3 units up from the *x*-axis.
Ⓓ It is 3 units to the right of the *y*-axis.

5. Garth drew a Venn diagram to classify different kinds of polygons.

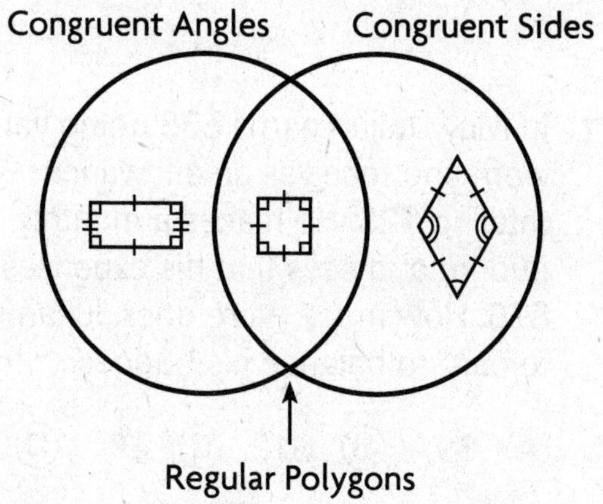

Which figure belongs in the section of the Venn diagram labeled Regular Polygons?

Ⓐ 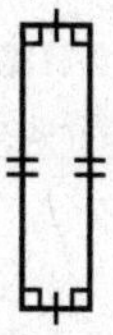

Ⓒ 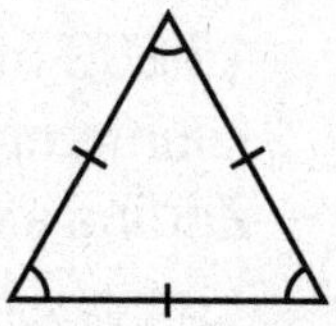

Ⓑ 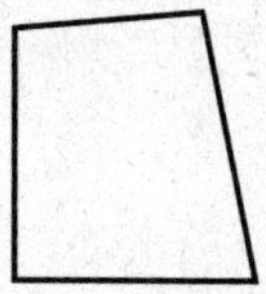

Ⓓ 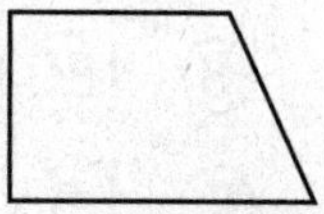

GO ON

6. The owner of an electronics store records the relationship between the outside temperature and the number of air-conditioning units he sells. He wants to plot the information on a scatter plot.

Air-Conditioning Units Sold						
Number of air-conditioning units	15	20	50	45	25	40
Temperature (°F)	65	70	90	85	70	80

Which is the best scale for both the *x*-axis and the *y*-axis in a scatter plot of the data?

Ⓐ 1 Ⓑ 2 Ⓒ 80 Ⓓ 5

7. In May, Julian earns $38 doing yard work and receives an allowance totaling $25. He makes a monthly budget and sees that his expenses are $76. How much more does Julian need to earn to balance his budget?

Ⓐ $9 Ⓑ $13 Ⓒ $6 Ⓓ $23

8. Zerlina estimates the distance between her house and the ocean to be about 18,000 meters. About how many kilometers away from the ocean is Zerlina's house?

Ⓐ 18 kilometers

Ⓑ 180 kilometers

Ⓒ 1.8 kilometers

Ⓓ 1,800 kilometers

9. Emily uses the rule $a = 3b$ to plot points in a graph. She uses a to represent the output and b to represent the input.

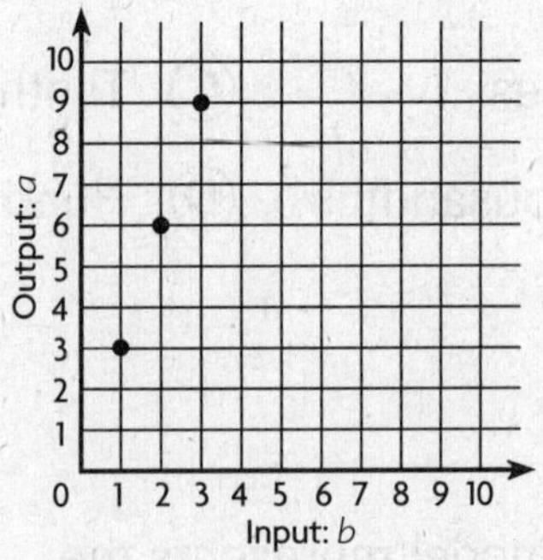

When the input is 3, what is the coordinate pair that represents the point?

Ⓐ (3, 9) Ⓒ (1, 3)

Ⓑ (9, 3) Ⓓ (3, 1)

10. Heather adds $\frac{1}{4}$ and $\frac{2}{3}$. Which model could she use to help find the sum?

Ⓐ
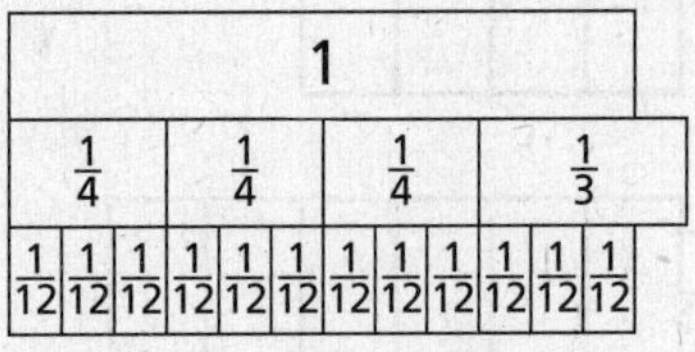

Ⓑ
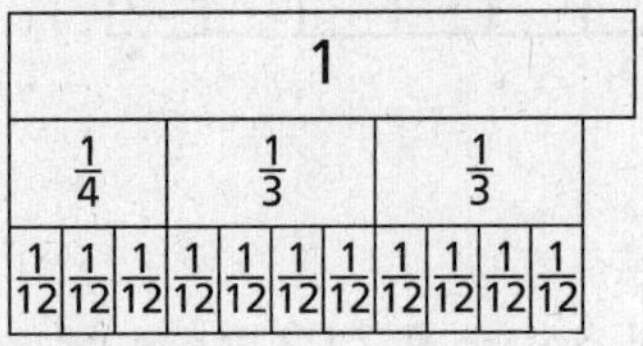

Ⓒ
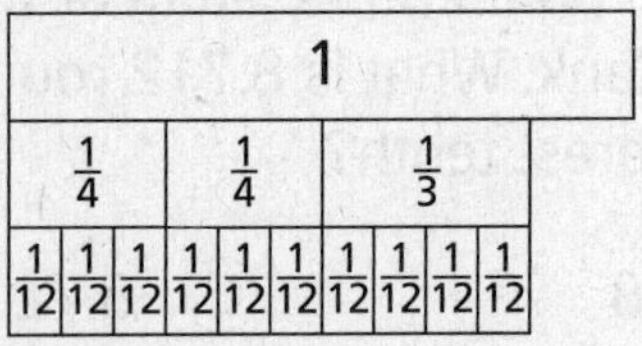

Ⓓ
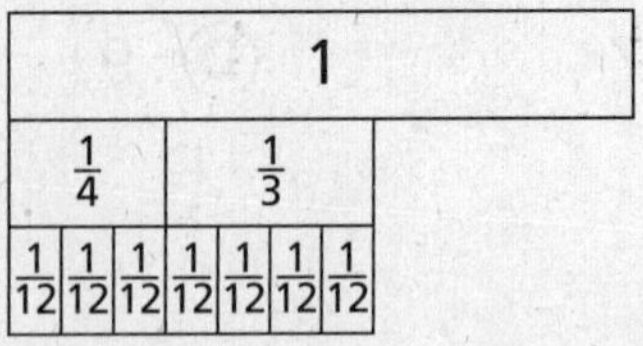

GO ON

11. What is the expanded form of 0.23?

Ⓐ 0.02 + 0.3

Ⓑ 2 + 0.3

Ⓒ 0.2 + 0.03

Ⓓ 0.02 + 0.03

12. The stem-and-leaf plot shows the number of minutes health-club members spent exercising during one visit.

Minutes Members Exercised

Stem	Leaf
3	0 0 2
4	0 0 5 5 7
6	2 3 5
7	0 5 5 8
9	0 5

Members who exercised for more than 60 minutes received a $2 coupon for a yogurt smoothie. Members who exercised for fewer than 60 minutes received a $0.50 coupon for a yogurt smoothie. How many more members received $2 coupons than $0.50 coupons?

Ⓐ 8　　Ⓒ 9

Ⓑ 17　　Ⓓ 1

13. What is the volume of the rectangular prism?

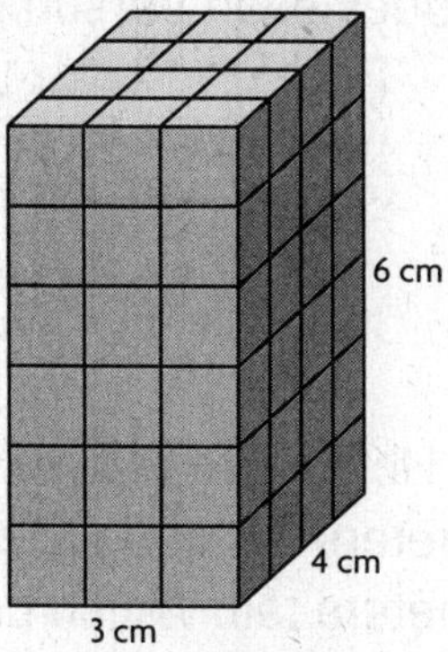

Ⓐ 18 cubic centimeters

Ⓑ 30 cubic centimeters

Ⓒ 13 cubic centimeters

Ⓓ 72 cubic centimeters

14. Victor built a rectangular prism with centimeter cubes. He used 9 centimeter cubes to make the bottom layer. If the prism was built with a total of 36 cubes, how many layers does the prism have?

Ⓐ 4　　Ⓒ 3

Ⓑ 8　　Ⓓ 6

15. Patrice walks from her classroom to the gym. She has walked 32.25 meters so far and has 52.85 meters left to walk. How far is Patrice's classroom from the gym?

Ⓐ 844.10 meters　　Ⓒ 84.50 meters

Ⓑ 85.10 meters　　Ⓓ 20.60 meters

GO ON

16. Two friends share $\frac{1}{3}$ of a pitcher of lemonade equally. What fraction of the pitcher does each person get?

Ⓐ $\frac{1}{4}$ Ⓑ $1\frac{1}{2}$ Ⓒ $\frac{1}{12}$ Ⓓ $\frac{1}{6}$

17. Avi and Helen are sisters. Avi is 1.249 meters tall and Helen is 1.429 meters tall. Which correctly compares the heights of the sisters?

Ⓐ $1.249 < 1.429$

Ⓑ $1.249 > 1.429$

Ⓒ $1.429 < 1.249$

Ⓓ $1.429 = 1.249$

18. Which model represents the expression?

$$\frac{3}{8} \times 16$$

Ⓐ 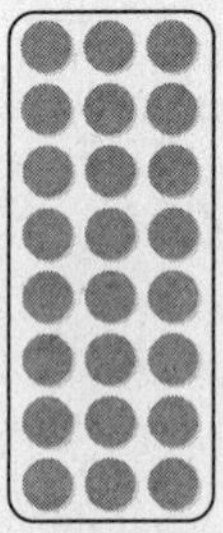

Ⓑ 

Ⓒ 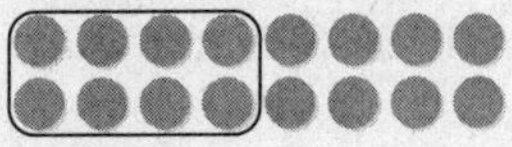

Ⓓ 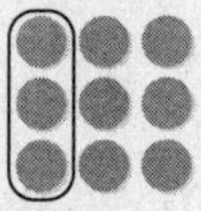

19. A carpenter uses 3 feet of wood to make each of 2 small stools and 5 feet of wood to make each of 3 medium stools. Then she uses 10 feet of wood to make a bench.

Which equation shows how to find *w*, the number of feet of wood used in all?

Ⓐ $2 \times 3 + 3 \times 5 \times 10 = w$

Ⓑ $2 \times 3 + 3 \times 5 - 10 = w$

Ⓒ $2 \times 3 + 3 \times 5 + 10 = w$

Ⓓ $2 + 3 \times 3 + 5 + 10 = w$

20. The rule for the pattern in the table is $p = f + 2$, where p is the output, the number of pentagons, and f is the input, the figure number.

Figure Number, *f*	1	2	3	4
Number of Pentagons, *p*	3	4	5	6

Rashad graphs the data from the table. Which ordered pair represents the point showing the number of pentagons in Figure 3?

Ⓐ (1, 3)

Ⓑ (4, 3)

Ⓒ (3, 5)

Ⓓ (3, 3)

GO ON

21. Which expression has a value of 4?

Ⓐ $(18 \div 3) + (6 \times 2)$

Ⓑ $(18 + 6) \div (2 \times 3)$

Ⓒ $6 + (18 \div 3) \times 2$

Ⓓ $(6 \times 3) + (18 \div 2)$

22. Which is the best estimate of $2.09 - 0.82$?

Ⓐ 4

Ⓑ 3

Ⓒ 0.5

Ⓓ 1

23. Which rule describes the pattern in the graph?

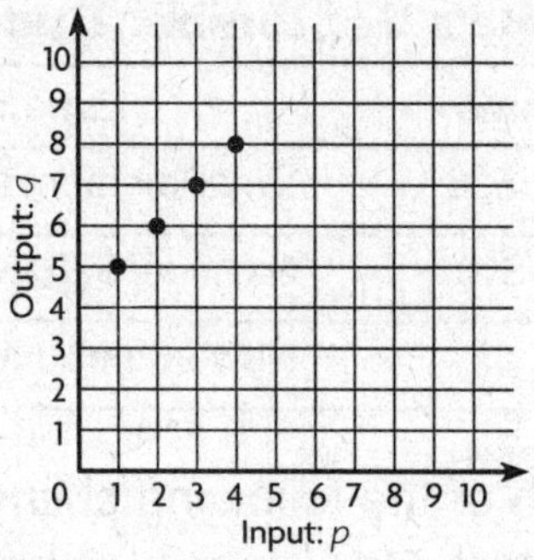

Ⓐ $p = q + 4$

Ⓑ $q = p + 4$

Ⓒ $p = 4q$

Ⓓ $q = 4p$

24. Sita and 3 friends gave a presentation that lasted a total of 5.40 minutes. If each presenter spoke for the same amount of time, which quick picture shows the amount of time each person spoke?

Ⓐ 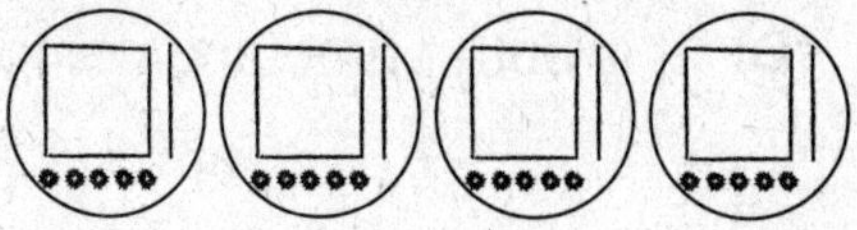

Ⓑ 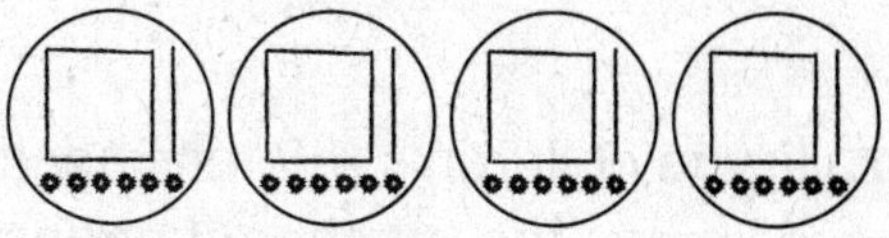

Ⓒ 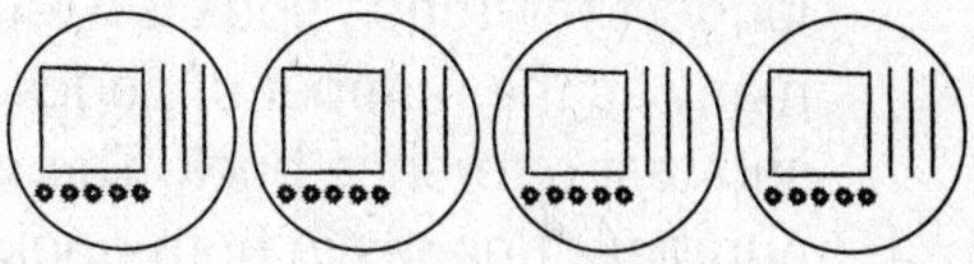

Ⓓ 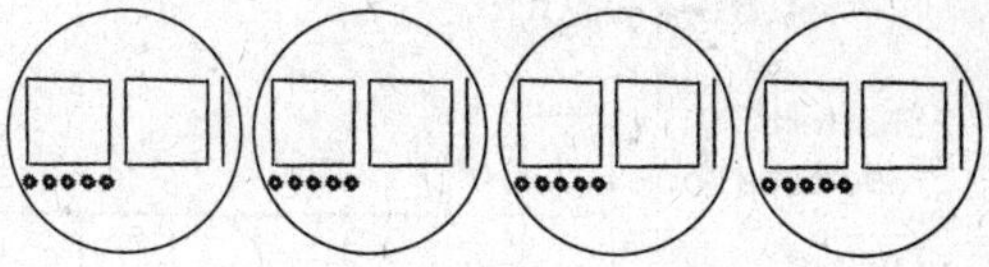

25. Yuri has 8 cups of raisins. He uses $\frac{1}{3}$ cup of raisins for each bag of snack mix. How many bags of snack mix can Yuri make with the raisins?

Ⓐ 16

Ⓑ 18

Ⓒ 11

Ⓓ 24

GO ON

26. Which statement about 51 is true?

Ⓐ It is prime.

Ⓑ It is composite.

Ⓒ It is neither prime nor composite.

Ⓓ It is both prime and composite.

27. In the children's reference section of a library, the number of pages in the longest reference book is 13 times as many as the number of pages in the shortest reference book. The combined number of pages in both books is 1,904 pages.

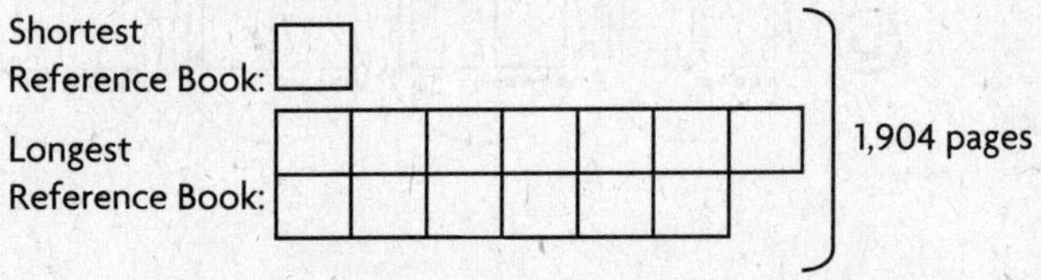

How many pages are in the shortest reference book?

Record your answer and fill in the bubbles on the grid. Be sure to use the correct place value.

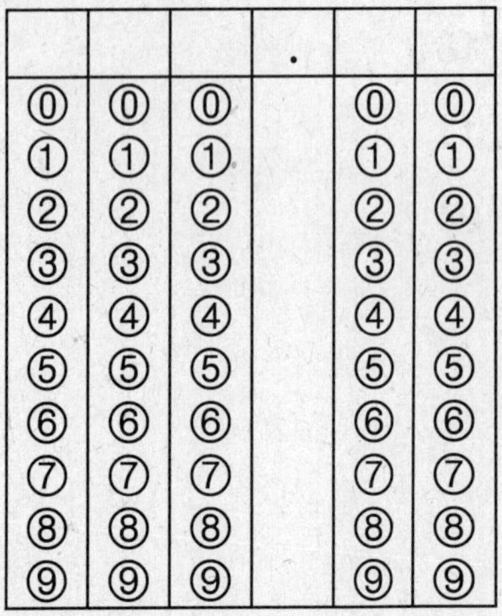

28. Javier earned $820 dollars this week. His net income was $683.20. He paid $95.60 in federal income tax. How much did Javier pay in state income taxes if only federal and state income taxes were taken out of his check?

Ⓐ $95.60 Ⓒ $820.00

Ⓑ $778.80 Ⓓ $41.20

29. Bo used $\frac{3}{10}$ of a package of notepaper to write a history report. He used $\frac{2}{5}$ of the same package of notepaper to write a science report. How much of the package of notepaper did Bo use to write reports?

Ⓐ $\frac{5}{10}$ Ⓑ $\frac{1}{10}$ Ⓒ $\frac{7}{10}$ Ⓓ $\frac{6}{10}$

30. Cole made a chart to keep track of his money.

Cole's September Budget	
Income	**Expenses**
Allowance: $36	Entertainment fund: $12
Yard work: $10	Savings: $20
	New swim trunks: $18

Which of the following changes should Cole make to balance his budget?

Ⓐ Increase yard work income by $4.

Ⓑ Decrease allowance by $2.

Ⓒ Increase savings by $4.

Ⓓ Decrease entertainment fund by $2.

GO ON

31. Hannah plots a point to represent the ordered pair (2, 9). Which describes how to locate this point on a coordinate grid?

Ⓐ Move 2 units to the right of the origin and then 9 units up.

Ⓑ Move 9 units up from the origin and then 2 units to the right.

Ⓒ Move 9 units up from the origin and then 2 units to the left.

Ⓓ Move 2 units to the right of the origin and then 9 units down.

32. Kyle uses inch cubes to build a rectangular prism.

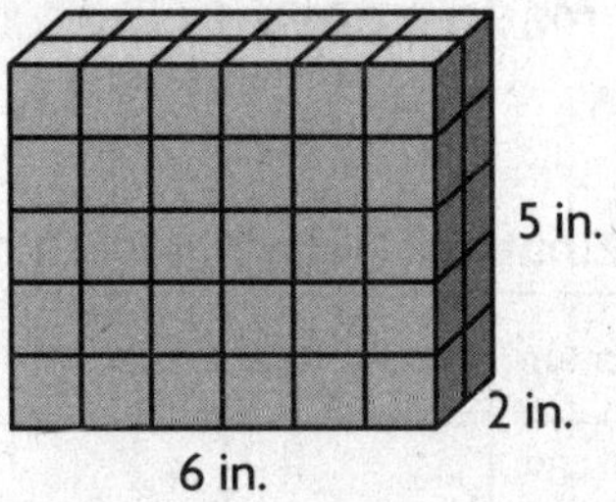

Which equation can Kyle use to find the volume of the rectangular prism?

Ⓐ $V = 6 + 2 + 5$

Ⓑ $V = 6 \times 2 \times 5$

Ⓒ $V = 6 \times 2$

Ⓓ $V = 8 \times 5$

33. Earl read about a pinecone that measured 9.267 centimeters long. What is the length of the pinecone rounded to the nearest hundredth?

Ⓐ 9.26 centimeters

Ⓑ 9 centimeters

Ⓒ 9.27 centimeters

Ⓓ 9.3 centimeters

34. Members of a nature club hiked 98.23 miles during an 11-day hiking trip. What was the average distance the members hiked daily?

Ⓐ 8.93 miles

Ⓑ 11 miles

Ⓒ 0.8 mile

Ⓓ 19 miles

35. Volunteers pack 6,045 donated books in boxes. They put 93 books in each box. How many boxes were packed with books?

Record your answer and fill in the bubbles on the grid. Be sure to use the correct place value.

			.		
⓪	⓪	⓪		⓪	⓪
①	①	①		①	①
②	②	②		②	②
③	③	③		③	③
④	④	④		④	④
⑤	⑤	⑤		⑤	⑤
⑥	⑥	⑥		⑥	⑥
⑦	⑦	⑦		⑦	⑦
⑧	⑧	⑧		⑧	⑧
⑨	⑨	⑨		⑨	⑨

GO ON

Name ________________________________

36. Jan draws a picture of a rectangular prism.

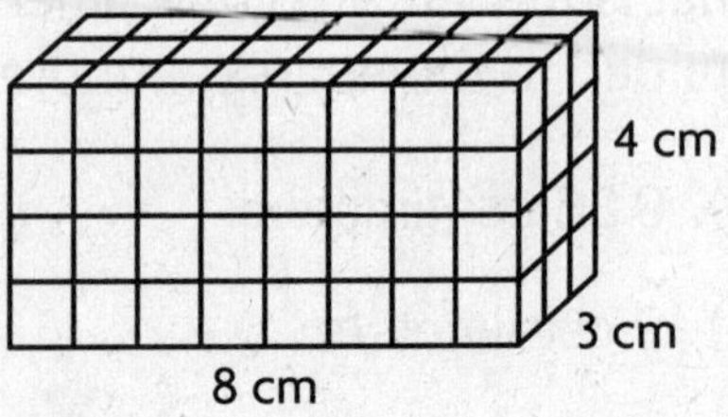

Which equation can Jan use to find the volume of the prism?

Ⓐ $V = 24 \times 4$

Ⓑ $V = (2 \times 8) + (2 \times 3)$

Ⓒ $V = 11 \times 4$

Ⓓ $V = 8 + 3 + 4$

37. What is the value of *m* in the equation?

$$2 \times 9 + 6 - 4 = m$$

Record your answer and fill in the bubbles on the grid. Be sure to use the correct place value.

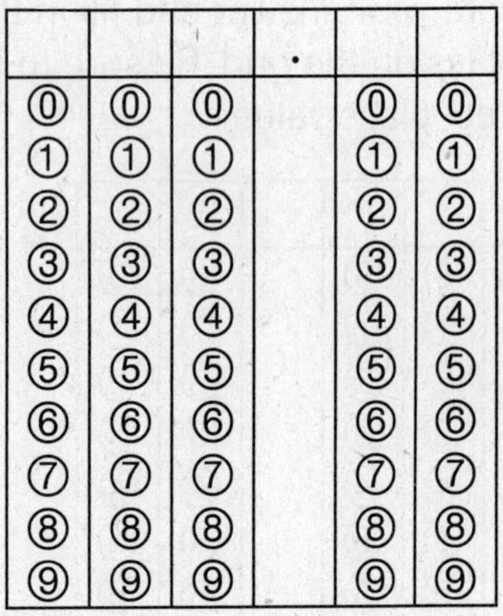

38. Which decimal is greater than 7.314?

Ⓐ 7.031 Ⓒ 7.301

Ⓑ 7.321 Ⓓ 7.187

39. Nigel's net monthly income is $2,100. He pays $450 each month in income tax. If only income tax is taken out of his check, what is his gross monthly income?

Ⓐ $900 Ⓒ $1,650

Ⓑ $2,550 Ⓓ $2,100

40. Clara made a chart to keep track of her money.

Clara's Financial Record: Month of October

Date	Description	Received ($)	Expenses ($)	Available Funds ($)
	Balance: end of September			0
7	allowance	40		40
10	prize	5		45
11	gift		8.37	36.63
12	party supplies		11.25	25.38
15	running errands	?		44.13

How much money does Clara earn from running errands?

Ⓐ $25.38 Ⓒ $18.75

Ⓑ $14.13 Ⓓ $44.13

GO ON

41. Eric made $\frac{3}{4}$ pound of potato salad for dinner. After dinner, $\frac{1}{3}$ pound of the potato salad is left. How much potato salad was eaten at dinner?

Ⓐ $\frac{1}{2}$ pound

Ⓑ $\frac{5}{12}$ pound

Ⓒ $\frac{4}{12}$ pound

Ⓓ $\frac{2}{3}$ pound

42. An intern at an animal shelter serves 36 eight-ounce portions of dog food to the dogs boarded at the shelter. How many pounds of dog food does the intern serve?

Ⓐ 9 pounds

Ⓑ 4 pounds

Ⓒ 72 pounds

Ⓓ 18 pounds

43. A cookie recipe calls for $\frac{7}{8}$ cup of peanuts and $\frac{4}{5}$ cup of walnuts. Which is the best estimate for the total amount of nuts used in the recipe?

Ⓐ 4 cups

Ⓑ $\frac{1}{2}$ cup

Ⓒ 2 cups

Ⓓ 3 cups

Use the data for 44–45.

Books Read

mystery	history	science	mystery	science
science	science	poetry	how-to	poetry
science	poetry	history	history	science
history	mystery	science	mystery	poetry
poetry	science	poetry	mystery	history
history	history	how-to	science	how-to

Books Read

Type of Book	Frequency
History	7
How-To	3
Mystery	5
Poetry	6
Science	?

44. Amina kept track of the types of books she read over the year. She uses the data to create a frequency table. How many science books did Amina read?

Ⓐ 9

Ⓑ 8

Ⓒ 10

Ⓓ 6

45. How many more history and poetry books did Amina read than how-to and mystery books?

Ⓐ 13

Ⓑ 5

Ⓒ 21

Ⓓ 8

GO ON

46. A bakery displays 24 oatmeal cookies and three times as many chocolate chip cookies. The cookies are arranged on 6 different display shelves with the same number of cookies on each shelf.

Which expression represents the number of cookies displayed on each shelf?

Ⓐ [24 × (6 × 24)] ÷ 3

Ⓑ [24 + (3 × 24)] ÷ 6

Ⓒ [24 × (6 + 24)] ÷ 3

Ⓓ 24 + [(3 × 24)] ÷ 6

47. Ms. Sarabhai wants to purchase a watch online. If she pays using an online payment method, she will need to make 3 payments of $40 each, with a $1.50 fee for each payment. What does Ms. Sarabhai pay in fees if she uses the online payment method?

Ⓐ $124.50

Ⓑ $1.50

Ⓒ $4.50

Ⓓ $120.00

48. Tal is making breakfast for his family. He has 5 cartons of eggs. He uses $\frac{1}{4}$ of the cartons. How many total cartons of eggs does Tal use?

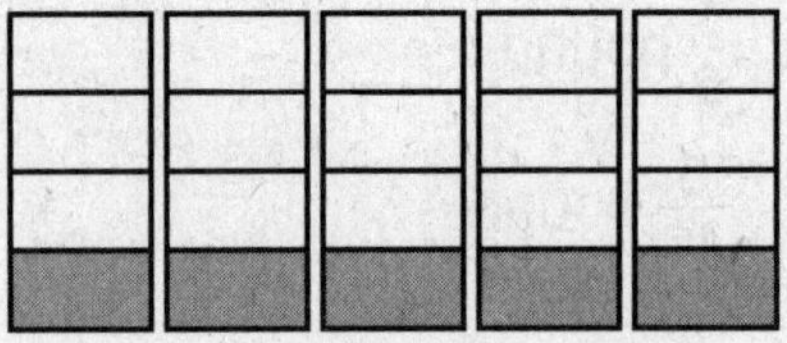

Ⓐ $1\frac{1}{4}$

Ⓑ $\frac{3}{4}$

Ⓒ $1\frac{1}{2}$

Ⓓ 2

49. Which multiplication problem can be solved using the quick picture?

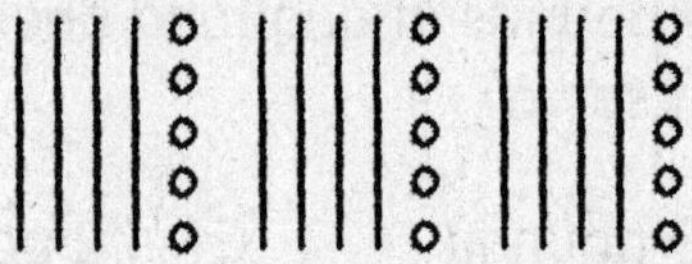

Ⓐ 4 × 0.35

Ⓑ 0.3 × 45

Ⓒ 0.3 × 0.45

Ⓓ 3 × 0.45

50. There are 237 yards of twine on one spool. If each spool contains the same amount of twine, how many yards of twine are there on 18 spools?

Ⓐ 4,266 yards

Ⓑ 3,176 yards

Ⓒ 1,896 yards

Ⓓ 3,526 yards

STOP

Fill in the bubble for the correct answer.

1. Xiu used the Distributive Property to find the product 3×0.74. Which expression did Xiu write?

Ⓐ $(3 \times 0.07) + (3 \times 0.04)$

Ⓑ $(3 \times 0.7) + (3 \times 0.04)$

Ⓒ $(3 \times 1) + (3 \times 0.74)$

Ⓓ $(3 \times 7) + (3 \times 4)$

2. Chris drew a model to represent a problem. Which division expression does his model represent?

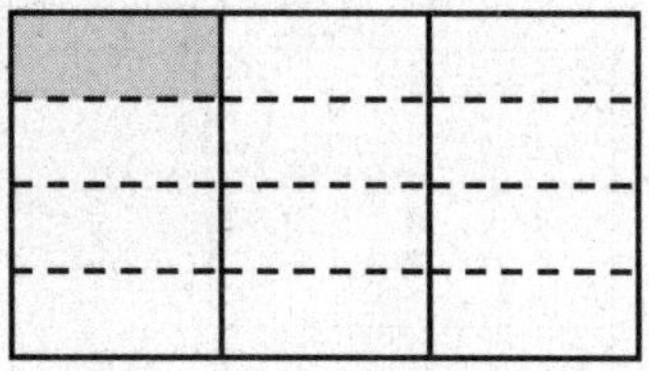

Ⓐ $\frac{1}{3} \div 4$

Ⓑ $\frac{1}{12} \div 4$

Ⓒ $1 \div \frac{1}{3}$

Ⓓ $\frac{1}{3} \div 2$

3. Wendy's puppy weighs 5.273 ounces. What is 5.273 rounded to the nearest tenth?

Ⓐ 5.28

Ⓑ 5.26

Ⓒ 5.2

Ⓓ 5.3

4. Which statement about a coordinate grid is true?

Ⓐ The vertical number line is the *x*-axis.

Ⓑ The horizontal number line is the *y*-axis.

Ⓒ The *x*-axis and *y*-axis intersect at the origin.

Ⓓ The origin is located at the point (1, 1).

5. Erin drew a Venn diagram to classify different kinds of polygons.

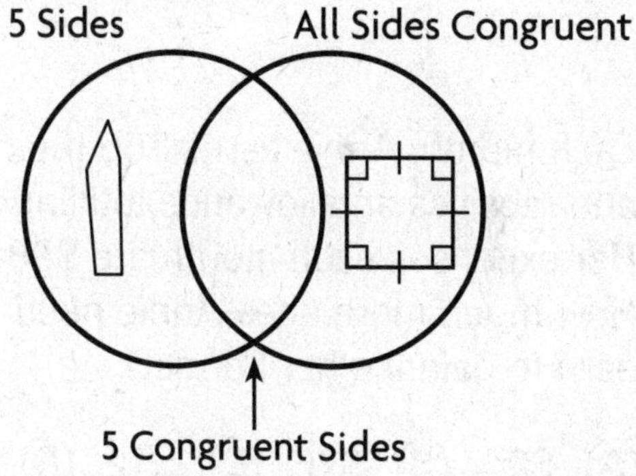

Which figure belongs in the section of the Venn diagram labeled "5 Congruent Sides"?

Ⓐ 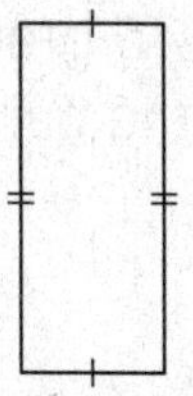

Ⓒ 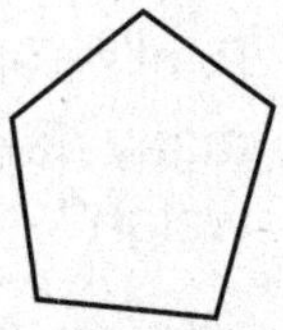

Ⓑ 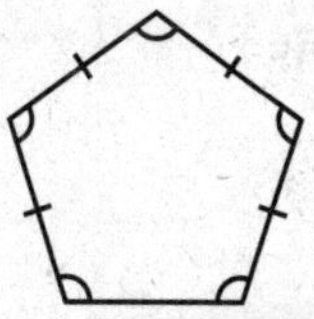

Ⓓ 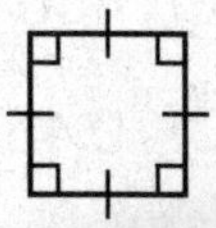

GO ON

Name ____________________________________

6. A food vendor interviews visitors at a state fair. He records the time they spent at the fair and the amount of money they spent on food. He wants to display the information on a scatter plot.

Spending at the State Fair						
Amount of Time (hr)	1	4	3	1	2	3
Amount of Money ($)	15	96	58	18	30	52

Which ordered pair would **NOT** be plotted on a scatter plot of the data?

Ⓐ (4, 96) Ⓒ (2, 30)

Ⓑ (1, 18) Ⓓ (3, 55)

7. Each month, Annie earns $56 tutoring and receives an allowance totaling $20. Her expenses each month are $88. How much more does Annie need to earn to balance her budget?

Ⓐ $24 Ⓑ $76 Ⓒ $12 Ⓓ $40

8. Paul's parakeet weighs 45 grams. How many dekagrams does the parakeet weigh?

Ⓐ 4.5 dekagrams

Ⓑ 450 dekagrams

Ⓒ 0.45 dekagrams

Ⓓ 45 dekagrams

9. The table uses the rule $u = v + 5$.

Input	v	1	2	3	4
Output	u				

Which set of numbers correctly completes the output values in the table?

Ⓐ 5, 10, 15, 20 Ⓒ 8, 9, 10, 11

Ⓑ 4, 3, 2, 1 Ⓓ 6, 7, 8, 9

10. Jen subtracts $\frac{1}{8}$ from $\frac{1}{2}$. Which model could she use to help find the difference?

Ⓐ
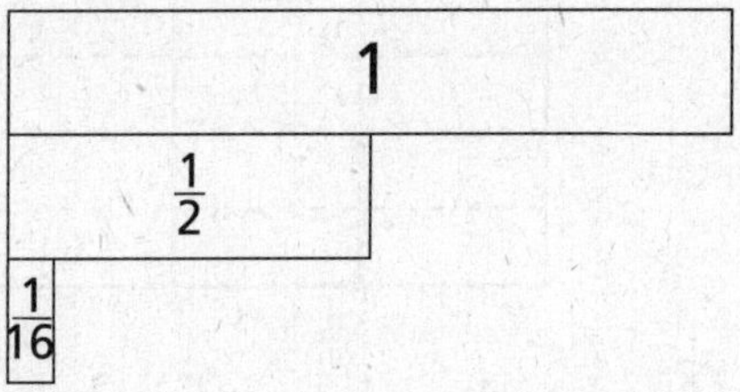

Ⓑ
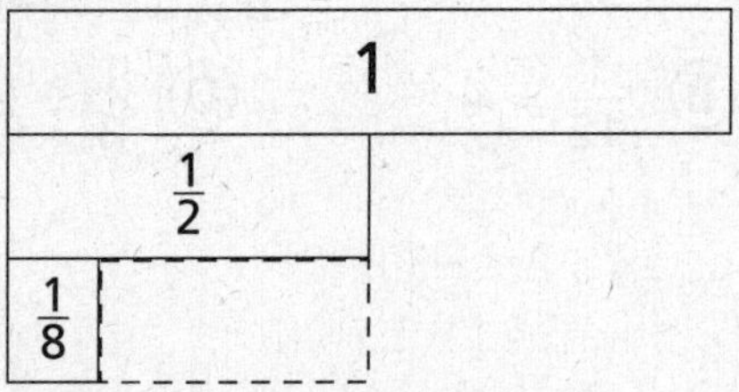

Ⓒ
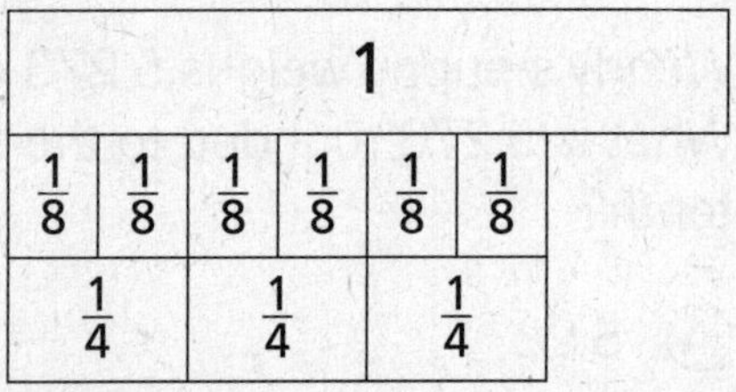

Ⓓ
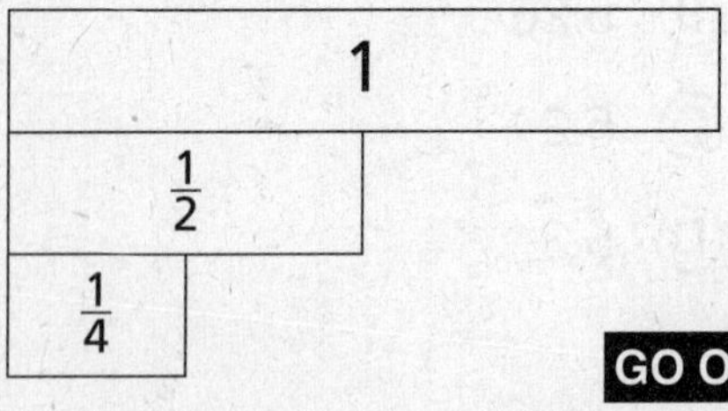

GO ON

11. A dime has a mass of about 0.002 kilograms. What is the value of 2 in 0.002?

Ⓐ 2 thousandths

Ⓑ 2 hundredths

Ⓒ 2 tenths

Ⓓ 2 hundreds

12. Ms. Campbell asked students to vote on their favorite type of movie. She made a frequency table of the data.

Favorite Type of Movie	
Type of Movie	**Frequency**
Adventure	15
Comedy	11
Documentary	4
Animated	7
Science Fiction	18

How many more students voted for Science Fiction and Animated than for Comedy and Documentary?

Record your answer and fill in the bubbles on the grid. Be sure to use the correct place value.

			.		
⓪	⓪	⓪		⓪	⓪
①	①	①		①	①
②	②	②		②	②
③	③	③		③	③
④	④	④		④	④
⑤	⑤	⑤		⑤	⑤
⑥	⑥	⑥		⑥	⑥
⑦	⑦	⑦		⑦	⑦
⑧	⑧	⑧		⑧	⑧
⑨	⑨	⑨		⑨	⑨

13. What is the perimeter of the square?

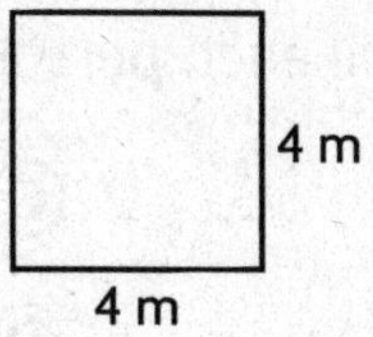

Ⓐ 16 meters

Ⓑ 32 meters

Ⓒ 8 meters

Ⓓ 12 meters

14. Greg built a rectangular prism with inch cubes. He used 12 inch cubes to make the bottom layer. If the prism was built with a total of 72 cubes, how many layers does Greg's prism have?

Ⓐ 40

Ⓑ 60

Ⓒ 4

Ⓓ 6

15. Ms. Green had a starting balance of $593.27 in her bank account. How much money does Ms. Green have left after she spends $81.75 of the money in her account?

Ⓐ $675.02

Ⓑ $502.72

Ⓒ $511.52

Ⓓ $312.48

GO ON

Name ____________________

16. Four friends share $\frac{1}{4}$ of a bag of baby carrots. What fraction of the bag of carrots will each person get?

Ⓐ $\frac{1}{16}$

Ⓑ $\frac{3}{4}$

Ⓒ $\frac{1}{7}$

Ⓓ $\frac{1}{12}$

17. Which correctly compares the decimals 4.279 and 4.28?

Ⓐ $4.279 > 4.28$

Ⓑ $4.28 < 4.279$

Ⓒ $4.28 > 4.279$

Ⓓ $4.28 = 4.279$

18. Dean draws a model to help him multiply a whole number and a fraction. Which multiplication expression does his model represent?

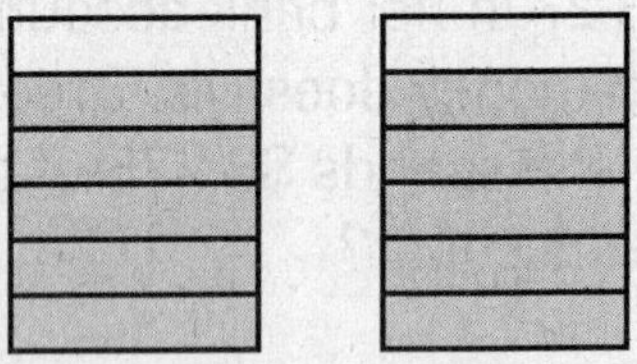

Ⓐ $6 \times \frac{2}{5}$

Ⓑ $2 \times \frac{10}{6}$

Ⓒ $2 \times \frac{5}{6}$

Ⓓ $2 \times \frac{1}{5}$

19. Maria buys 4 sheets of 10 stamps each and 5 sheets of 8 stamps each. She uses 34 of the stamps on envelopes.

Which equation shows how to find *s*, the number of stamps Maria has left?

Ⓐ $4 + 10 \times 5 + 8 + 34 = s$

Ⓑ $4 \times 10 + 5 \times 8 - 34 = s$

Ⓒ $4 + 10 \times 5 + 8 - 34 = s$

Ⓓ $4 \times 10 + 5 \times 8 + 34 = s$

20. The rule for the pattern in the table is $b = l + 3$, where *b* is the output, the number of bonus points, and *l* is the input, the level of the game.

Game Level, *l*	1	2	3	4
Number of Bonus Points, *b*	4	5	6	7

Carolyn graphs the data from the table. Which ordered pair represents the point showing the number of bonus points awarded at Level 4?

Ⓐ (2, 10)

Ⓑ (7, 7)

Ⓒ (4, 1)

Ⓓ (4, 7)

GO ON

21. What is the value of the expression?

16 ÷ [(13 + 7) − (12 + 4)]

Ⓐ 4
Ⓑ 28
Ⓒ 2
Ⓓ 16

22. Which is the best estimate of 2.8 × 1.2?

Ⓐ 1
Ⓑ 3
Ⓒ 30
Ⓓ 7

23. Which rule describes the pattern in the graph?

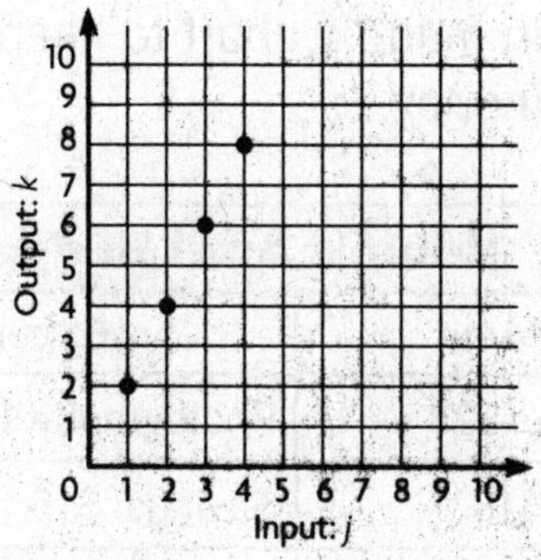

Ⓐ $j = k + 2$
Ⓑ $k = j + 2$
Ⓒ $k = 2j$
Ⓓ $j = 2k$

24. Wes has a length of hose that is 7.16 meters long. He cuts the hose into 4 equal pieces.

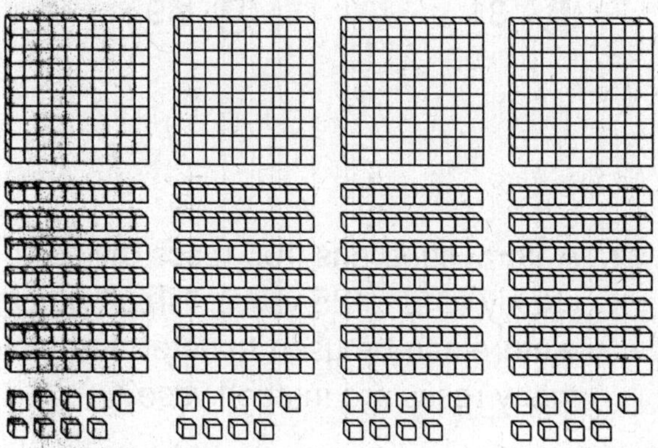

How long is each piece of hose?

Ⓐ 3.16 meters
Ⓑ 4.97 meters
Ⓒ 1.79 meters
Ⓓ 1.37 meters

25. Gina has 7 cups of apple juice. She uses $\frac{1}{4}$ cup of apple juice in each serving of fruit punch. How many servings of punch can Gina make with the apple juice?

Ⓐ 3
Ⓑ 28
Ⓒ 11
Ⓓ 16

GO ON

26. Which is a prime number?

Ⓐ 27 Ⓒ 39

Ⓑ 81 Ⓓ 89

27. A floral shop has 400 roses divided evenly among 25 vases. Which quick picture can be used to determine how many roses are in each vase?

Ⓐ
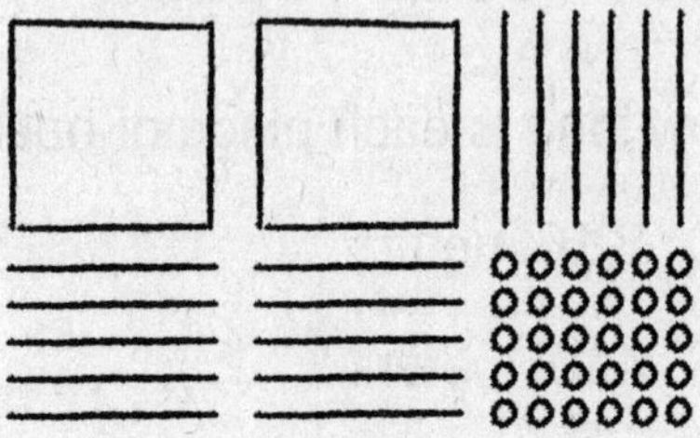

Ⓑ
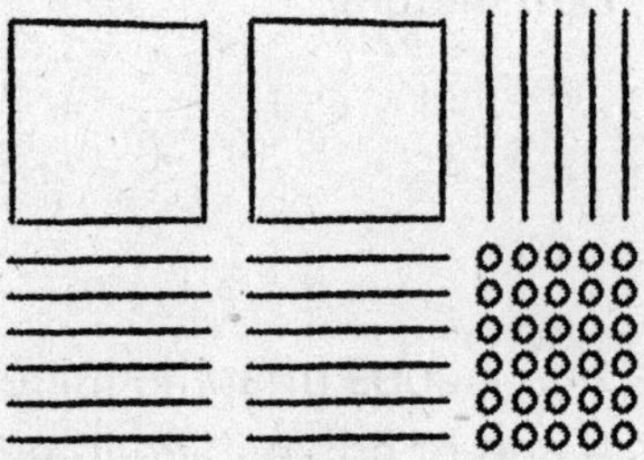

Ⓒ
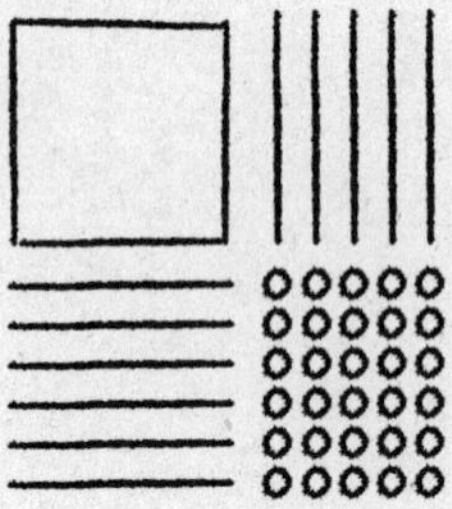

Ⓓ
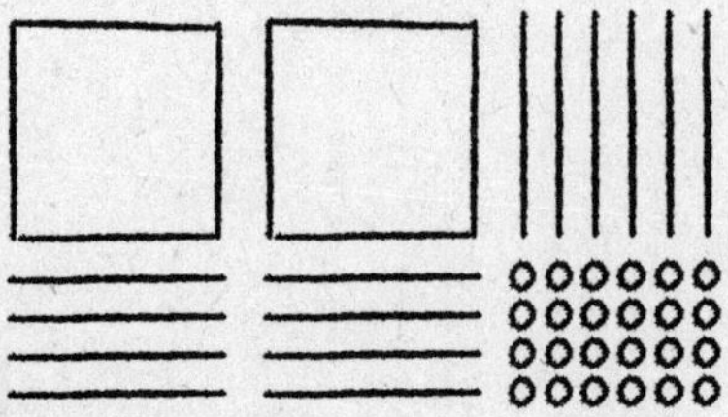

28. Tony pays $0.08 in sales tax for every $1 that he spends. If Tony spends $70, how much will he pay, including sales tax?

Ⓐ $75.60 Ⓒ $5.60

Ⓑ $70.08 Ⓓ $64.40

29. Noah filled $\frac{1}{3}$ of his plate with pasta and $\frac{1}{2}$ of the plate with vegetables. He left the rest of the plate empty. How much of his plate did Noah fill with food?

Ⓐ $\frac{5}{6}$ Ⓑ $\frac{2}{5}$ Ⓒ $\frac{1}{6}$ Ⓓ $\frac{1}{5}$

30. Robin made a chart to keep track of her money.

Robin's April Budget	
Income	**Expenses**
Allowance: $28	Photography supplies: $27
Tutoring: $18	Savings: $15
	Stationery: $9

Which of the following changes should Robin make to balance her budget?

Ⓐ Increase savings by $5.

Ⓑ Decrease allowance by $5.

Ⓒ Decrease photography supplies purchase by $5.

Ⓓ Decrease tutoring income by $5.

GO ON

31. Amanda plots a point to represent the ordered pair (4, 6). Which describes how to locate this point on a coordinate grid?

Ⓐ Move 4 units to the right of the origin and then 6 units to the left.

Ⓑ Move 4 units up from the origin and then 6 units to the right.

Ⓒ Move 4 units to the right of the origin and then 6 units up.

Ⓓ Move 6 units to the right of the origin and then 4 units down.

32. Rebekah drew a rectangle.

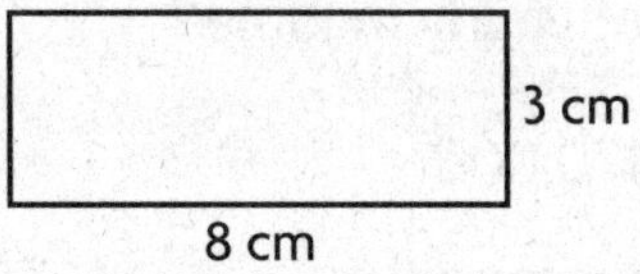

Which equation represents the area of the rectangle?

Ⓐ $A = 2 \times 8 + 3$

Ⓑ $A = 8 + 3 + 8 + 3$

Ⓒ $A = 8 + 3$

Ⓓ $A = 8 \times 3$

33. A young Monarch caterpillar measures about 0.236 inch long. What is the length of the caterpillar rounded to the nearest hundredth?

Ⓐ 0.24 inch　　Ⓒ 0.23 inch

Ⓑ 0.2 inch　　Ⓓ 0.3 inch

34. Mr. Cortez spent 17.4 minutes folding 100 flyers. If he spent the same amount of time folding each flyer, how many minutes did it take Mr. Cortez to fold 10 flyers?

Ⓐ 1.74 minutes　　Ⓒ 17.4 minutes

Ⓑ 0.174 minute　　Ⓓ 174 minutes

35. Pet store workers need to place 2,204 fish into fish tanks with 58 fish in each tank. How many tanks are needed to hold all of the fish?

Record your answer and fill in the bubbles on the grid. Be sure to use the correct place value.

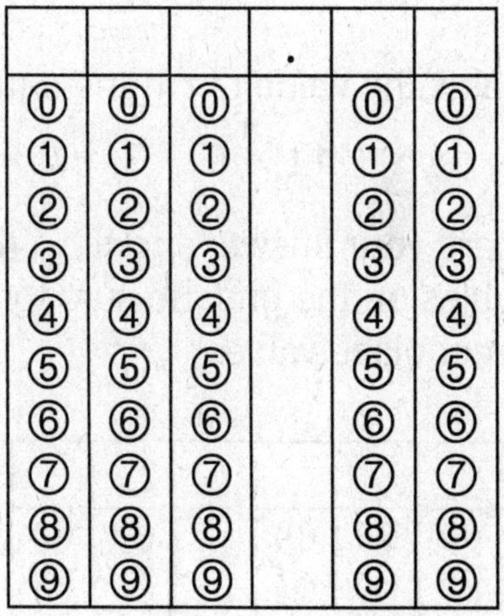

GO ON

Name ____________________

36. Ned uses centimeter cubes to build a rectangular prism.

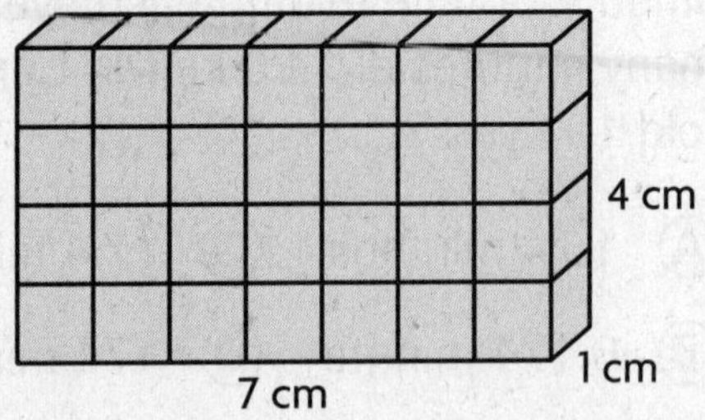

Which equation can Ned use to find the volume of the rectangular prism?

Ⓐ $V = 7 + 1 + 4$

Ⓑ $V = (2 \times 7) + (2 \times 4)$

Ⓒ $V = 7 \times 1 \times 4$

Ⓓ $V = 7 \times 1$

37. What is the value of *t* in the equation?

$$5 + 11 \times 6 - 3 = t$$

Record your answer and fill in the bubbles on the grid. Be sure to use the correct place value.

			.		
⓪	⓪	⓪		⓪	⓪
①	①	①		①	①
②	②	②		②	②
③	③	③		③	③
④	④	④		④	④
⑤	⑤	⑤		⑤	⑤
⑥	⑥	⑥		⑥	⑥
⑦	⑦	⑦		⑦	⑦
⑧	⑧	⑧		⑧	⑧
⑨	⑨	⑨		⑨	⑨

38. Team A traveled 21.459 miles to the game. Team B traveled 21.542 miles to the same game. Which expression correctly compares the distances the teams traveled?

Ⓐ $21.459 > 21.542$

Ⓑ $21.542 < 21.459$

Ⓒ $21.542 = 21.459$

Ⓓ $21.459 < 21.542$

39. Sharon's gross yearly income is $55,000. She pays $15,000 in taxes each year. If this is the only money taken out of Sharon's checks, what is her net yearly income?

Ⓐ $70,000

Ⓑ $40,000

Ⓒ $50,000

Ⓓ $15,000

GO ON

40. Ravi made a chart to keep track of his money.

Ravi's Financial Record: Month of February

Date	Description	Received ($)	Expenses ($)	Available Funds ($)
	Balance: end of January			0
1	allowance	50		50
5	hat		12.59	37.41
8	shovel snow	15		52.41
11	art supplies		8.37	44.04
17	music downloads		11.93	32.11

Which expression can be used to find how much Ravi has in available funds after he receives payment for shoveling snow?

Ⓐ \$12.59 + \$15 Ⓒ \$37.41 + \$15

Ⓑ \$37.41 − \$15 Ⓓ \$52.41 − \$15

41. Elise wants to add $\frac{1}{3} + \left(\frac{1}{3} + \frac{3}{4}\right)$. She rewrites the problem as $\left(\frac{1}{3} + \frac{1}{3}\right) + \frac{3}{4}$. Which property does Elise use to find the sum?

Ⓐ Identity Ⓒ Commutative

Ⓑ Associative Ⓓ Distributive

42. Ms. Perkins needs to fill 19 fish tanks that each hold 2 gallons of water. How many quarts of water does she need?

Ⓐ 76 quarts Ⓒ 152 quarts

Ⓑ 38 quarts Ⓓ 57 quarts

43. It is 15.952 miles from Kate's house to the soccer stadium. Kate and her family have driven 10.708 miles so far. About how many more miles do they need to drive to reach the soccer stadium?

Ⓐ 5 miles Ⓒ 27 miles

Ⓑ 15 miles Ⓓ 1 mile

Use the stem-and-leaf plot for 44–45.

Lengths of Cats (cm)

Stem	Leaf
3	
4	2 4 6 6 7 9
5	0 1 1

4|2 represents 42.

44. At the animal shelter, Megan records the lengths of the cats. In centimeters, the lengths are: 46, 42, 38, 50, 33, 46, 47, 51, 30, 44, 51, 37, 49. Megan is making a stem-and-leaf plot of the data.

What are the leaves for stem 3?

Ⓐ 0, 3, 8 Ⓒ 0, 3, 7, 8

Ⓑ 3, 4, 5 Ⓓ 6, 6, 7, 9

45. How many more cats are longer than 46 centimeters than are exactly 46 centimeters?

Ⓐ 5 Ⓑ 2 Ⓒ 8 Ⓓ 3

GO ON

46. Tina collects 12 eggs from her family's chickens and gives 4 of the eggs to a neighbor. She does this every day for 6 days.

Which expression matches the words?

Ⓐ $(12 - 4) \times 6$

Ⓑ $(12 - 4) + 6$

Ⓒ $(6 \times 12) - 4$

Ⓓ $6 \times (12 + 4)$

47. Ms. Ching sees a stereo she would like to buy. If Ms. Ching pays for the stereo with her credit card, she will pay \$890 plus \$71 in interest. If she pays with her debit card, she will pay \$890 with no interest fee. How much will Ms. Ching save by paying for the stereo with her debit card?

Ⓐ \$142 Ⓒ \$961

Ⓑ \$819 Ⓓ \$71

48. Ellen is making placemats. She has 8 rolls of lace. She uses $\frac{1}{6}$ of the rolls of lace to decorate the placemats. How much of the lace does Ellen use in all?

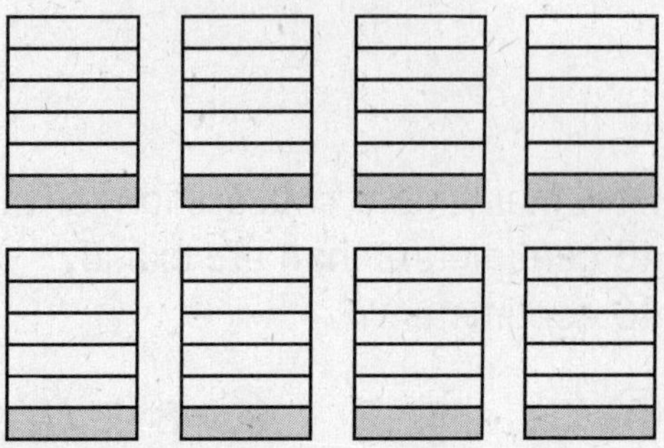

Ⓐ 3 rolls Ⓒ $1\frac{1}{4}$ rolls

Ⓑ $1\frac{2}{6}$ rolls Ⓓ 8 rolls

49. Jon swims for 0.45 minutes. Thea swims 3 times as long as Jon. Which model can be used to find the total amount of time Thea swims?

Ⓐ 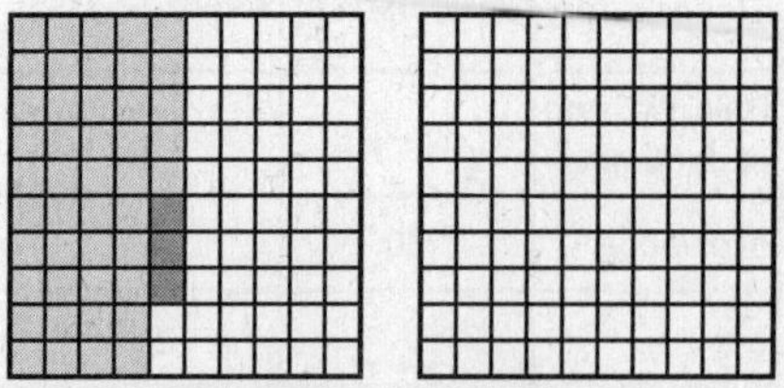

Ⓑ 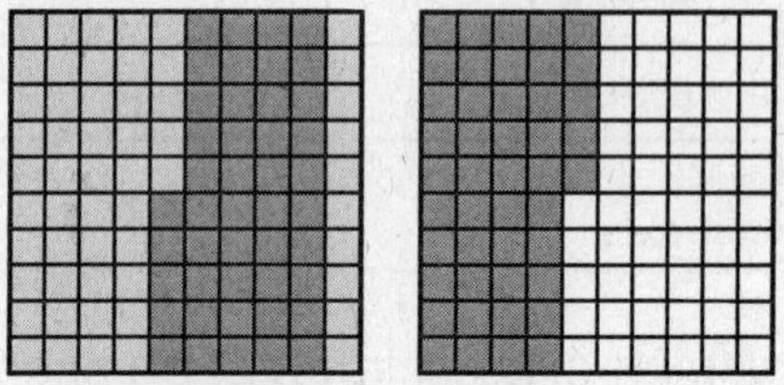

Ⓒ 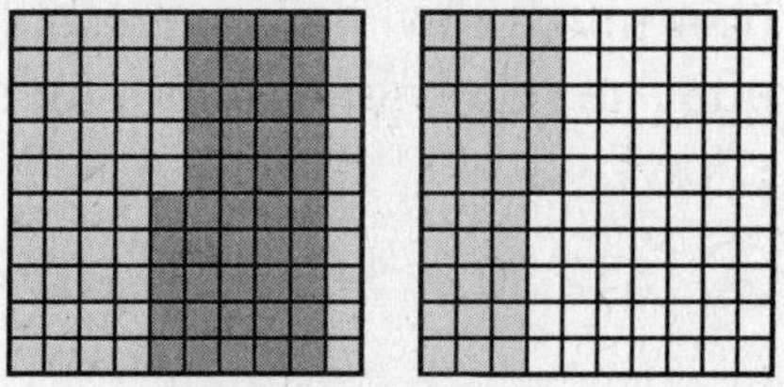

Ⓓ 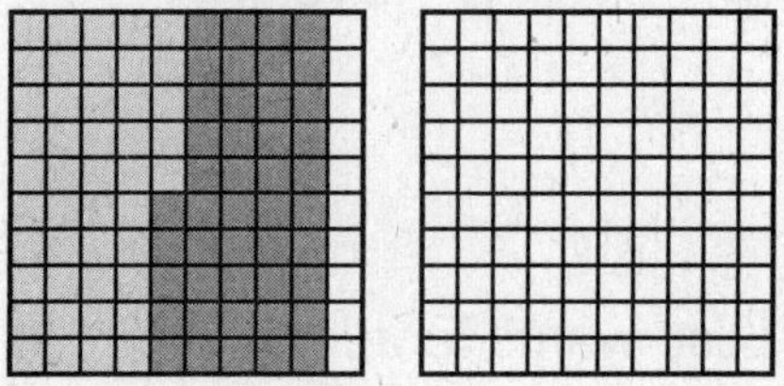

50. There are 249 calories in one serving of crackers. How many calories are there in 31 servings of crackers?

Ⓐ 996 calories

Ⓑ 7,500 calories

Ⓒ 7,719 calories

Ⓓ 9,086 calories

STOP

Name ______________________________

Fill in the bubble for the correct answer.

1. Which decimal is greater than 0.883?

Ⓐ 0.88

Ⓑ 0.338

Ⓒ 0.888

Ⓓ 0.833

2. Volunteers at a food pantry collected $575.26 in cash donations. They spent $95.15 on food. How much money from the donations is left?

Ⓐ $375.85

Ⓑ $225.11

Ⓒ $480.11

Ⓓ $105.75

3. Jaden biked 0.372 miles with his father. What is the distance biked rounded to the nearest hundredth?

Ⓐ 0.37 mile

Ⓑ 0.38 mile

Ⓒ 0.4 mile

Ⓓ 0.3 mile

4. Mr. Chang has $405.62 in his checking account. How much does he have after he spends $37.84?

Ⓐ $615.62

Ⓑ $367.78

Ⓒ $443.46

Ⓓ $247.84

5. Hiro builds a scale model of a bridge that measures 0.572 meter tall. What is 0.572 rounded to the nearest tenth?

Ⓐ 0.57

Ⓑ 0.5

Ⓒ 0.6

Ⓓ 1

GO ON

6. Which addition property is shown?
(6.17 + 2.35) + 9.65 = 6.17 + (2.35 + 9.65)

Ⓐ Associative Property of Addition

Ⓑ Commutative Property of Addition

Ⓒ Identity Property of Addition

Ⓓ Distributive Property

7. On Saturday Izzy hiked 4.252 kilometers, Laura hiked 4.214 kilometers, and Anna hiked 4.403 kilometers.

Which lists the girls in order of the distance they hiked from longest to shortest distance?

Ⓐ Anna, Laura, Izzy

Ⓑ Izzy, Laura, Anna

Ⓒ Laura, Izzy, Anna

Ⓓ Anna, Izzy, Laura

8. At her first swim lesson, Leah swam for 15.218 seconds without stopping. After her second lesson she could swim for 57.907 seconds without stopping. About how many more seconds could Leah swim without stopping after her second lesson?

Ⓐ 60 seconds

Ⓑ 33 seconds

Ⓒ 43 seconds

Ⓓ 55 seconds

9. A teacher's desk is 0.725 meter long. What is the length of the desk rounded to the nearest hundredth?

Ⓐ 0.73 meter

Ⓑ 0.72 meter

Ⓒ 0.8 meter

Ⓓ 0.7 meter

10. It is 10.85 miles from Fred's house to the beach. Fred and his family have driven 8.10 miles so far. How many more miles do they need to drive before they reach the beach?

Ⓐ 18.95 miles

Ⓑ 2.75 miles

Ⓒ 12.65 miles

Ⓓ 7.25 miles

GO ON

11. A badminton shuttlecock has a mass of about 0.005 kilogram. What is the value of the digit 5 in this number?

Ⓐ 5 tenths

Ⓑ 5 thousandths

Ⓒ 5 hundredths

Ⓓ 5 ones

12. Dan has $50. At the camping store, he buys a water bottle, a cooler, and a can of bug spray.

Item	Price
Water bottle	$4.25
Bug spray	$11.90
Cooler	$18.34

Which is the best estimate of how much money Dan has left?

Ⓐ $20

Ⓑ $35

Ⓒ $25

Ⓓ $16

13. Which correctly compares the decimals 7.200 and 7.2?

Ⓐ $7.200 = 7.2$

Ⓑ $7.2 < 7.200$

Ⓒ $7.200 < 7.2$

Ⓓ $7.2 > 7.200$

14. Gilda rounds 0.258 to 0.26. To what place value does Gilda round?

Ⓐ Tenths

Ⓑ Ones

Ⓒ Thousandths

Ⓓ Hundredths

15. Which shows 1.267 written in expanded form?

Ⓐ $1 + 0.267$

Ⓑ $1.2 + 1.06 + 1.007$

Ⓒ $1 + 0.2 + 0.06 + 0.007$

Ⓓ $0.1 + 0.2 + 0.06 + 0.007$

GO ON

16. Mark used the Commutative Property to solve an equation.

$25 + (38 + 12) = 25 + (12 + \blacksquare)$

What is the unknown number in the equation?

Record your answer and fill in the bubbles on the grid. Be sure to use the correct place value.

			.		
0	0	0		0	0
1	1	1		1	1
2	2	2		2	2
3	3	3		3	3
4	4	4		4	4
5	5	5		5	5
6	6	6		6	6
7	7	7		7	7
8	8	8		8	8
9	9	9		9	9

17. Which shows 0.125 written in expanded form?

Ⓐ 0.1 + 0.02 + 0.005

Ⓑ 1.0 + 0.2 + 0.05

Ⓒ 0.1 + 0.02 + 0.05

Ⓓ 0.1 + 0.002 + 0.005

18. Ed has 3.75 pieces of pizza. He eats 1.50 slices. About how many slices of pizza does Ed have left?

Ⓐ 0.5 Ⓒ 5

Ⓑ 2 Ⓓ 2.75

19. Mr. Evans bought 4.55 pounds of green grapes and 2.65 pounds of red grapes. How many pounds of grapes did Mr. Evans buy in all?

Ⓐ 5.20 pounds

Ⓑ 9.25 pounds

Ⓒ 6.50 pounds

Ⓓ 7.20 pounds

20. Jenna used the Associative Property to write an expression equivalent to (0.32 + 4.55) + 6.45. Which expression did Jenna write?

Ⓐ $(6.4 \times 0.32) + (6.05 \times 4.55)$

Ⓑ 0.32 + (4.55 + 6.45)

Ⓒ 6.45 + 0.32 + 4.55

Ⓓ $0.32 \times (4.55 + 6.45)$

STOP

Fill in the bubble for the correct answer.

1. Mike uses 22 ounces of lemon juice to make one pitcher of lemonade. He has 572 ounces of lemon juice. How many pitchers of lemonade can Mike make?

Ⓐ 260 Ⓒ 132

Ⓑ 21 Ⓓ 26

2. A concert hall has 6 sections. There are 515 seats in each section. About how many seats are in the concert hall?

Ⓐ 36,000

Ⓑ 300

Ⓒ 3,000

Ⓓ 520

3. There are 321 visitors at the library. Each library table seats 12 people. How many tables are needed to seat all of the visitors?

Ⓐ 20

Ⓑ 30

Ⓒ 27

Ⓓ 9

4. A tailor has 9 glass jars on a shelf. Each jar holds 242 buttons. How many buttons does the tailor have in all?

Ⓐ 1,868

Ⓑ 1,800

Ⓒ 2,360

Ⓓ 2,178

5. There are 165 apples divided evenly into 11 containers at a store. Which quick picture can be used to determine how many apples are in each container?

Ⓐ 

Ⓑ 

Ⓒ 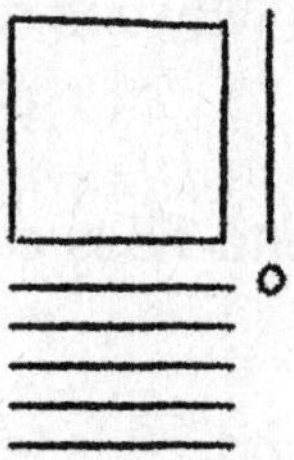

Ⓓ 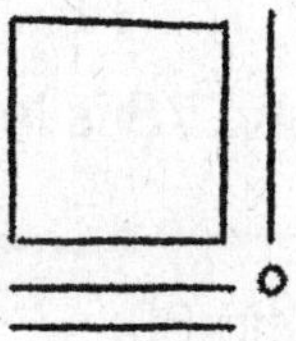

GO ON

6. What is the best way to estimate the quotient of 7,713 divided by 18?

Ⓐ 7,000 ÷ 10 = 700

Ⓑ 8,000 ÷ 20 = 400

Ⓒ 10,000 ÷ 50 = 200

Ⓓ 6,000 ÷ 20 = 300

7. Amy's older brother works 35 hours each week. If he earns $18 an hour, how much does he earn in one week?

Ⓐ $350 Ⓒ $900

Ⓑ $130 Ⓓ $630

8. Tami used estimation to place the first digit of the quotient.

$$\begin{array}{r} 3 \\ 24\overline{)7{,}458} \end{array}$$

Which best explains why she chose this digit?

Ⓐ 75 ÷ 3 = 25, and 75 is close to 74

Ⓑ 60 ÷ 3 = 20, and 20 is less than 75

Ⓒ 75 ÷ 25 = 3, and 75 is less than 7,458

Ⓓ 80 ÷ 20 = 4, and 80 is about 74

9. A store owner orders 3,360 pens. He decides to sell the pens in packages of 12. How many packages of pens does the store owner make from the order?

Record your answer and fill in the bubbles on the grid. Be sure to use the correct place value.

			.		
⓪	⓪	⓪		⓪	⓪
①	①	①		①	①
②	②	②		②	②
③	③	③		③	③
④	④	④		④	④
⑤	⑤	⑤		⑤	⑤
⑥	⑥	⑥		⑥	⑥
⑦	⑦	⑦		⑦	⑦
⑧	⑧	⑧		⑧	⑧
⑨	⑨	⑨		⑨	⑨

10. What is the best estimate for the product of 37 and 19?

Ⓐ 300

Ⓑ 400

Ⓒ 200

Ⓓ 800

GO ON

Name ______________________________________

11. A city bus driver drives 189 miles in one week. If she drives the same distance each week, how many miles does she drive in 4 weeks?

Ⓐ 493 miles

Ⓑ 756 miles

Ⓒ 726 miles

Ⓓ 800 miles

12. At the county fair's giant pumpkin contest, the weight of the prize-winning pumpkin was 11 times the weight of the smallest pumpkin. The combined weight of both pumpkins was 2,028 pounds.

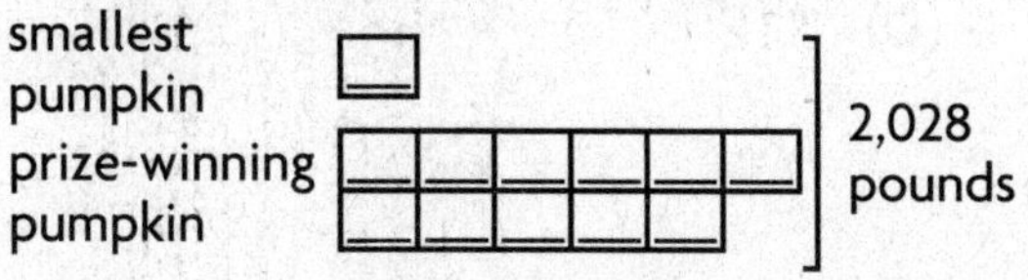

How much did the smallest pumpkin weigh?

Ⓐ 1,859 pounds

Ⓑ 22,308 pounds

Ⓒ 169 pounds

Ⓓ 284 pounds

13. Mary used partial quotients to divide 1,224 by 51. What is the sum of the partial quotients used to solve the problem?

Ⓐ 14

Ⓑ 4

Ⓒ 20

Ⓓ 24

14. A farmer buys 1,920 herb plants each year. He buys the herbs in crates of 48 plants per crate. How many crates does the farmer buy?

Ⓐ 80 Ⓒ 40

Ⓑ 60 Ⓓ 75

15. Mr. Cho has $325 to spend during a 5-day trip to Austin. He wants to spend about the same amount each day. Which shows the best estimate of how much Mr. Cho can spend each day?

Ⓐ $60

Ⓑ $80

Ⓒ $25

Ⓓ $50

GO ON

16. Mrs. Sanchez drives a bookmobile 194 miles each week. If she drives the same distance each week, about how many miles will she drive in 52 weeks?

Ⓐ 10,000 miles

Ⓑ 500 miles

Ⓒ 1,000 miles

Ⓓ 5,000 miles

17. Rob's cat weighs 12 times as much as his parakeet. The combined weight of the cat and parakeet is 468 grams. How much does the cat weigh?

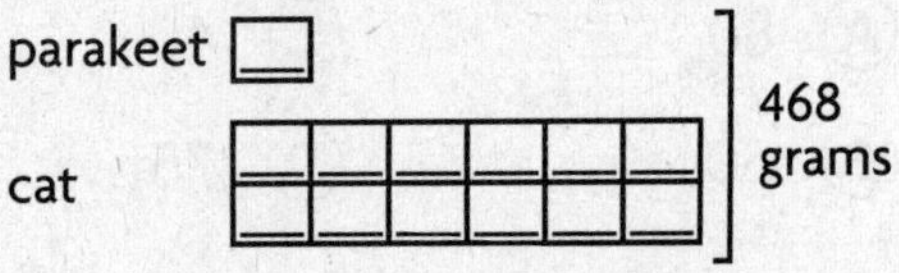

Ⓐ 360 grams

Ⓑ 432 grams

Ⓒ 120 grams

Ⓓ 178 grams

18. Which is the best estimate for the product of 8 and 6,136?

Ⓐ 48,000

Ⓑ 56,000

Ⓒ 480,000

Ⓓ 40,000

19. It costs $216 for 18 tickets to the zoo. How much does it cost for one ticket if all the tickets are the same price?

Ⓐ $10

Ⓑ $16

Ⓒ $36

Ⓓ $12

20. A small bag of nuts contains 427 calories. What is the number of calories in 24 small bags of nuts?

Ⓐ 16,000 calories

Ⓑ 1,708 calories

Ⓒ 10,248 calories

Ⓓ 8,572 calories

Name ______________________________

Fill in the bubble for the correct answer.

1. Tina's water bottle holds 0.24 liter of water. During basketball practice, Tina drinks 3 bottles of water. Which model can be used to find how much water Tina drinks during practice?

Ⓐ 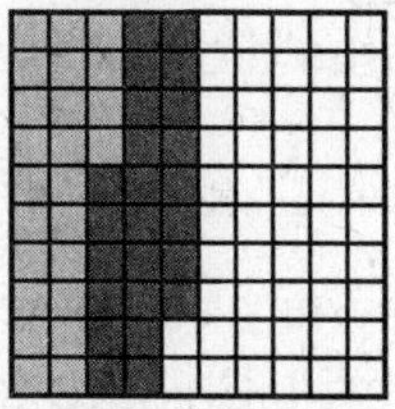

Ⓑ 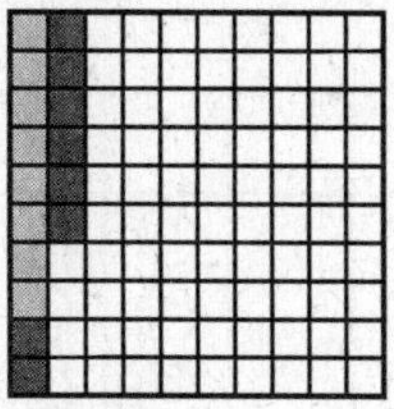

Ⓒ 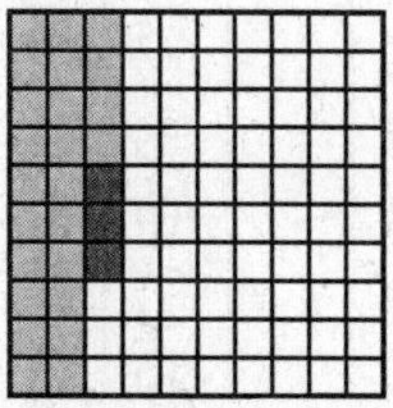

Ⓓ 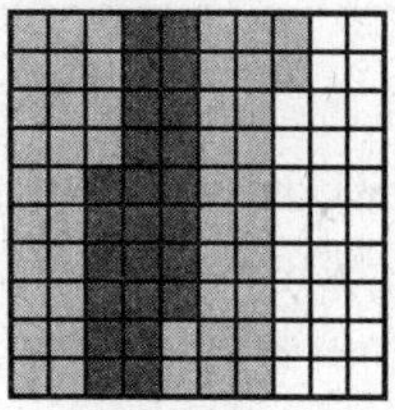

2. Ernie spends $12.86 on school supplies. Stella spends 3 times as much as Ernie. How much money does Stella spend?

Ⓐ $38.58

Ⓑ $24.86

Ⓒ $32.58

Ⓓ $18.58

3. Lara uses 0.34 meter of ribbon in her art project. Nate uses 10 times as much ribbon as Lara. How much ribbon does Nate use?

Ⓐ 34 meters

Ⓑ 13.40 meters

Ⓒ 3.40 meters

Ⓓ 340 meters

4. Gary's mother drives him 4.25 miles to school each day. If she drives Gary to school for 5 days, how many miles will she have driven?

Ⓐ 2.125 miles

Ⓑ 0.21 mile

Ⓒ 212 miles

Ⓓ 21.25 miles

GO ON

5. Leena knows that the mass of one dime is about 2.3 grams. She needs to find the mass of 4 dimes.

Which equation shows how to use the Distributive Property to solve?

Ⓐ $(4 \times 2.3) + (4 \times 2.3) = 18.4$ grams

Ⓑ $(4 \times 2) + (4 \times 0.3) = 9.2$ grams

Ⓒ $(4 \times 3) + (4 \times 0.2) = 12.08$ grams

Ⓓ $(4 \times 2) + (4 \times 0.03) = 8.12$ grams

6. Which expression uses the expanded form of the factors to rewrite the expression 24×0.37?

Ⓐ $(20 + 4) \times (3 + 0.7)$

Ⓑ $(2 + 4) \times (0.3 + 0.07)$

Ⓒ $(20 + 4) \times (0.3 + 0.07)$

Ⓓ $(20 + 4) \times (0.3 + 0.7)$

7. Gia multiplies 2.3 by 1.65. What is the place value of the decimal in the product?

Ⓐ Thousandths

Ⓑ Hundredths

Ⓒ Tenths

Ⓓ Ones

8. In the first few years of its life, a Saguaro cactus grows an average of 0.02 inch each month.

Javier shaded a decimal model to find the average number of inches a Saguaro cactus grows in 6 months. How many squares did Javier shade in his model?

Record your answer and fill in the bubbles on the grid. Be sure to use the correct place value.

			.		
0	0	0		0	0
1	1	1		1	1
2	2	2		2	2
3	3	3		3	3
4	4	4		4	4
5	5	5		5	5
6	6	6		6	6
7	7	7		7	7
8	8	8		8	8
9	9	9		9	9

9. To solve $0.2 \times \$0.06$, Pilar multiplies whole numbers. She writes $2 \times 6 = 12$. Which shows where Pilar should place the decimal point in the product?

Ⓐ $12.00

Ⓑ $0.012

Ⓒ $0.12

Ⓓ $1.20

GO ON

10. A hiking path is 1.6 miles long. Vin hikes 5 tenths of the path. Which model can be used to find how far Vin hikes?

Ⓐ 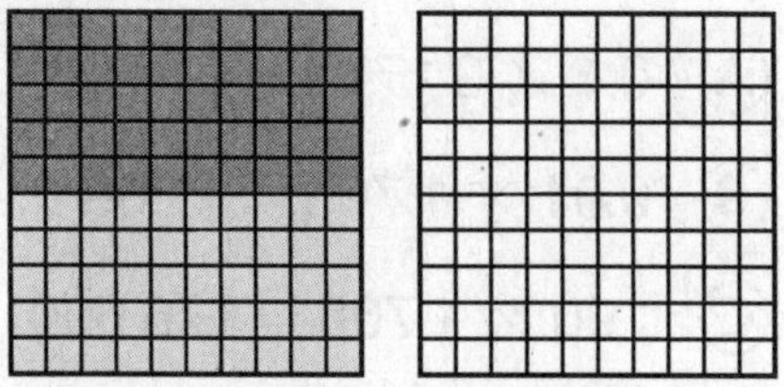

Ⓑ 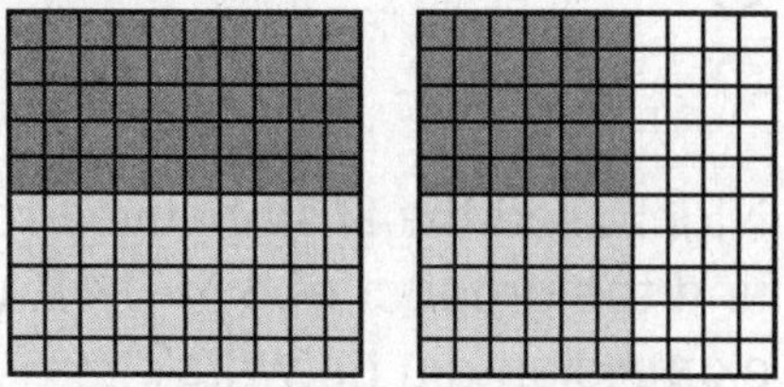

Ⓒ 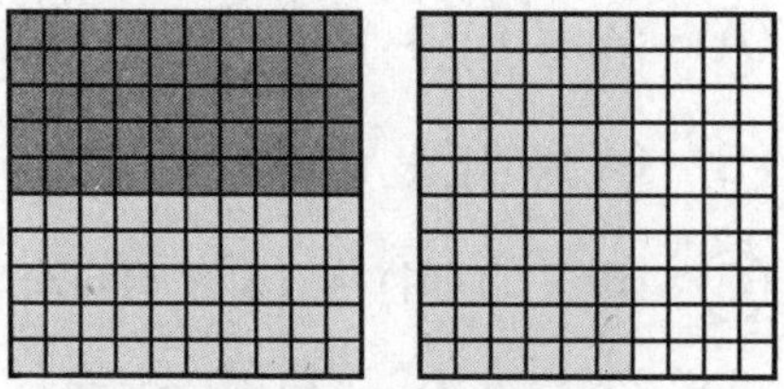

Ⓓ 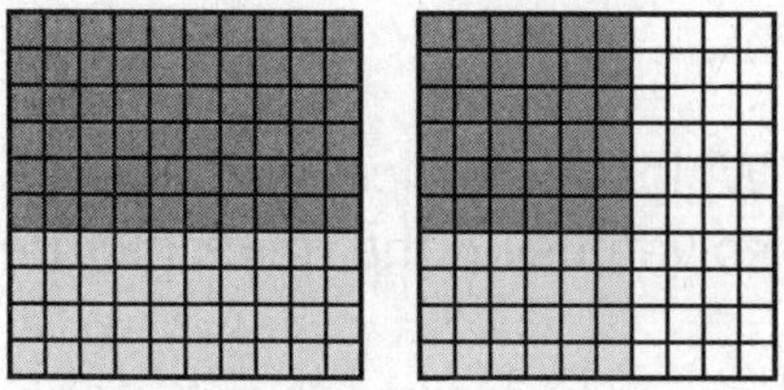

11. Bernie drew a model to solve for the product of a decimal and a whole number.

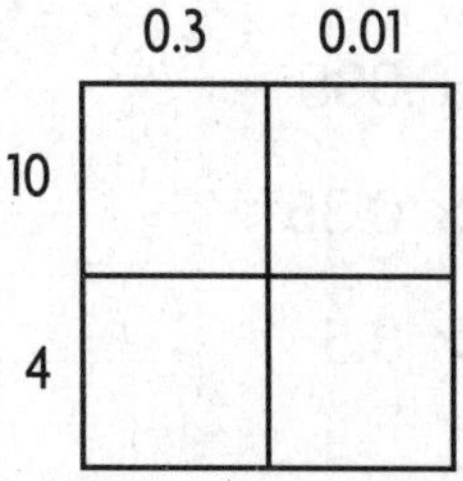

What does Bernie's model show?

Ⓐ 10.3 × 4.01

Ⓑ 1.4 × 31

Ⓒ 10.4 × 13

Ⓓ 14 × 0.31

12. Mr. Logan runs 3.7 miles each day. If he runs the same distance each day, about how many miles will Mr. Logan run in 7 days?

Ⓐ 28

Ⓑ 1

Ⓒ 259

Ⓓ 49

13. A ceramic tile has an area of 0.25 square inch. Darlene uses 100 ceramic tiles to design an art project. Which equation can Darlene use to find the area of her design covered by the tiles?

Ⓐ $100 \times 0.25 = 25$

Ⓑ $10 \times 2.5 = 25$

Ⓒ $10 \times 25 = 250$

Ⓓ $100 \times 0.025 = 2.5$

14. Matt uses 0.5 of a 0.9-ounce tube of red dye to color his fabric design. How much red dye does Matt use?

Ⓐ 4.5 ounces

Ⓑ 45.0 ounces

Ⓒ 0.45 ounce

Ⓓ 0.045 ounce

GO ON

Name ___________________________________

15. Sam has $5.65. Hallie has 3 times as much money as Sam. Which model can be used to find the amount of money Hallie has?

Ⓐ
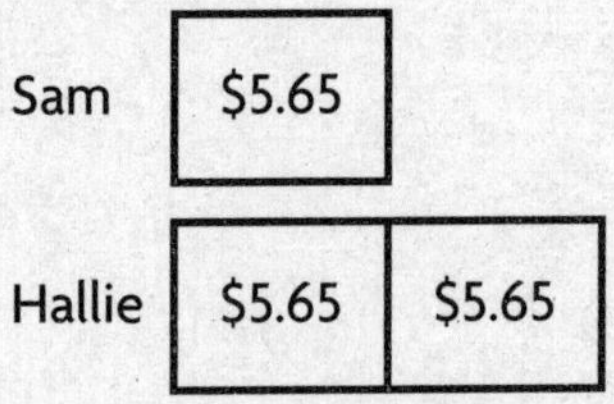

Ⓑ
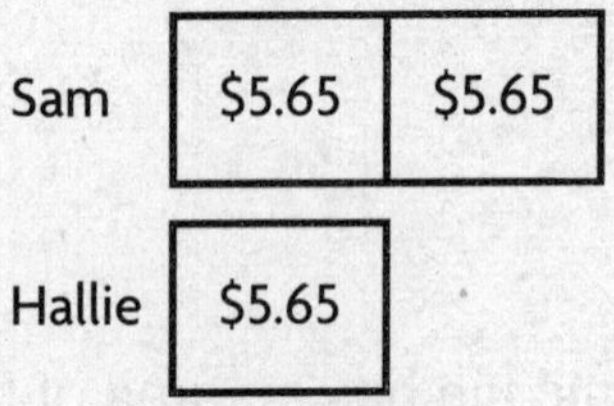

Ⓒ
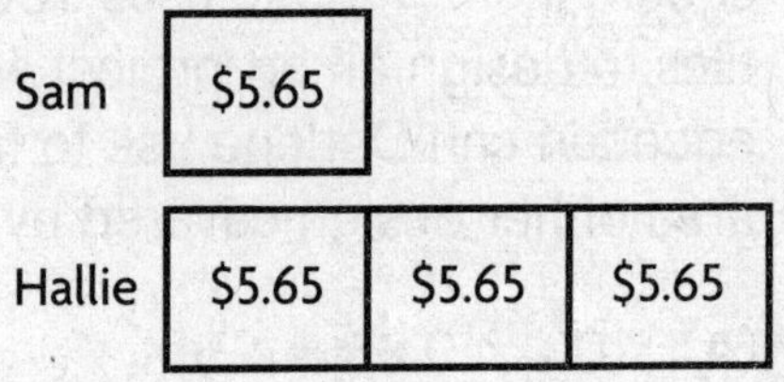

Ⓓ
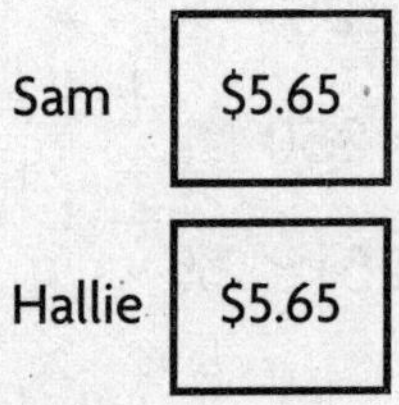

16. Which equation provides the best estimate of the product of 1.7 and 3.2?

Ⓐ $2 \times 3 = 6$
Ⓑ $1 \times 4 = 4$
Ⓒ $3 \times 3 = 9$
Ⓓ $2 \times 2 = 4$

17. The admission at a museum is $5.50 for an adult ticket. The price of a child's ticket is 0.1 that of the adult price. How much is a child's ticket?

Ⓐ $5.00
Ⓑ $0.05
Ⓒ $0.55
Ⓓ $5.05

18. Gold paint will be used to paint $\frac{1}{100}$ of a 1,766 square foot mural. Which equation shows how much of the mural will be covered in gold paint?

Ⓐ $0.1 \times 0.1766 = 0.1766$
Ⓑ $0.01 \times 1{,}766 = 17.66$
Ⓒ $100 \times 1{,}766 = 176{,}600$
Ⓓ $1.0 \times 1{,}766 = 1{,}766$

19. Nigel used the Distributive Property to find the product of 4×0.47. Which expression did he write?

Ⓐ $(4 \times 0) + (4 \times 0.47)$
Ⓑ $(4 \times 4) + (4 \times 7)$
Ⓒ $(4 \times 0.04) + (4 \times 0.07)$
Ⓓ $(4 \times 0.4) + (4 \times 0.07)$

20. Which multiplication problem can be solved using the quick picture?

Ⓐ 3×0.35
Ⓑ 3×0.035
Ⓒ 0.3×0.35
Ⓓ 0.3×3.5

STOP

Fill in the bubble for the correct answer.

1. Which is the best estimate of the quotient of 4.7 divided by 7?

Ⓐ 1.4

Ⓑ 0.7

Ⓒ 6

Ⓓ 7

2. Mary biked 95.25 kilometers in 15 days. Which shows the average distance Mary biked each day?

Ⓐ 6.35 kilometers

Ⓑ 0.63 kilometer

Ⓒ 65 kilometers

Ⓓ 16 kilometers

3. Claude cuts a piece of paper that is 8.25 inches wide into 5 pieces of equal width. Which shows the width of each piece of paper?

Ⓐ 16.5 inches

Ⓒ 0.165 inch

Ⓑ 0.65 inch

Ⓓ 1.65 inches

4. Marcos used 16 cups of flour to make 100 muffins. He divides to find how many cups of flour are needed for one muffin. Which shows the decimal point placed correctly in the quotient?

Ⓐ 1.6 cups

Ⓑ 0.016 cup

Ⓒ 0.16 cup

Ⓓ 16.0 cups

5. Fiona has a banner that is 1.8 meters long. She draws a line dividing the banner into 2 equal parts. What is the length of each part of the banner?

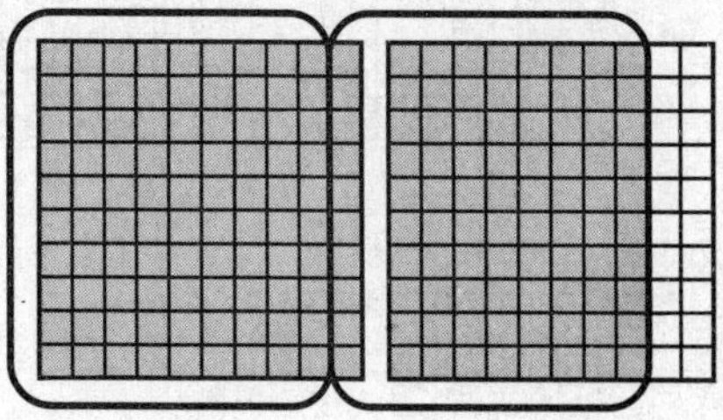

Ⓐ 0.90 meter

Ⓑ 0.20 meter

Ⓒ 0.80 meter

Ⓓ 0.09 meter

GO ON

6. A carpenter had a log that measured 35.5 meters long. He cut the log into 5 equal lengths. Which represents the length of each piece of the log if a flat represents 1 unit?

Ⓐ 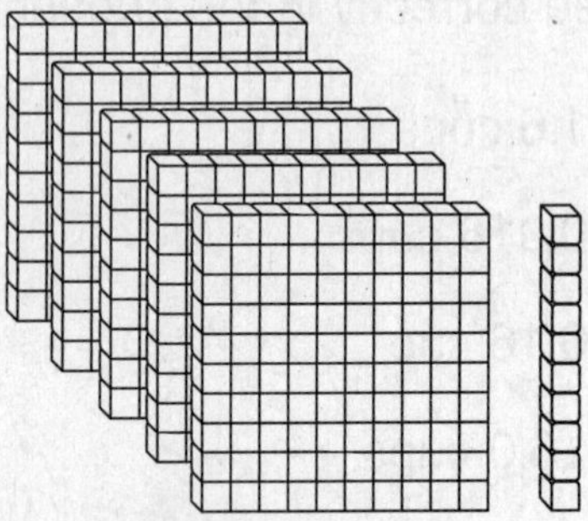

Ⓑ 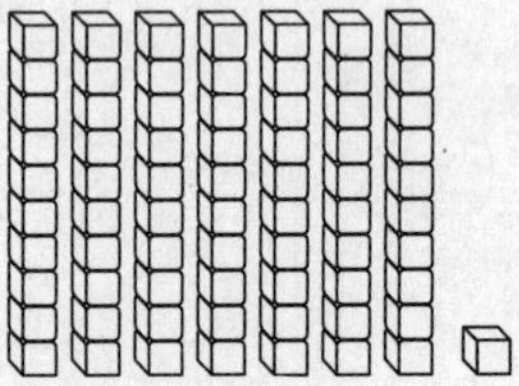

Ⓒ 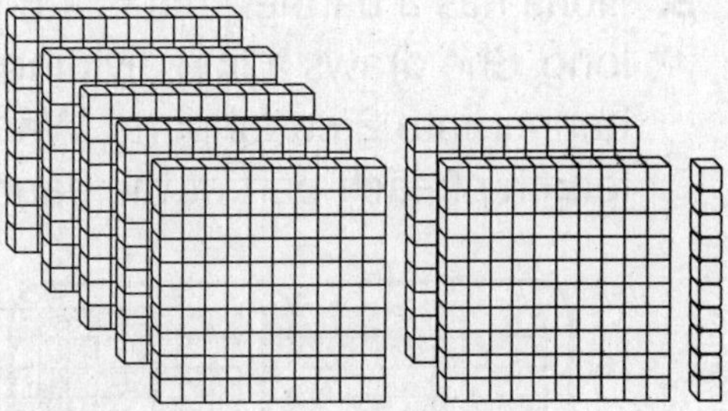

Ⓓ 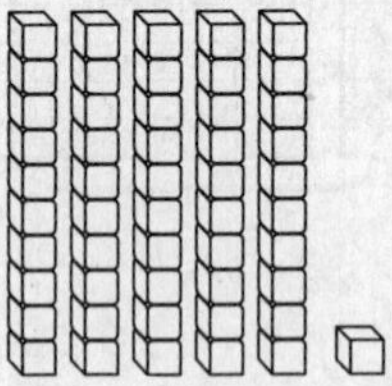

7. A class of 32 students decorated a banner measuring 29.44 feet long. If they divided the banner into 32 sections of equal length and each student decorated a section, how much of the banner did each student decorate?

Ⓐ 9.20 feet
Ⓑ 0.92 foot
Ⓒ 12 feet
Ⓓ 0.09 foot

8. It costs $96.85 for 13 tickets to the aquarium. All the tickets cost the same amount. Which shows the best estimate for the cost of one ticket?

Ⓐ $15.00
Ⓑ $3.00
Ⓒ $25.00
Ⓓ $10.00

9. Which equation can be used to find one-tenth of 119.9?

Ⓐ $119.9 \div 10 = 11.99$

Ⓑ $119.9 \div 100 = 1.2$

Ⓒ $119.9 \div 9 = 13.32$

Ⓓ $119.9 \div 1.0 = 119.9$

10. A gardener has 3.69 pounds of plant food. If he divides it into equal portions for 3 tomato plants, which quick picture shows how much plant food he has for each plant?

Ⓐ 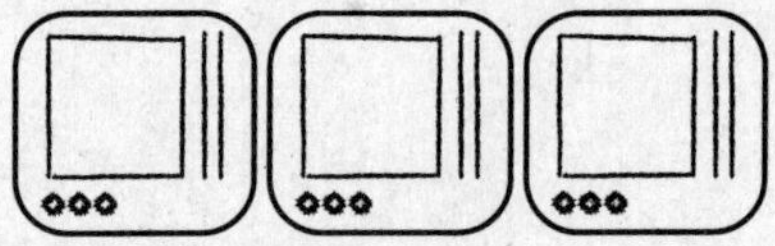

Ⓑ 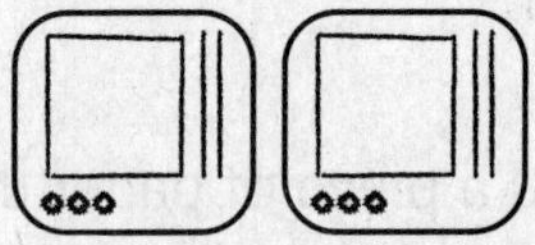

Ⓒ 

Ⓓ 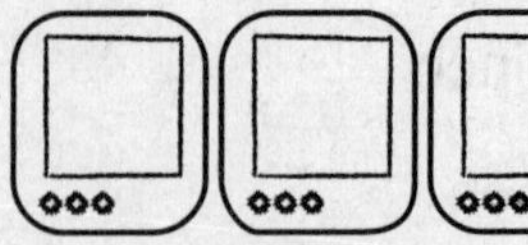

GO ON

11. A plumber cuts 21.48 meters of pipe into 3 pieces of equal length. How long is each piece of pipe?

Ⓐ 0.716 meter

Ⓑ 14 meters

Ⓒ 7.16 meters

Ⓓ 2 meters

12. Pat's Pizza Shop uses 44 pounds of flour to make 100 pizzas. Which equation shows the amount of flour needed to make 10 pizzas?

Ⓐ $440 \div 10 = 44$ pounds

Ⓑ $44 \div 10 = 4.4$ pounds

Ⓒ $44 \div 100 = 0.44$ pound

Ⓓ $44 \div 1 = 44$ pounds

13. In 12 months a town received 44.52 inches of rain. What was the average monthly rainfall?

Ⓐ 0.0371 inch

Ⓑ 13.7 inches

Ⓒ 0.371 inch

Ⓓ 3.71 inches

14. Matt cut a 2.50-foot submarine sandwich into five pieces of equal length. How long is each piece?

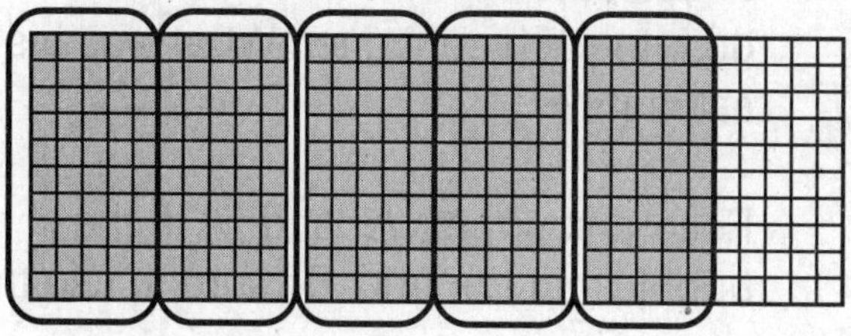

Ⓐ 0.25 foot

Ⓑ 0.50 foot

Ⓒ 2.5 feet

Ⓓ 0.09 foot

15. Which is the best estimate of the quotient of 2.2 divided by 4?

Ⓐ 0.5

Ⓒ 0.1

Ⓑ 0.9

Ⓓ 2

GO ON

16. Joe divided 41.16 pounds of sugar into 4 containers. He rounds the number of pounds of sugar to the nearest 10 to estimate how much sugar should go into each container. What was his estimate?

Record your answer and fill in the bubbles on the grid. Be sure to use the correct place value.

			.		
⓪	⓪	⓪		⓪	⓪
①	①	①		①	①
②	②	②		②	②
③	③	③		③	③
④	④	④		④	④
⑤	⑤	⑤		⑤	⑤
⑥	⑥	⑥		⑥	⑥
⑦	⑦	⑦		⑦	⑦
⑧	⑧	⑧		⑧	⑧
⑨	⑨	⑨		⑨	⑨

17. Over 5 days, Sina's family drove 215.5 kilometers. If they drove the same distance each day, about how many kilometers did the family drive each day?

Ⓐ 10 kilometers

Ⓑ 40 kilometers

Ⓒ 120 kilometers

Ⓓ 100 kilometers

18. Bonita cuts 2.80 yards of rope into 4 pieces of equal length. How long is each piece?

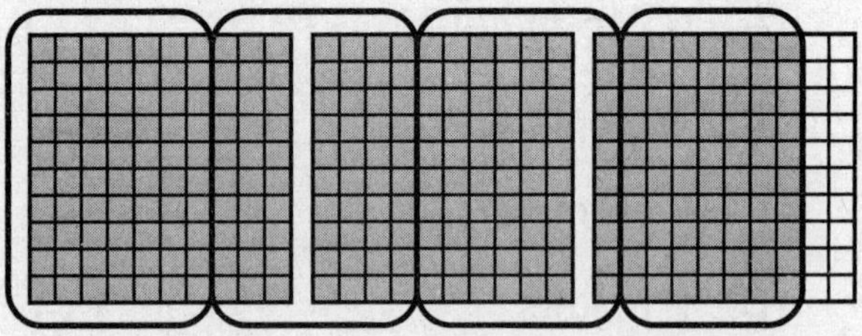

Ⓐ 4 yards　　Ⓒ 0.28 yard

Ⓑ 3 yards　　Ⓓ 0.7 yards

19. A mountain climber eats 43.8 ounces of trail mix during an 8-day climb. Which is the best estimate of the average number of ounces of trail mix the mountain climber eats each day?

Ⓐ 5 ounces　　Ⓒ 2 ounces

Ⓑ 10 ounces　　Ⓓ 3 ounces

20. A baker used 80.5 ounces of cornmeal to make 10 pans of cornbread. Each pan contains the same amount of cornmeal. How many ounces of cornmeal are in each pan of cornbread?

Ⓐ 0.08 ounce　　Ⓒ 0.80 ounce

Ⓑ 85 ounces　　Ⓓ 8.05 ounces

STOP

Name ____________________

Fill in the bubble for the correct answer.

1. What is the value of the digit 1 in 0.001?

Ⓐ 1 thousandth

Ⓑ 1 one

Ⓒ 1 hundredth

Ⓓ 1 tenth

2. What is the best estimate for the quotient of 1.3 ÷ 6?

Ⓐ 0.8

Ⓑ 0.2

Ⓒ 0.6

Ⓓ 0.4

3. Which shows 0.268 rounded to the nearest hundredth?

Ⓐ 0.26

Ⓑ 0.2

Ⓒ 0.3

Ⓓ 0.27

4. What is the product of 0.9 and 3.5?

Ⓐ 3.15 Ⓒ 31.5

Ⓑ 0.315 Ⓓ 3.015

5. There are 165 arrowheads displayed in 11 display cases at a museum, with the same number of arrowheads in each case. Which quick picture can be used to determine how many arrowheads are in each case?

Ⓐ 

Ⓑ 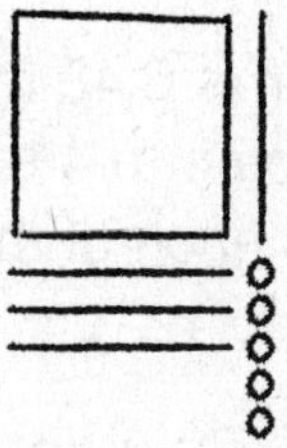

Ⓒ 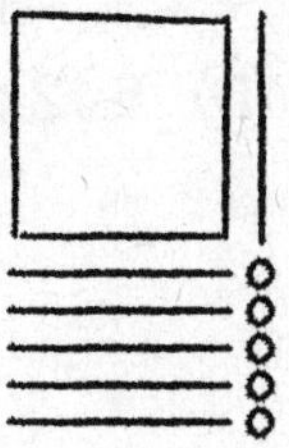

Ⓓ 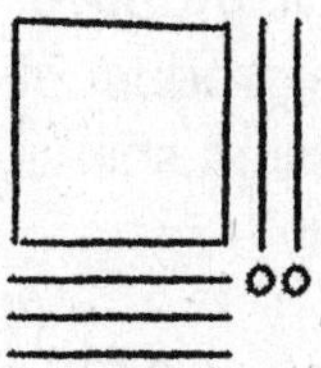

GO ON

6. Rose has a piece of wood that is 2.13 meters long. She paints 0.75 meter of the wood. About how many meters are not painted?

Ⓐ 3 meters
Ⓑ 1 meter
Ⓒ 4 meters
Ⓓ 2 meters

7. Use the model to answer the question. A flat represents 1 unit.

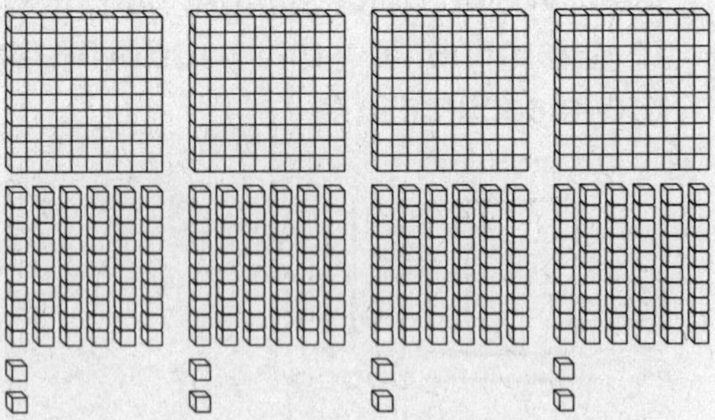

Eddie has a rope that is 6.48 meters long. He cuts the rope into 4 equal lengths. How long is each of the 4 pieces?

Ⓐ 4.16 meters
Ⓑ 1.26 meters
Ⓒ 1.62 meters
Ⓓ 6.12 meters

8. Marlene used the Distributive Property to find the product of 6 and 0.82. Which expression shows the Distributive Property?

Ⓐ $(6 \times 0.08) + (6 \times 0.02)$
Ⓑ $(6 \times 0.8) + (6 \times 0.02)$
Ⓒ $(6 \times 0) + (6 \times 0.82)$
Ⓓ $(6 \times 8) + (6 \times 2)$

9. Which multiplication problem can be solved using the quick picture?

Ⓐ 0.2×6.7
Ⓑ 0.2×0.67
Ⓒ 2×6.7
Ⓓ 2×0.67

10. Helen used blocks to build a scale model of a tower. The model is 949 millimeters tall. Each block is 32 millimeters tall. About how many blocks tall is the tower?

Ⓐ 50
Ⓑ 40
Ⓒ 30
Ⓓ 60

GO ON

11. Which correctly compares 4.602 and 4.62?

Ⓐ $4.602 < 4.62$

Ⓑ $4.62 < 4.602$

Ⓒ $4.602 > 4.62$

Ⓓ $4.62 = 4.602$

12. A tablespoon of honey contains 64 calories. How many calories are in 14 tablespoons of honey?

Record your answer and fill in the bubbles on the grid. Be sure to use the correct place value.

			.		
0	0	0		0	0
1	1	1		1	1
2	2	2		2	2
3	3	3		3	3
4	4	4		4	4
5	5	5		5	5
6	6	6		6	6
7	7	7		7	7
8	8	8		8	8
9	9	9		9	9

13. Which is the best estimate for the product of 5 and 382?

Ⓐ 900

Ⓑ 500

Ⓒ 2,000

Ⓓ 3,000

14. A path around a lake is 0.38 mile long. Mike walks the path 2 times. Which model can be used to find how far Mike walks?

Ⓐ 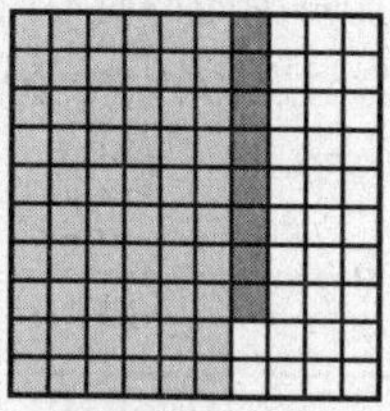

Ⓑ 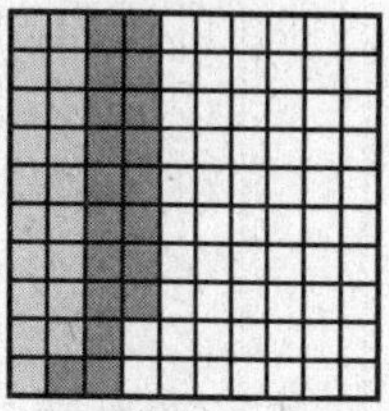

Ⓒ 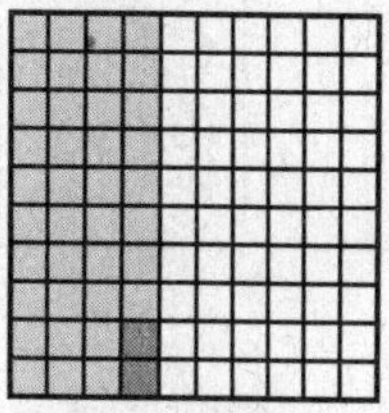

Ⓓ 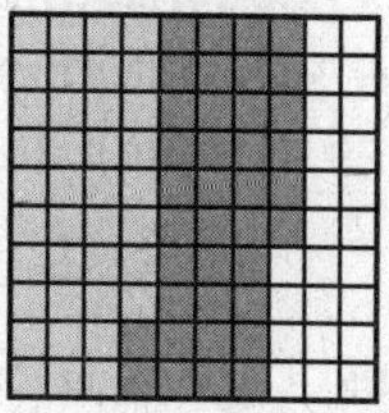

15. Mira has a toy chest that measures 0.829 meter tall. What is 0.829 rounded to the nearest tenth?

Ⓐ 0.9

Ⓑ 0.8

Ⓒ 0.82

Ⓓ 0.83

GO ON

16. Miles used partial quotients to divide 5,376 by 84. What is the sum of the partial quotients used to solve the problem?

Record your answer and fill in the bubbles on the grid. Be sure to use the correct place value.

			.		
⓪	⓪	⓪		⓪	⓪
①	①	①		①	①
②	②	②		②	②
③	③	③		③	③
④	④	④		④	④
⑤	⑤	⑤		⑤	⑤
⑥	⑥	⑥		⑥	⑥
⑦	⑦	⑦		⑦	⑦
⑧	⑧	⑧		⑧	⑧
⑨	⑨	⑨		⑨	⑨

17. The school cooks used 161.5 ounces of beans to make 100 servings of soup. How many ounces of beans are in 10 servings of soup?

Ⓐ 16.15 ounces
Ⓑ 0.165 ounce
Ⓒ 1.615 ounces
Ⓓ 1,615 ounces

18. Mt. Pelée is 1.396 kilometers high. Mt. Vesuvius is 1.281 kilometers high. Mt. Pinatubo is 1.484 kilometers high.

Which lists the volcanoes in order from shortest to highest?

Ⓐ Pelée, Vesuvius, Pinatubo

Ⓑ Pelée, Pinatubo, Vesuvius

Ⓒ Vesuvius, Pelée, Pinatubo

Ⓓ Vesuvius, Pinatubo, Pelée

19. Which expression uses the expanded form of the factors to rewrite 35×0.18?

Ⓐ $(30 + 5) \times (1 + 0.8)$

Ⓑ $(3 + 5) \times (0.1 + 0.08)$

Ⓒ $(30 + 5) \times (0.1 + 0.8)$

Ⓓ $(30 + 5) \times (0.1 + 0.08)$

20. What property is shown by the equation?

$(32.21 + 14.8) + 11.2$
$= 32.21 + (14.8 + 11.2)$

Ⓐ Identity Property of Addition

Ⓑ Commutative Property of Addition

Ⓒ Associative Property of Addition

Ⓓ Not here

21. Anita had \$22.67 in a savings account in April. By July, she had 4 times as much in the account as she did in April. How much money did Anita have in the savings account in July?

Ⓐ \$90.68
Ⓑ \$80.48
Ⓒ \$88.48
Ⓓ \$68.01

GO ON

22. Karel used 43.68 liters of water during a 12-day camping trip. On average, how many liters of water did Karel use each day?

Ⓐ 3.59 liters

Ⓑ 3.64 liters

Ⓒ 0.364 liter

Ⓓ 5.36 liters

23. Ms. Lopez had $618.54 in her checking account. She deposits $50.25 into her account. How much will she have left in the account after she spends $47.29?

Ⓐ $621.50

Ⓑ $571.25

Ⓒ $565.73

Ⓓ $248.33

24. In June, Laura ran 200 yards in 38.82 seconds. In July she ran the same distance in 28.81 seconds. About how many seconds faster was Laura's time in July than in June?

Ⓐ 40 seconds

Ⓑ 20 seconds

Ⓒ 50 seconds

Ⓓ 10 seconds

25. Four teammates ran a relay race in 2.48 minutes. Which quick picture shows the average time for each team member?

Ⓐ 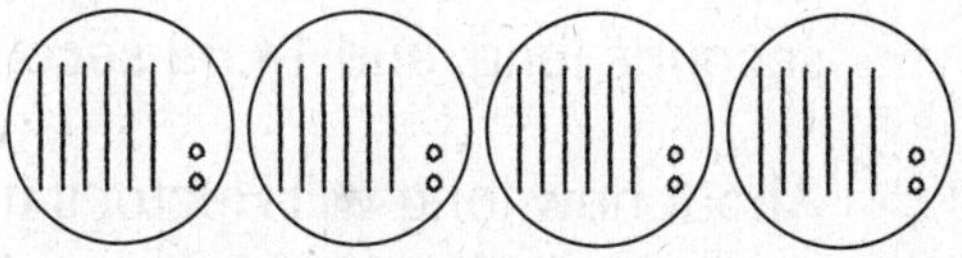

Ⓑ 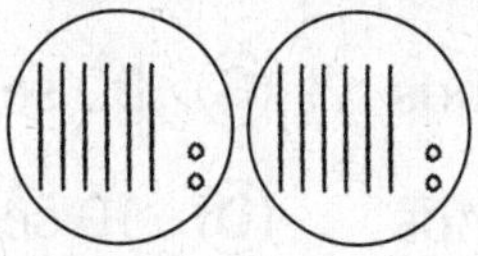

Ⓒ 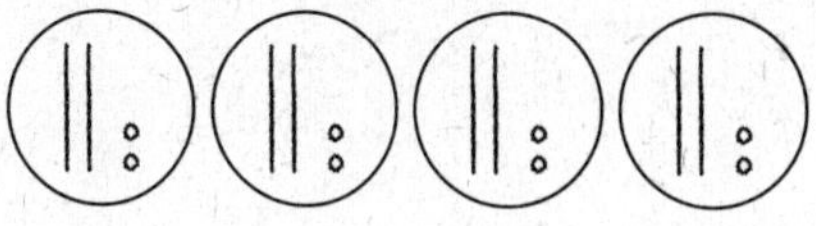

Ⓓ 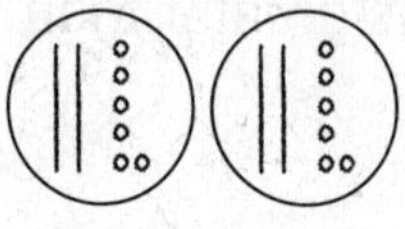

GO ON

26. There are 982 reference books in one school library. There are 17 libraries in the school system, and they all own the same number of reference books. About how many reference books are in the entire school library system?

Ⓐ 1,500

Ⓑ 20,000

Ⓒ 10,000

Ⓓ 2,000

27. Hector has three audio files on his phone. He wants to join the files together to make one audio file. The files are 16.22 seconds long, 9.31 seconds long, and 14.89 seconds long.

About how long will Hector's final audio file be?

Ⓐ 20 seconds

Ⓑ 40 seconds

Ⓒ 90 seconds

Ⓓ 10 seconds

28. Which decimal is greater than 1.434?

Ⓐ 1.443

Ⓑ 1.034

Ⓒ 1.340

Ⓓ 1.433

29. To solve 0.4×0.05 Mi-Yung multiplies whole numbers. She writes $4 \times 5 = 20$. Which shows where Mi-Yung should place the decimal point in the product?

Ⓐ 0.20

Ⓑ 2.00

Ⓒ 0.020

Ⓓ 20.00

30. Tanya raced on her bike 1.20 kilometers in 4 minutes. If she rode at the same speed throughout, how many kilometers did she ride each minute?

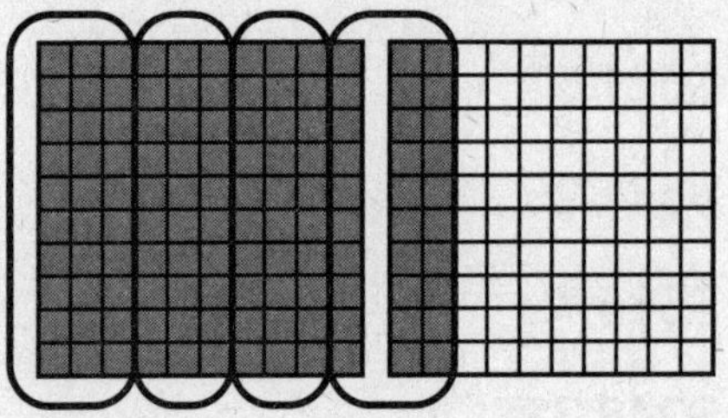

Ⓐ 0.03 kilometer

Ⓑ 0.12 kilometer

Ⓒ 34 kilometers

Ⓓ 0.3 kilometer

STOP

Fill in the bubble for the correct answer.

1. Jill's family divided a whole lasagna into 10 pieces of equal size. They ate $\frac{2}{5}$ of the lasagna. Which fraction represents the amount of lasagna remaining?

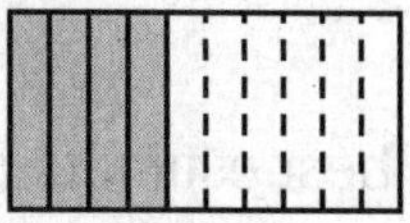

Ⓐ $\frac{6}{10}$

Ⓑ $\frac{7}{10}$

Ⓒ $\frac{5}{10}$

Ⓓ $\frac{3}{10}$

2. What is the least common denominator of the fractions $\frac{1}{4}$ and $\frac{2}{3}$?

Record your answer and fill in the bubbles on the grid. Be sure to use the correct place value.

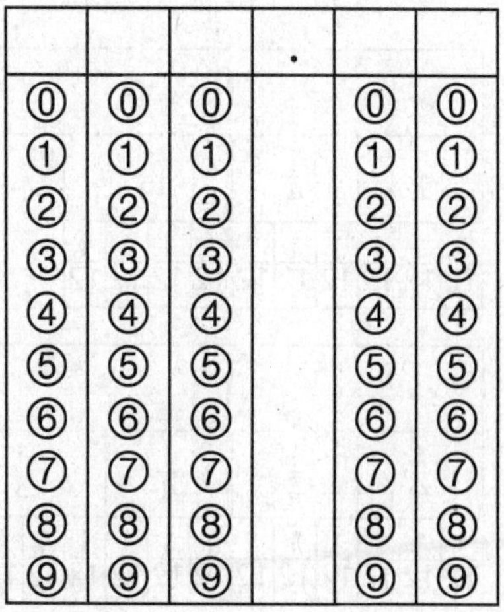

3. Devon combines $\frac{1}{3}$ cup of raisins and $\frac{1}{2}$ cup of granola to make a snack. How many cups of raisins and granola does Devon use?

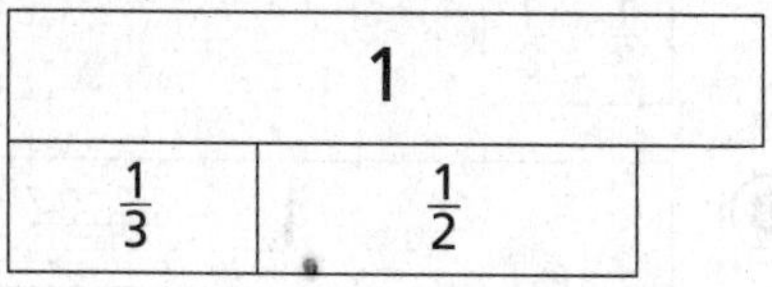

Ⓐ $\frac{2}{5}$ cup

Ⓑ $\frac{3}{6}$ cup

Ⓒ $\frac{2}{6}$ cup

Ⓓ $\frac{5}{6}$ cup

4. Ann spent $\frac{1}{8}$ of her allowance to buy paper and $\frac{3}{4}$ of her allowance to buy paint. How much of her allowance did Ann spend?

Ⓐ $\frac{4}{8}$

Ⓑ $\frac{7}{8}$

Ⓒ $\frac{4}{12}$

Ⓓ $\frac{1}{12}$

5. Harry filled a watering can with $\frac{3}{4}$ gallon of water. After watering a plant, he sees that $\frac{1}{8}$ gallon is left. How much water did Harry use to water the plant?

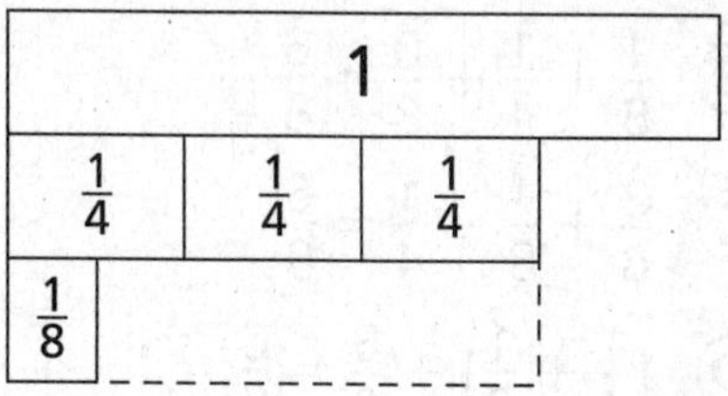

Ⓐ $\frac{1}{8}$ gallon

Ⓑ $\frac{3}{8}$ gallon

Ⓒ $\frac{5}{8}$ gallon

Ⓓ $\frac{1}{2}$ gallon

GO ON

Name ______________________________

6. Which shows how to use objects to model $\frac{1}{2} - \frac{1}{4}$?

Ⓐ 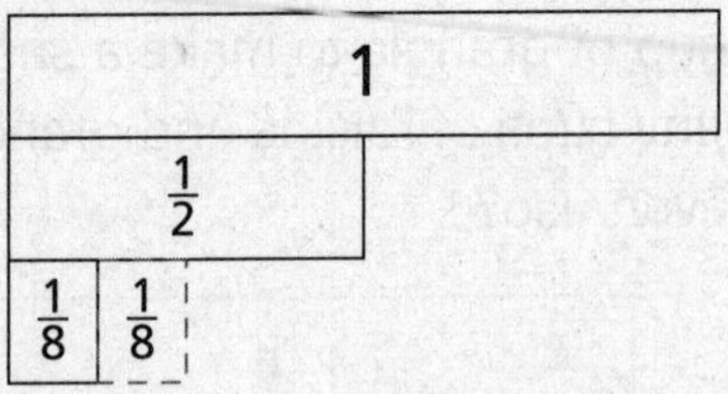

Ⓑ 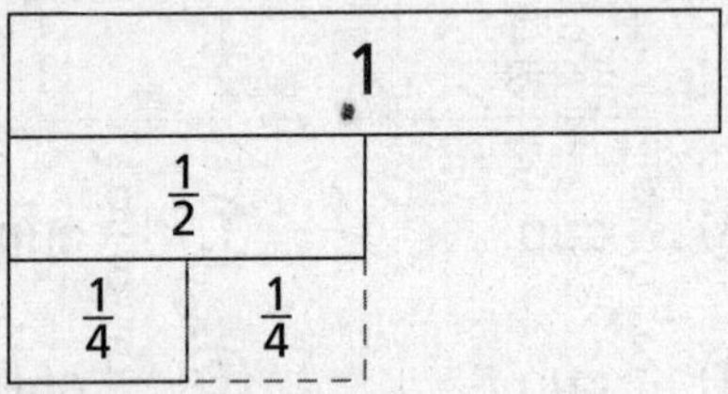

Ⓒ 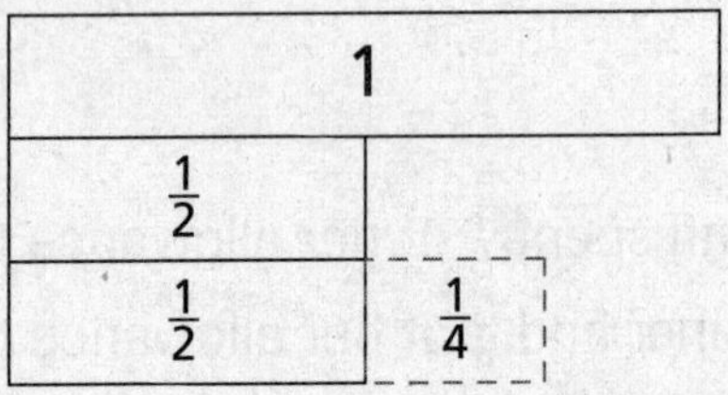

Ⓓ 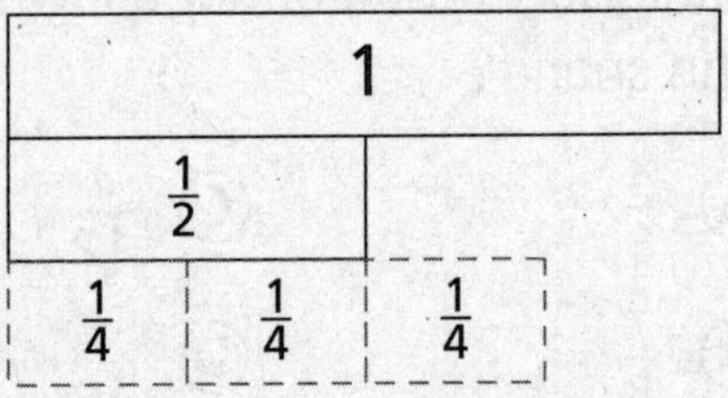

7. Xena used the Associative Property to rewrite the problem $(\frac{1}{4} + \frac{1}{8}) + \frac{3}{8}$. Which solution could she have written?

Ⓐ $\frac{1}{4} + \left(\frac{1}{8} + \frac{3}{8}\right) = \frac{6}{8}$

Ⓑ $\frac{1}{8} + \frac{1}{4} + \frac{3}{8} = \frac{6}{8}$

Ⓒ $\frac{3}{8} + \frac{1}{8} + \frac{1}{4} = \frac{6}{8}$

Ⓓ $\left(\frac{1}{4} + \frac{1}{8}\right) + \frac{3}{8} = \frac{6}{8}$

8. Which fractions are equivalent to $\frac{5}{6}$ and $\frac{2}{9}$ and show the least common denominator?

Ⓐ $\frac{10}{12}, \frac{4}{18}$ Ⓒ $\frac{15}{18}, \frac{4}{18}$

Ⓑ $\frac{10}{18}, \frac{4}{18}$ Ⓓ $\frac{10}{12}, \frac{6}{27}$

9. Which is the best estimate of the sum of $\frac{5}{6}$ and $\frac{3}{8}$?

Ⓐ 3 Ⓒ 2

Ⓑ $1\frac{1}{2}$ Ⓓ $\frac{1}{2}$

10. Tonya adds $\frac{3}{4}$ and $\frac{1}{3}$. Which model could she use to help find the sum?

Ⓐ 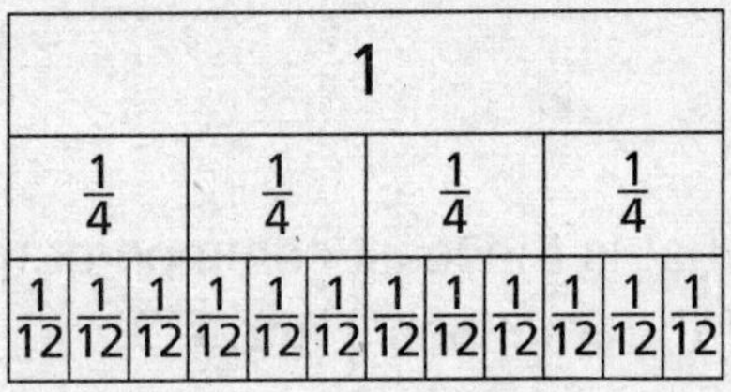

Ⓑ 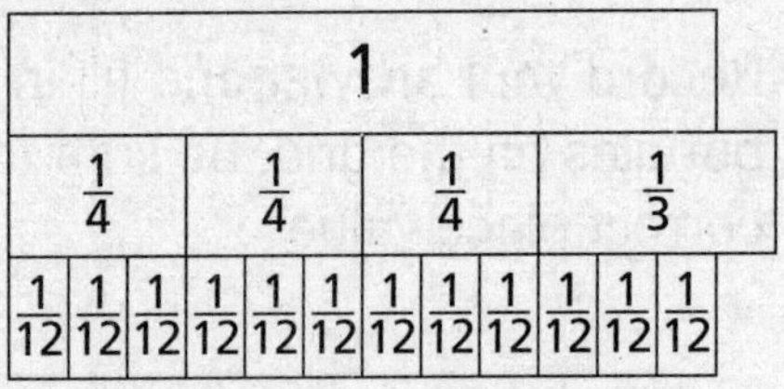

Ⓒ 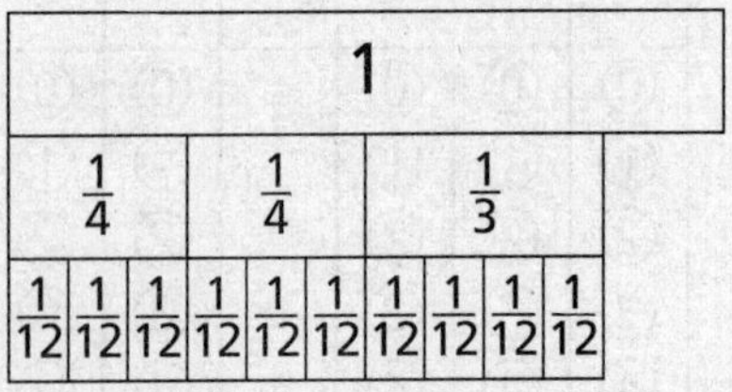

Ⓓ 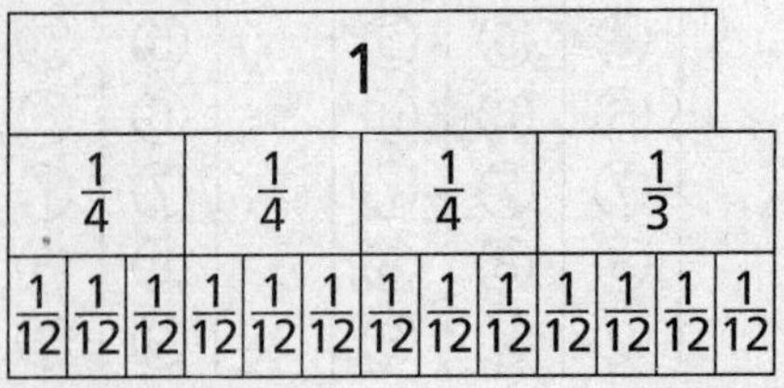

GO ON

11. Pia has $\frac{9}{10}$ meter of ribbon. She cuts off $\frac{3}{5}$ meter of the ribbon to use as a bow on a box. How much ribbon does Pia have left?

Ⓐ $\frac{1}{2}$ meter
Ⓑ $\frac{3}{10}$ meter
Ⓒ $\frac{5}{6}$ meter
Ⓓ $\frac{6}{15}$ meter

12. Ken uses $\frac{3}{4}$ yard of blue yarn and $\frac{3}{8}$ yard of red yarn for an art project. What is the total length of yarn Ken uses?

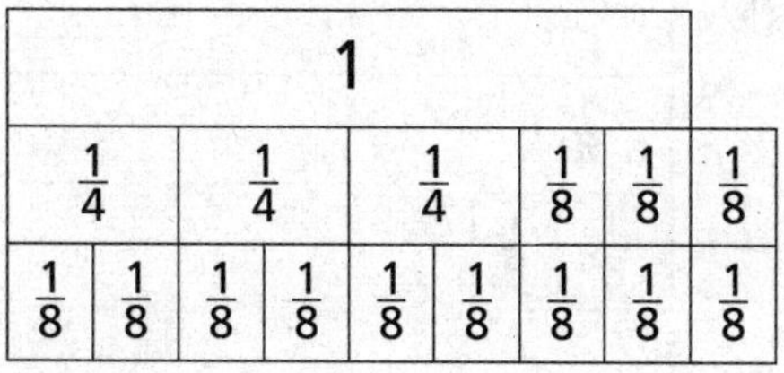

Ⓐ $\frac{7}{8}$ yard
Ⓑ $1\frac{1}{4}$ yards
Ⓒ 1 yard
Ⓓ $1\frac{1}{8}$ yards

13. Jose ran $3\frac{3}{10}$ miles and Syd ran $6\frac{1}{2}$ miles. How many more miles did Syd run than Jose?

Ⓐ $3\frac{1}{5}$ miles
Ⓑ $3\frac{1}{2}$ miles
Ⓒ $3\frac{1}{4}$ miles
Ⓓ $3\frac{1}{3}$ miles

14. Which shows how to use objects to model $\frac{1}{5} + \frac{1}{2}$?

Ⓐ
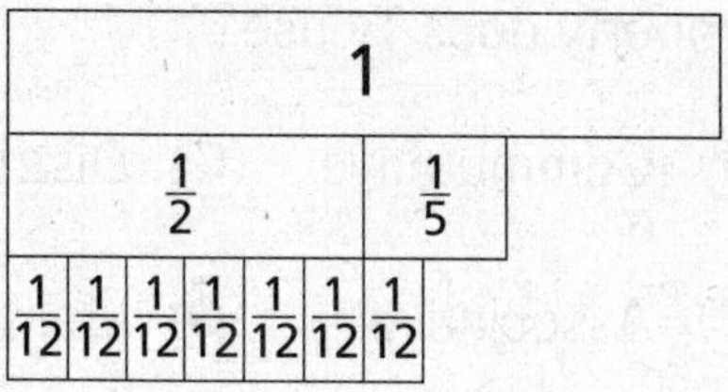

Ⓑ
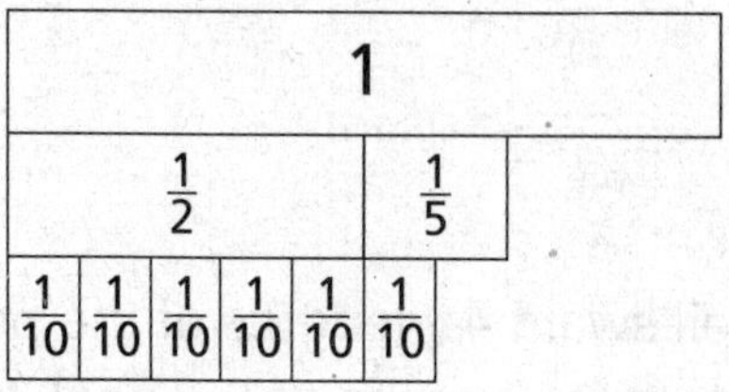

Ⓒ
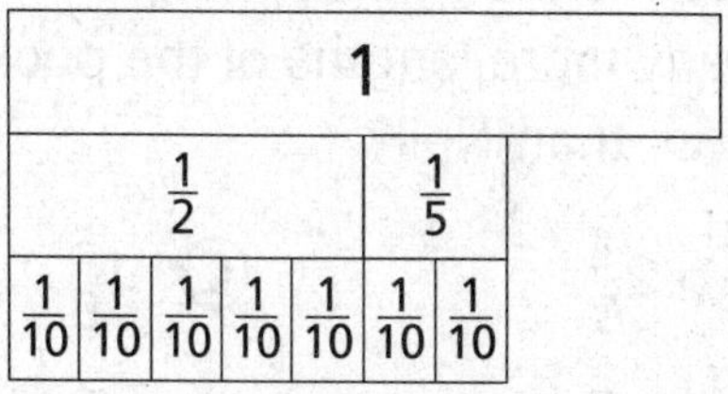

Ⓓ
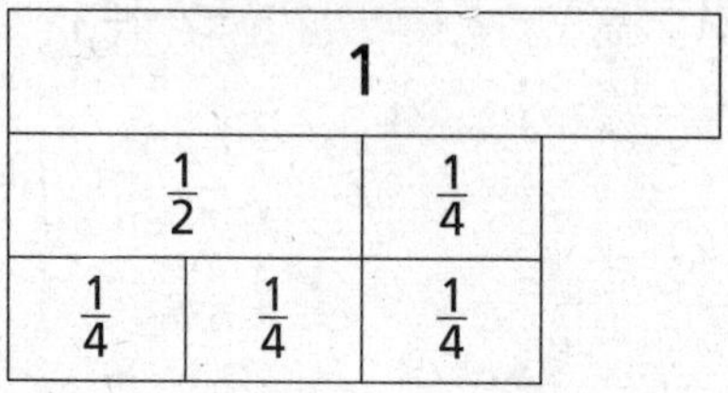

15. Gail made $\frac{7}{8}$ quart of lemonade. Her sister drank $\frac{1}{4}$ quart of the lemonade. How much lemonade is left?

Ⓐ $\frac{1}{2}$ quart
Ⓑ $\frac{2}{3}$ quart
Ⓒ 1 quart
Ⓓ $\frac{5}{8}$ quart

GO ON

Name ______________________________

16. Ty is adding $(\frac{1}{4} + \frac{2}{3}) + \frac{1}{4}$. He rewrites the problem as $\frac{1}{4} + \frac{1}{4} + \frac{2}{3}$. What property does Ty use?

Ⓐ Commutative
Ⓑ Associative
Ⓒ Distributive
Ⓓ Identity

17. Neil swam $4\frac{2}{3}$ lengths of the pool. Mia swam $6\frac{1}{2}$ lengths of the pool. How many more lengths of the pool did Mia swim than Neil?

Ⓐ $2\frac{1}{6}$
Ⓑ $1\frac{1}{6}$
Ⓒ $1\frac{5}{6}$
Ⓓ $2\frac{1}{2}$

18. Mikela uses $1\frac{1}{6}$ cups of rye flour and $2\frac{3}{4}$ cups of wheat flour to make bread. How much flour does Mikela use in all?

Ⓐ $3\frac{11}{12}$ cups
Ⓑ $3\frac{3}{4}$ cups
Ⓒ $1\frac{3}{4}$ cups
Ⓓ $3\frac{2}{5}$ cups

19. Anton is making a fruit salad. He uses $\frac{2}{3}$ cup of grapes and $\frac{1}{2}$ cup of strawberries. What is the total amount of fruit Anton uses?

Ⓐ 1 cup
Ⓑ $\frac{2}{6}$ cup
Ⓒ $\frac{4}{6}$ cup
Ⓓ $1\frac{1}{6}$ cups

20. Xiu subtracts $\frac{1}{6}$ from $\frac{1}{4}$. Which model could she use to help find the difference?

Ⓐ
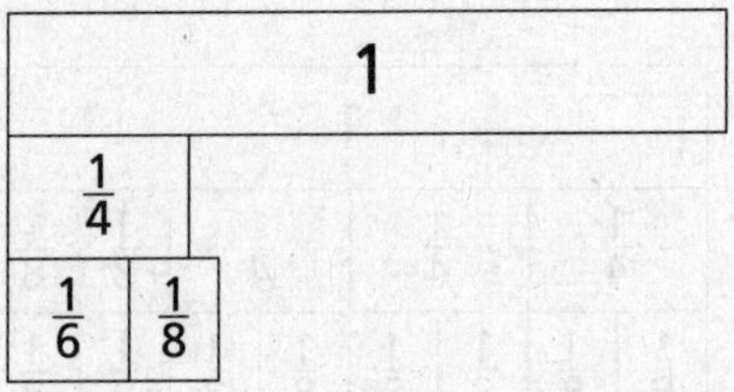

Ⓑ
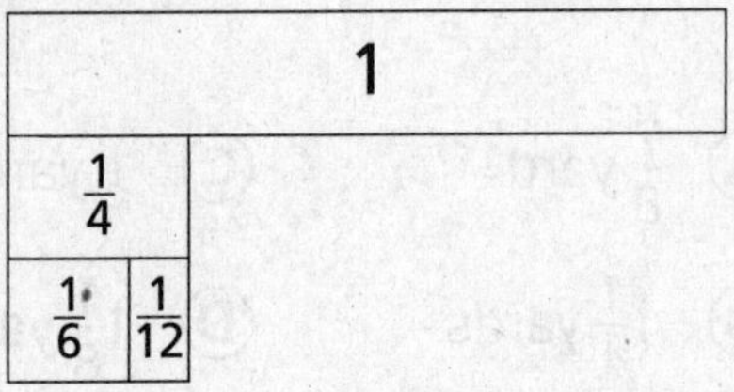

Ⓒ
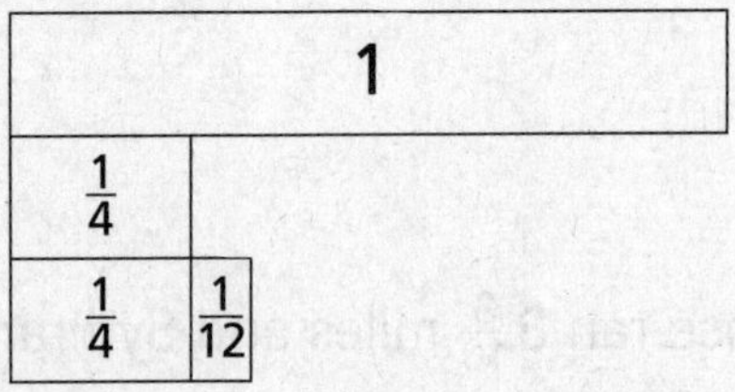

Ⓓ
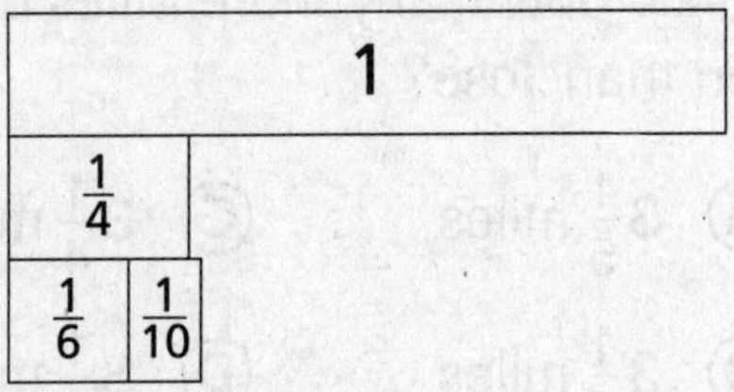

STOP

Name ________________________________

Fill in the bubble for the correct answer.

1. Ray has 12 baseball cards in his collection. Three-fourths of the cards have been autographed. Which shows how to find the number of cards that have been autographed?

Ⓐ 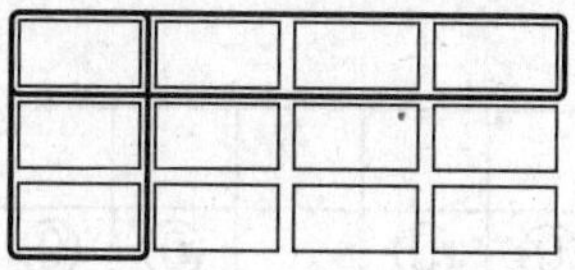

Ⓑ 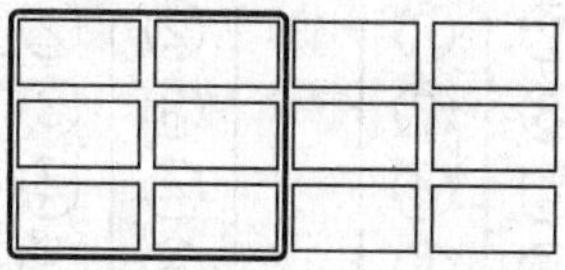

Ⓒ 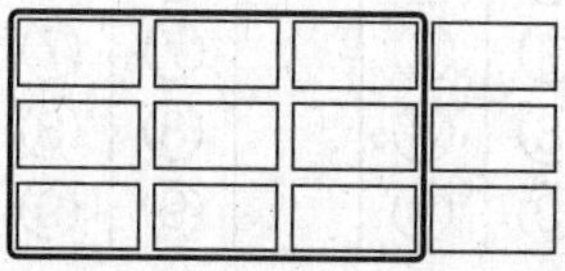

Ⓓ 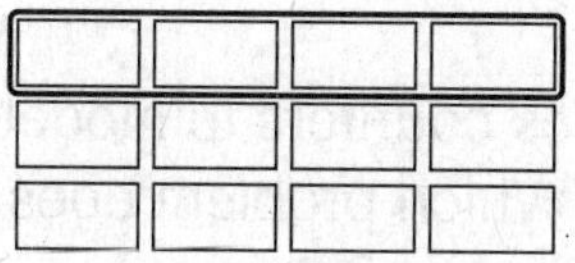

2. Millie uses 5 quarts of water for her plants. She uses $\frac{1}{4}$ quart of water for each plant. How many plants does Millie water?

Ⓐ 20

Ⓑ 9

Ⓒ 25

Ⓓ 10

3. Which division expression can be solved using the model?

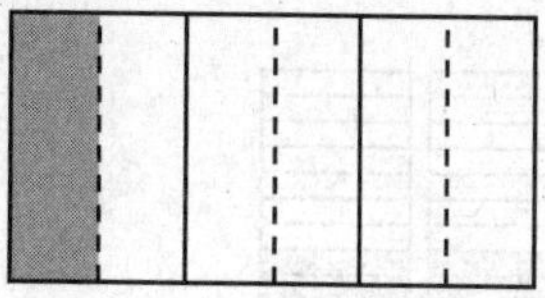

Ⓐ $\frac{1}{3} \div 3$ Ⓒ $\frac{1}{3} \div 2$

Ⓑ $\frac{1}{2} \div 3$ Ⓓ $2 \div \frac{1}{3}$

4. What is the product of $\frac{2}{3}$ and 18?

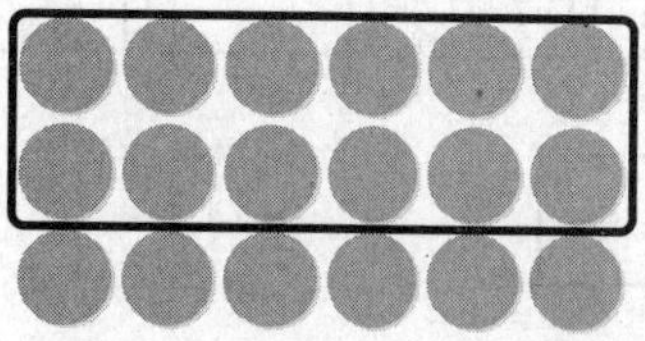

Ⓐ 6   Ⓑ 12   Ⓒ 9   Ⓓ 15

5. Adionte drew a model to help him multiply a whole number by a fraction. Which multiplication expression does his model represent?

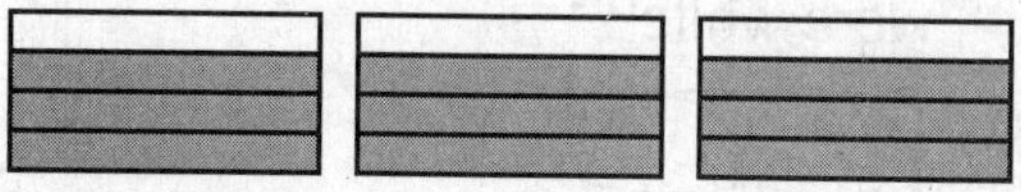

Ⓐ $3 \times \frac{1}{4}$

Ⓑ $3 \times \frac{3}{4}$

Ⓒ $3 \times \frac{1}{2}$

Ⓓ $3 \times \frac{1}{3}$

GO ON

6. Phil took 4 loaves of banana bread to a picnic. After the picnic, $\frac{3}{10}$ of each loaf was left. How many total loaves of banana bread were left after the picnic?

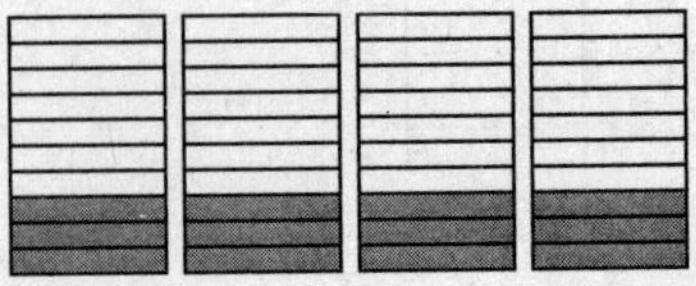

Ⓐ 3 Ⓑ $\frac{3}{5}$ Ⓒ 12 Ⓓ $1\frac{1}{5}$

7. A butcher grinds 4 pounds of beef. Which shows how many $\frac{1}{4}$-pound burgers can be made from the beef?

Ⓐ 

Ⓑ 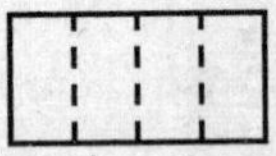

Ⓒ 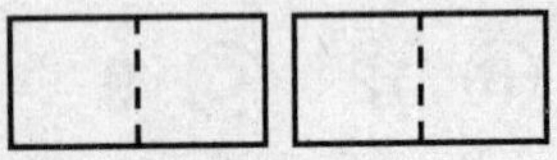

Ⓓ 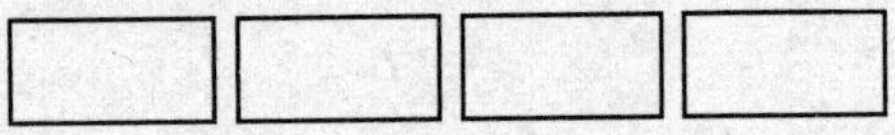

8. Zoe bought 6 marbles. Of those six, $\frac{1}{3}$ of them were white. How many marbles were white?

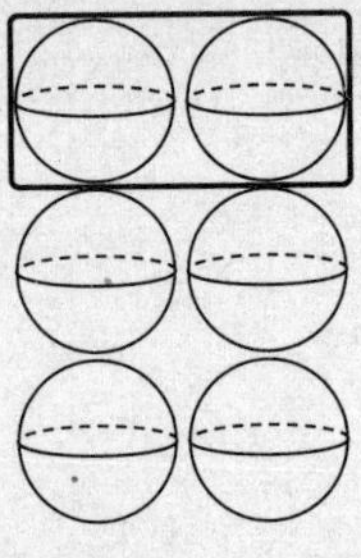

Ⓐ 3 Ⓒ 6

Ⓑ 4 Ⓓ 2

9. Kristin has 10 pipe cleaners. She cuts each pipe cleaner into fourths. How many pipe cleaner pieces does Kristen have?

Record your answer and fill in the bubbles on the grid. Be sure to use the correct place value.

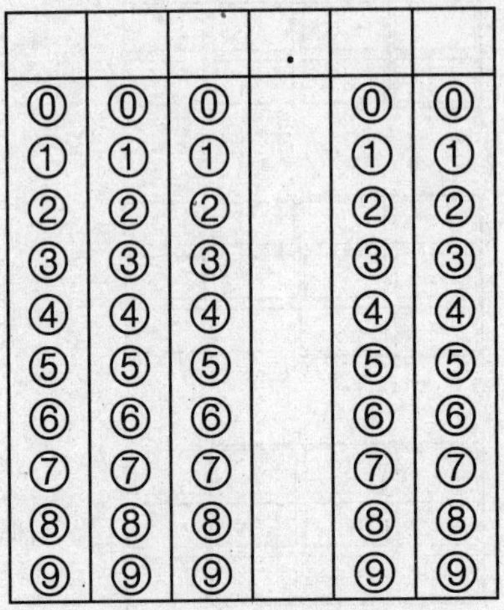

10. LaMia uses counters to model a problem. Which problem does LaMia's model represent?

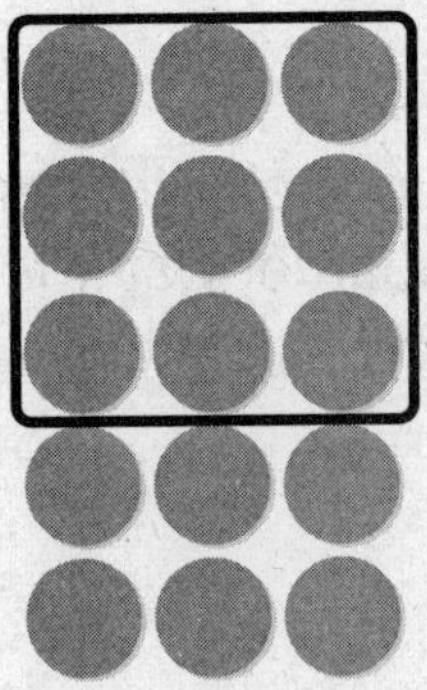

Ⓐ $\frac{3}{5} \times 15$

Ⓑ $\frac{1}{3} \times 9$

Ⓒ $\frac{1}{2} \times 15$

Ⓓ $\frac{2}{5} \times 15$

GO ON

Name ______________________________

11. Don divides $\frac{1}{4}$ of a pizza equally among himself and 2 friends. What fraction of the whole pizza should each person get?

Ⓐ $\frac{1}{8}$ Ⓑ $\frac{1}{12}$ Ⓒ $\frac{1}{2}$ Ⓓ $\frac{1}{3}$

12. Erin served 3 pies at her party. Her guests ate $\frac{2}{3}$ of each pie. Which model shows how to find the total amount of pie that was eaten?

Ⓐ 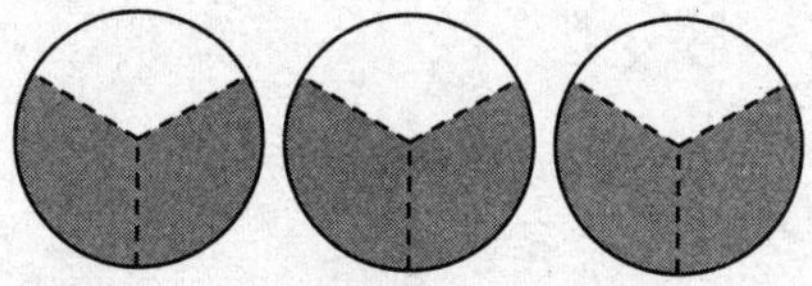

Ⓑ 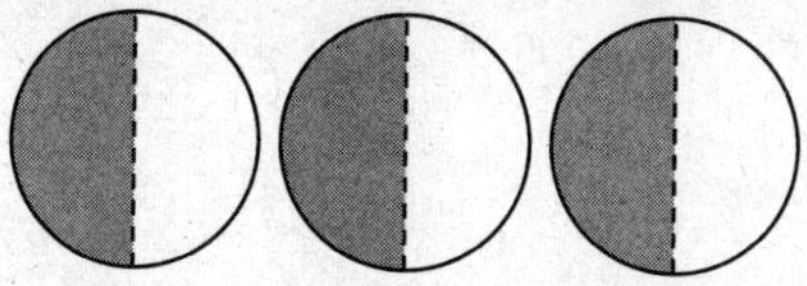

Ⓒ 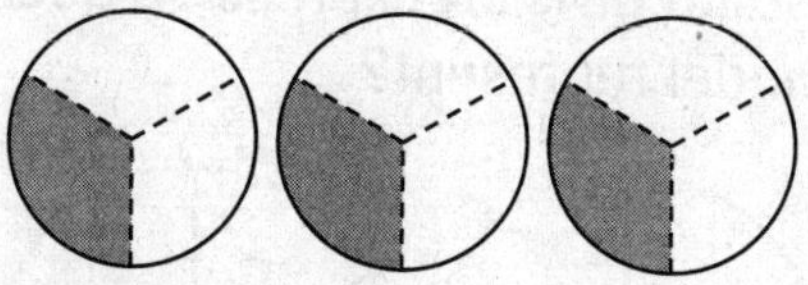

Ⓓ 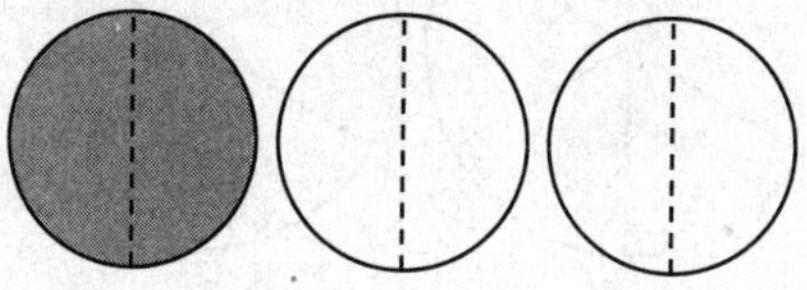

13. Six friends want to share a $\frac{1}{2}$-gallon of ice cream equally. What fraction of a gallon of ice cream should each friend receive?

Ⓐ $\frac{1}{4}$ gallon

Ⓑ $\frac{1}{10}$ gallon

Ⓒ $\frac{1}{8}$ gallon

Ⓓ $\frac{1}{12}$ gallon

14. Connie has 3 granola bars. She divides the bars into $\frac{1}{4}$-size pieces. Which picture represents the expression $3 \div \frac{1}{4}$?

Ⓐ 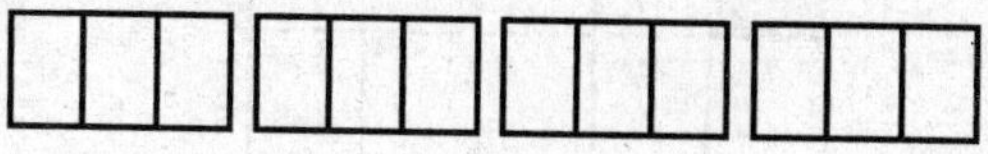

Ⓑ 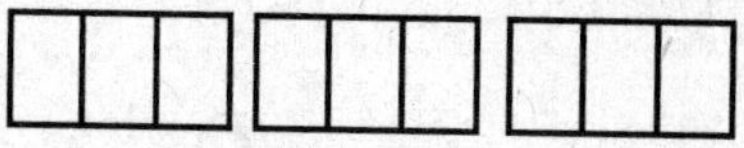

Ⓒ 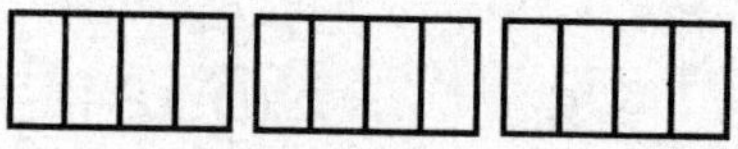

Ⓓ 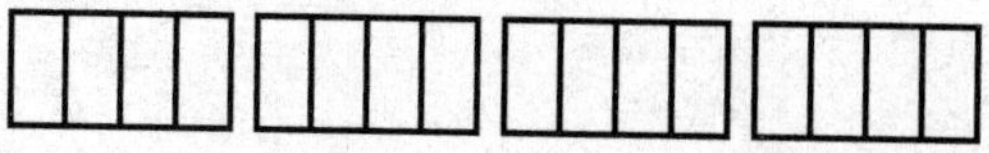

15. Raul has $\frac{1}{2}$ loaf of bread. He divides the half loaf into equal parts.

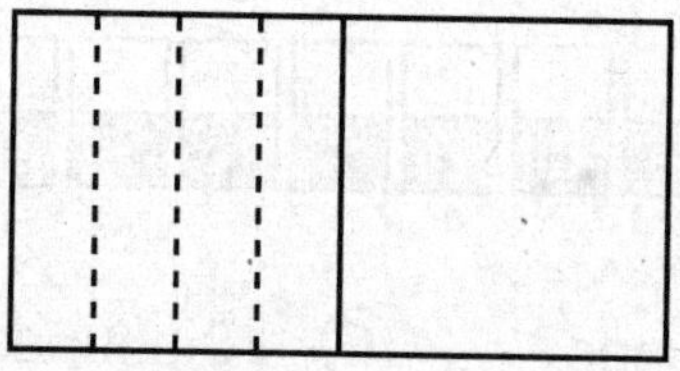

Which division expression does the model represent?

Ⓐ $\frac{1}{2} \div 4$

Ⓑ $\frac{1}{8} \div 4$

Ⓒ $1 \div \frac{1}{2}$

Ⓓ $\frac{1}{2} \div 2$

GO ON

Name ______________________________

16. Joss drew a model to help solve a problem. Which division expression does the model represent?

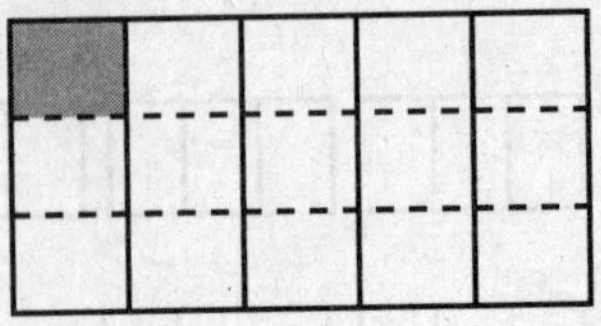

Ⓐ $\frac{1}{3} \div 5$ Ⓒ $\frac{1}{5} \div 3$

Ⓑ $\frac{1}{2} \div 5$ Ⓓ $5 \div \frac{1}{3}$

17. Ann's dad cooked dinner for 9 people. He cooked $\frac{1}{2}$ pound of turkey for each person. How many pounds of turkey did Ann's dad cook?

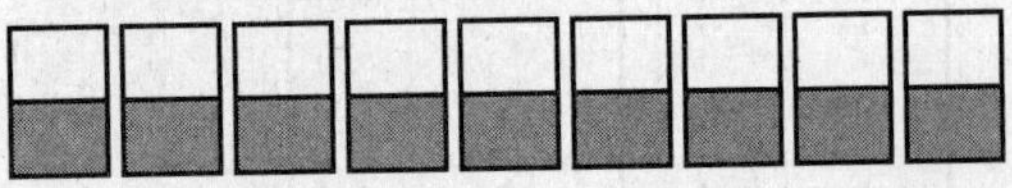

Ⓐ 4 pounds Ⓒ 18 pounds

Ⓑ $2\frac{1}{2}$ pounds Ⓓ $4\frac{1}{2}$ pounds

18. A shelf in a window is 4 feet long. Danny uses $\frac{3}{4}$ of the shelf for plants. How many feet of the shelf does Danny use for plants?

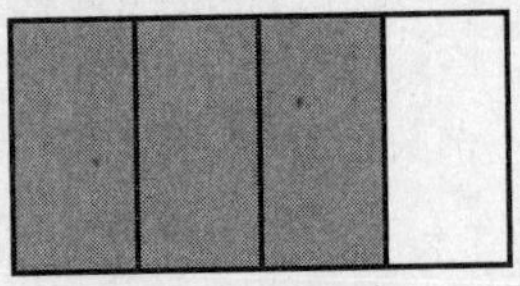

Ⓐ 2 feet Ⓒ 1 foot

Ⓑ 3 feet Ⓓ 4 feet

19. Vin makes a model to help him solve a problem. Which multiplication expression does his model represent?

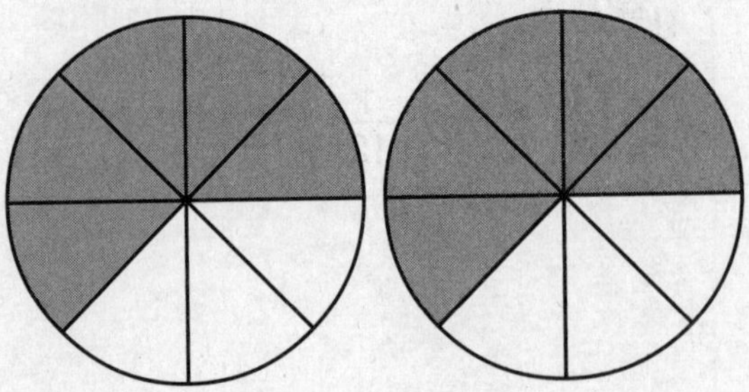

Ⓐ $2 \times \frac{3}{8}$

Ⓑ $2 \times \frac{1}{4}$

Ⓒ $2 \times \frac{5}{8}$

Ⓓ $10 \times \frac{1}{8}$

20. Which division expression does the model represent?

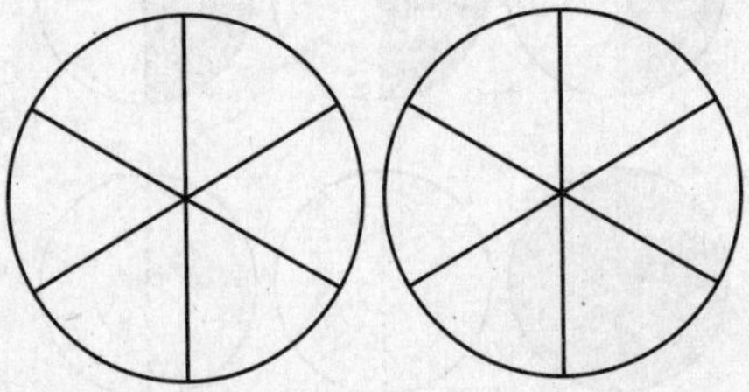

Ⓐ $2 \div \frac{1}{6}$

Ⓑ $2 \div \frac{1}{12}$

Ⓒ $12 \div \frac{1}{6}$

Ⓓ $6 \div \frac{1}{12}$

STOP

Name ______________________________

Fill in the bubble for the correct answer.

1. Which is the best estimate of the sum of $\frac{5}{8}$ and $\frac{7}{12}$?

Ⓐ 2 Ⓒ 3

Ⓑ 5 Ⓓ 1

2. George has 10 new books. Of those ten, $\frac{1}{5}$ of the books were gifts. How many books were gifts?

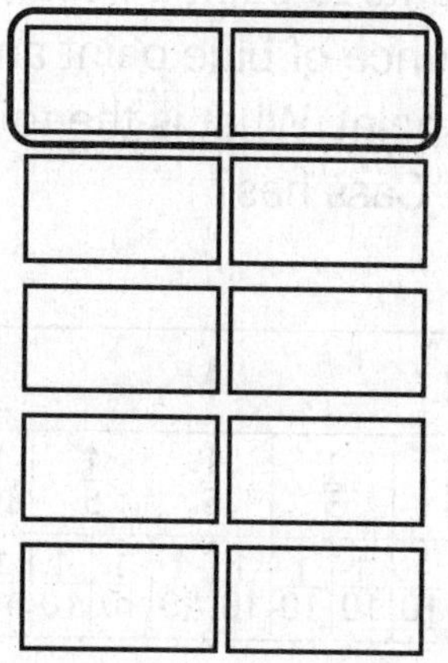

Ⓐ 6 Ⓑ 2 Ⓒ 5 Ⓓ 4

3. Eric uses the Associative Property to evaluate the expression $\frac{7}{10} + \frac{2}{3} + \frac{1}{3}$. Which equation does he write?

Ⓐ $\left(\frac{2}{3} + \frac{7}{10}\right) + \frac{1}{3} = 1\frac{7}{10}$

Ⓑ $\frac{2}{3} + \frac{7}{10} + \frac{1}{3} = 1\frac{7}{10}$

Ⓒ $\frac{1}{3} + \frac{7}{10} + \frac{2}{3} = 1\frac{7}{10}$

Ⓓ $\frac{7}{10} + \left(\frac{2}{3} + \frac{1}{3}\right) = 1\frac{7}{10}$

4. Two-thirds of a pie is left over after dinner. Meg takes $\frac{1}{6}$ of the whole pie to a neighbor. How much pie is left after Meg takes some to the neighbor?

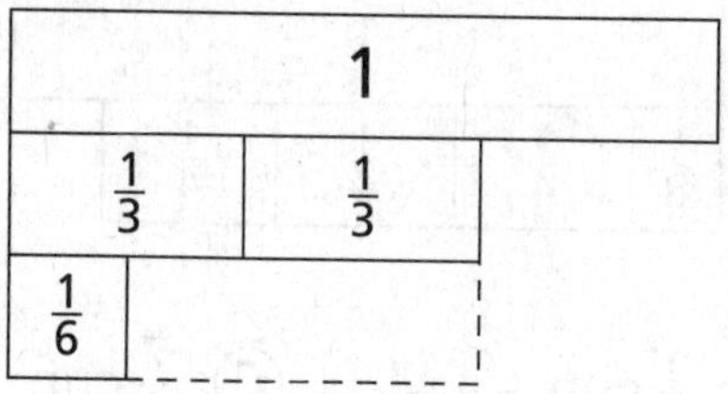

Ⓐ $\frac{5}{6}$ Ⓒ $\frac{3}{6}$

Ⓑ $\frac{2}{3}$ Ⓓ $\frac{1}{3}$

5. Sara used a model to help her multiply a whole number and a fraction. Which multiplication expression does her model represent?

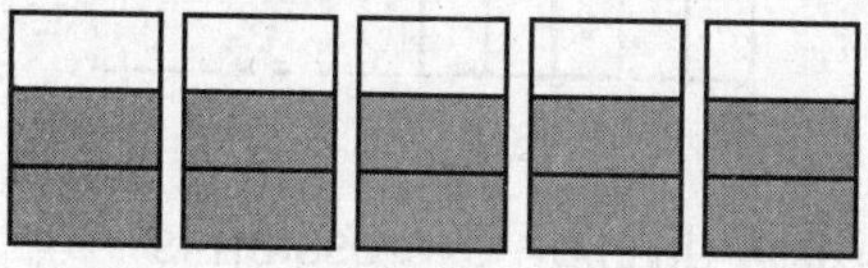

Ⓐ $5 \times \frac{2}{3}$

Ⓑ $2 \times \frac{3}{5}$

Ⓒ $5 \times \frac{1}{5}$

Ⓓ Not here

GO ON

Name ______________________________

6. Mona sprinkles $\frac{1}{8}$ cup of Parmesan cheese and $\frac{3}{4}$ cup of mozzarella cheese on top of a pizza. What is the total amount of cheese Mona sprinkles on her pizza?

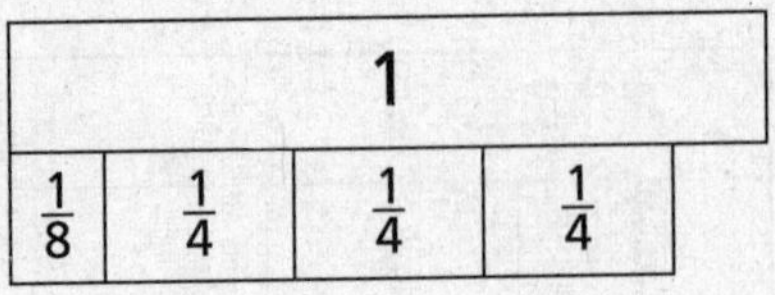

Ⓐ $\frac{1}{2}$ cup

Ⓑ 1 cup

Ⓒ $\frac{7}{8}$ cup

Ⓓ $\frac{3}{8}$ cup

7. Jake has $\frac{1}{2}$ pan of baked ziti. He divides the baked ziti into equal parts.

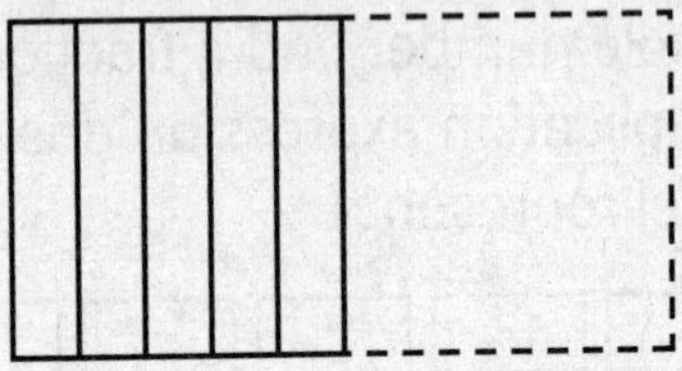

Which division expression is represented by the model?

Ⓐ $\frac{1}{10} \div 5$

Ⓑ $\frac{1}{2} \div 5$

Ⓒ $\frac{1}{5} \div 2$

Ⓓ $\frac{1}{2} \div 2$

8. Which division problem is shown by the model?

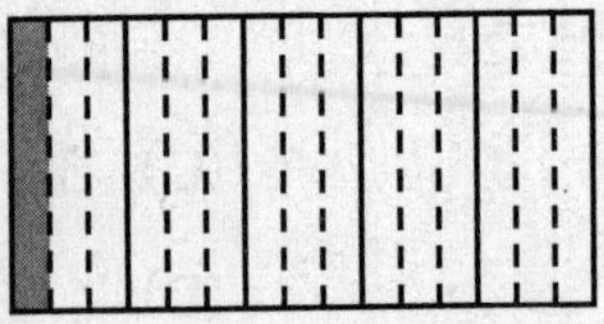

Ⓐ $\frac{1}{5} \div 3 = \frac{1}{15}$

Ⓑ $5 \div \frac{1}{3} = 15$

Ⓒ $\frac{1}{3} \div 5 = \frac{1}{15}$

Ⓓ $3 \div \frac{1}{5} = 15$

9. Cass wants to paint a postcard. He has $\frac{4}{5}$ ounce of blue paint and $\frac{3}{10}$ ounce of gold paint. What is the total amount of paint Cass has?

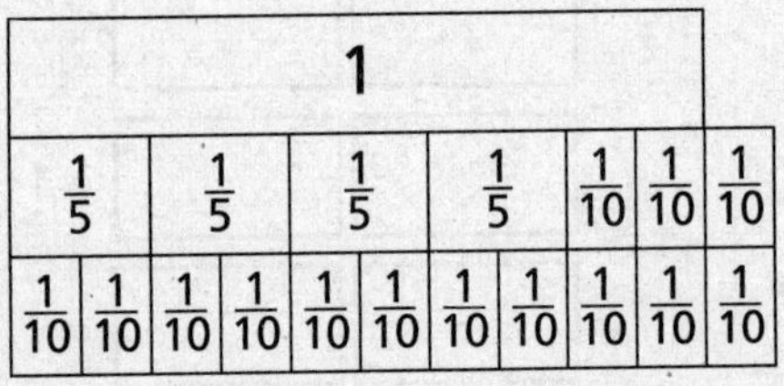

Ⓐ $1\frac{1}{10}$ ounce

Ⓑ 1 ounce

Ⓒ $\frac{7}{10}$ ounce

Ⓓ $1\frac{1}{5}$ ounce

10. Benji is adding $2\frac{1}{2} + (3\frac{1}{2} + 1\frac{1}{3})$. He rewrites the expression as $(2\frac{1}{2} + 3\frac{1}{2}) + 1\frac{1}{3}$. What property does Benji use?

Ⓐ Associative Property

Ⓑ Distributive Property

Ⓒ Commutative Property

Ⓓ Identity Property

GO ON

11. A tailor had $\frac{11}{12}$ foot of thread. He used $\frac{3}{4}$ foot to sew a button on a shirt. How much of the thread does the tailor have left?

Ⓐ $\frac{1}{5}$ foot
Ⓑ $\frac{1}{8}$ foot
Ⓒ $\frac{1}{2}$ foot
Ⓓ $\frac{1}{6}$ foot

12. Rob has 12 sandwiches. He cuts each sandwich into thirds. How many pieces of sandwich does Rob have?

Record your answer and fill in the bubbles on the grid. Be sure to use the correct place value.

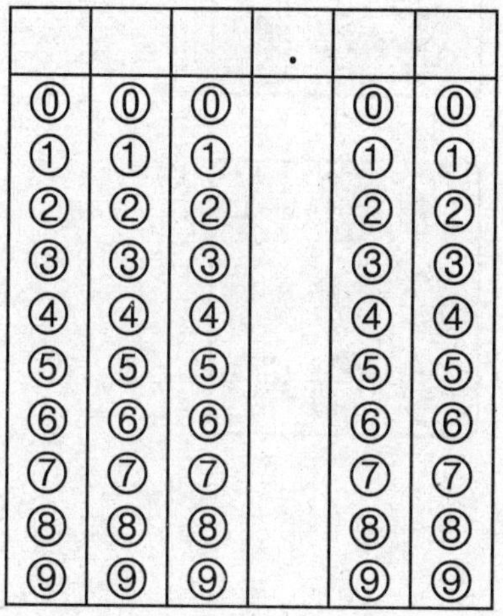

13. Which problem does the area model represent?

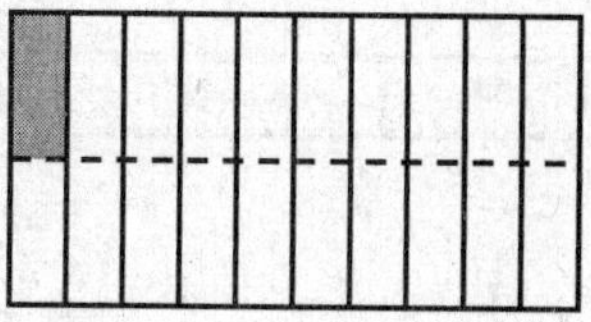

Ⓐ $\frac{1}{2} \div 5$
Ⓑ $\frac{1}{5} \div 2$
Ⓒ $\frac{1}{2} \div 5$
Ⓓ $\frac{1}{10} \div 2$

14. Fern adds $\frac{1}{4}$ and $\frac{5}{8}$. Which model could she use to help find the sum?

Ⓐ
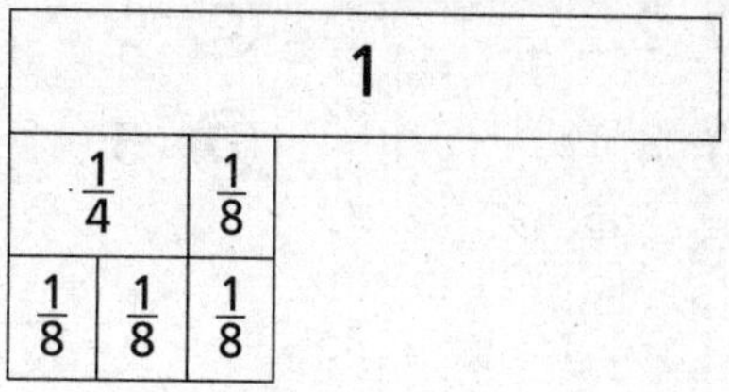

Ⓑ
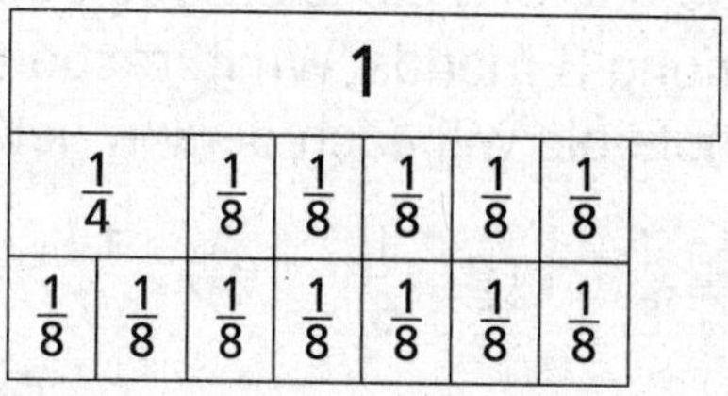

Ⓒ
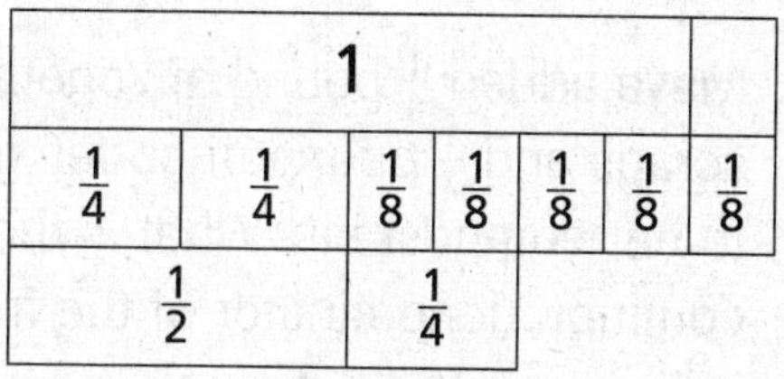

Ⓓ
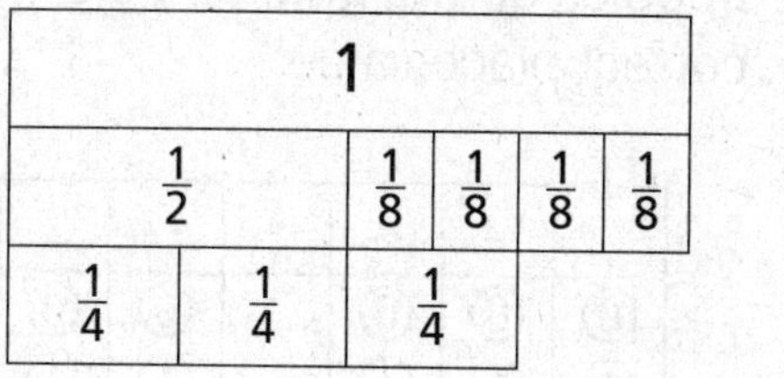

15. Paul jogged around a track $5\frac{1}{3}$ times. Sunita jogged around the same track $7\frac{1}{6}$ times. How many more times did Sunita jog around the track than Paul?

Ⓐ $1\frac{5}{6}$
Ⓑ $2\frac{1}{3}$
Ⓒ $2\frac{1}{6}$
Ⓓ $1\frac{1}{6}$

GO ON

Name ______________________________

16. Which is the best estimate of the sum of $\frac{4}{5}$ and $\frac{3}{4}$?

Ⓐ 2
Ⓑ 4
Ⓒ $\frac{1}{2}$
Ⓓ 5

17. One half of a pie is divided equally among 3 friends. What fraction of the whole pie will each person get?

Ⓐ $\frac{1}{8}$ Ⓑ $\frac{1}{6}$ Ⓒ $\frac{1}{10}$ Ⓓ $\frac{1}{4}$

18. Maya added $\frac{1}{4}$ pound of vegetable scraps and $\frac{1}{7}$ pound of coffee grounds to her compost bin. What is the least common denominator of the fractions?

Record your answer and fill in the bubbles on the grid. Be sure to use the correct place value.

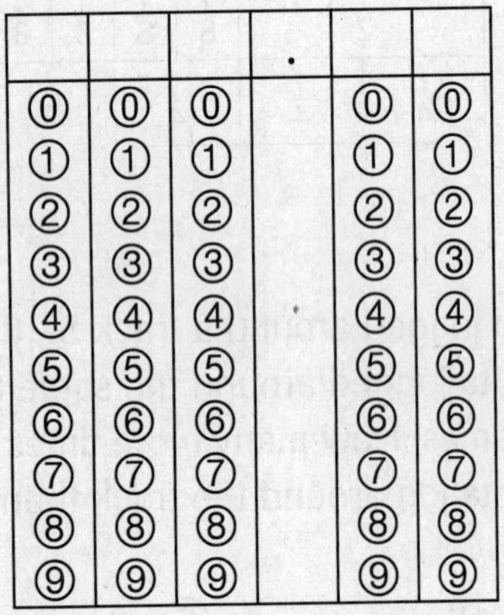

19. Todd used counters to model $\frac{2}{3} \times 9$. Which picture represents the expression?

Ⓐ
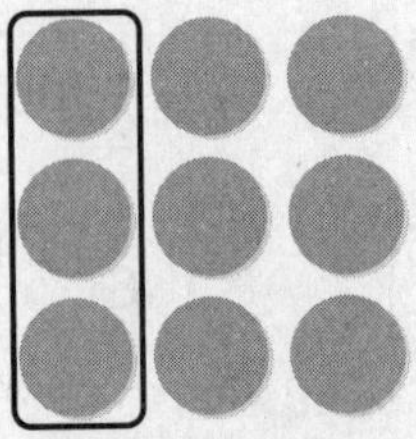

Ⓑ
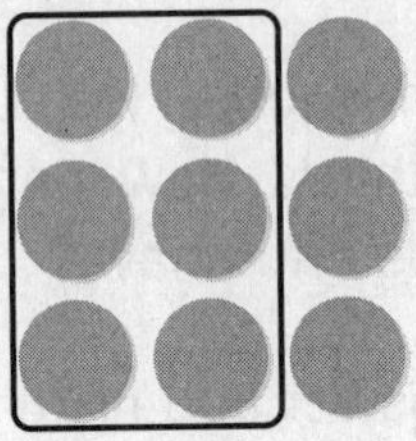

Ⓒ
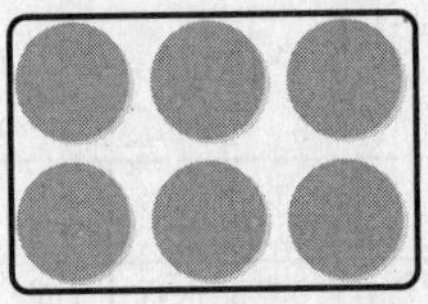

Ⓓ
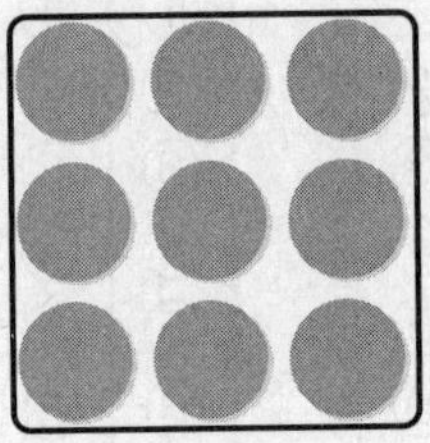

20. Which multiplication expression does the model represent?

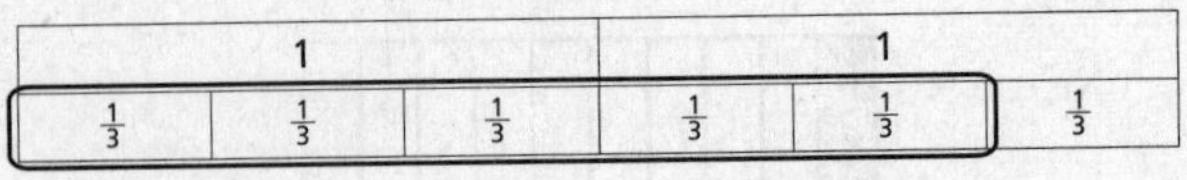

Ⓐ $\frac{1}{3} \times 2$
Ⓑ $\frac{5}{6} \times 6$
Ⓒ $\frac{5}{6} \times 2$
Ⓓ $\frac{5}{3} \times 2$

GO ON

21. Alice's mother took 2 cheesecakes to a party. After the party, $\frac{3}{8}$ of each cheesecake was left. How much cheesecake was left in all?

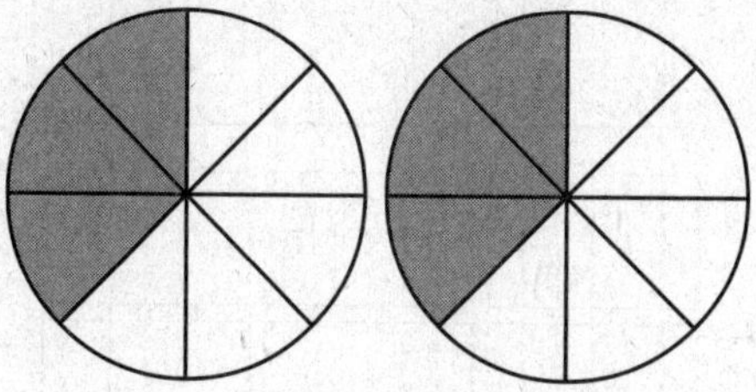

Ⓐ $\frac{6}{8}$ Ⓑ $\frac{2}{6}$ Ⓒ $\frac{2}{8}$ Ⓓ $\frac{3}{6}$

22. Kayla made $\frac{8}{12}$ gallon of iced tea for a picnic. The guests at the picnic drank $\frac{1}{4}$ gallon of the iced tea. Which shows the amount of iced tea remaining?

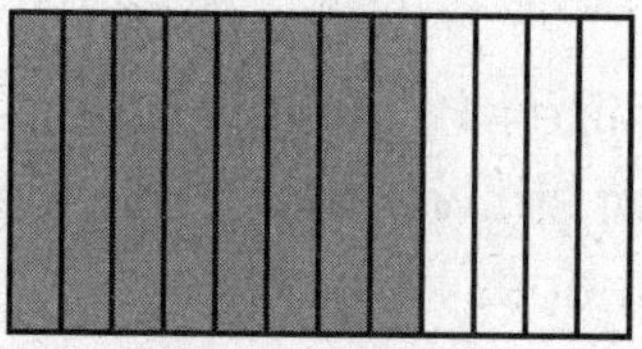

Ⓐ $\frac{1}{12}$ gallon

Ⓑ $\frac{2}{12}$ gallon

Ⓒ $\frac{5}{12}$ gallon

Ⓓ $\frac{9}{12}$ gallon

23. Marvin painted $\frac{1}{6}$ of his clay pot yellow and $\frac{3}{5}$ of it green. What fraction of his clay pot did Marvin paint?

Ⓐ $\frac{4}{30}$ Ⓑ $\frac{23}{30}$ Ⓒ $\frac{1}{30}$ Ⓓ $\frac{18}{30}$

24. Victor has 2 fruit bars. He divides the bars into $\frac{1}{3}$-size pieces. Which represents the expression $2 \div \frac{1}{3}$?

Ⓐ 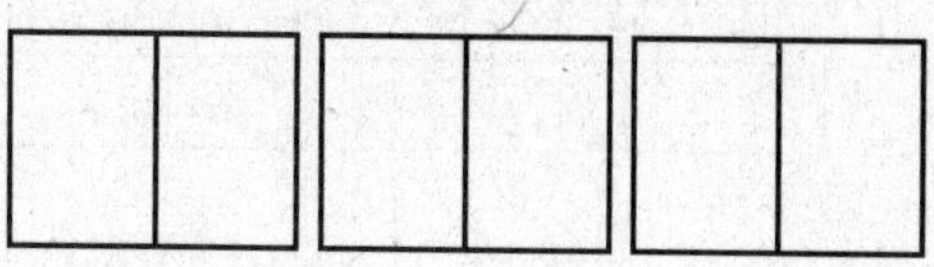

Ⓑ 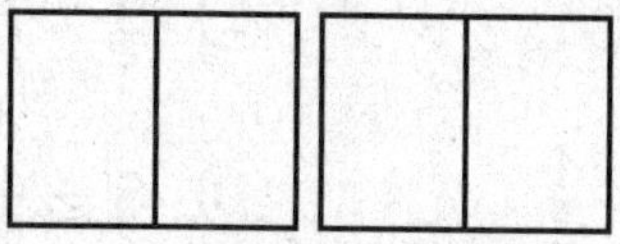

Ⓒ 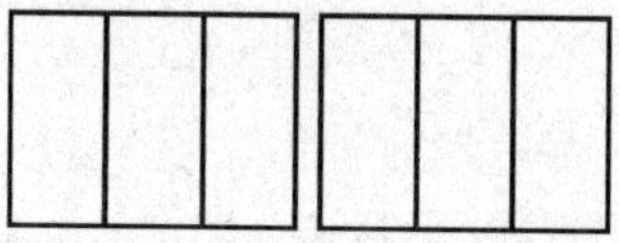

Ⓓ 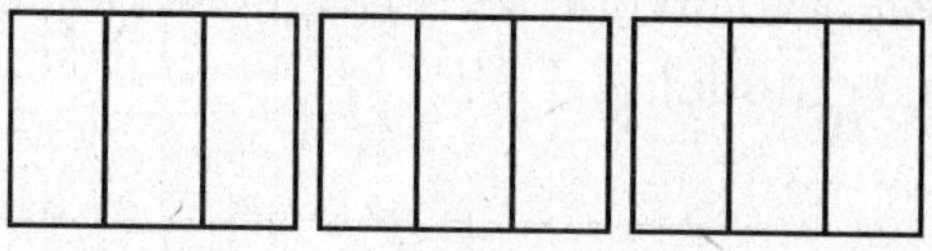

25. Which shows how to use objects to model $\frac{1}{2} + \frac{1}{3}$?

Ⓐ 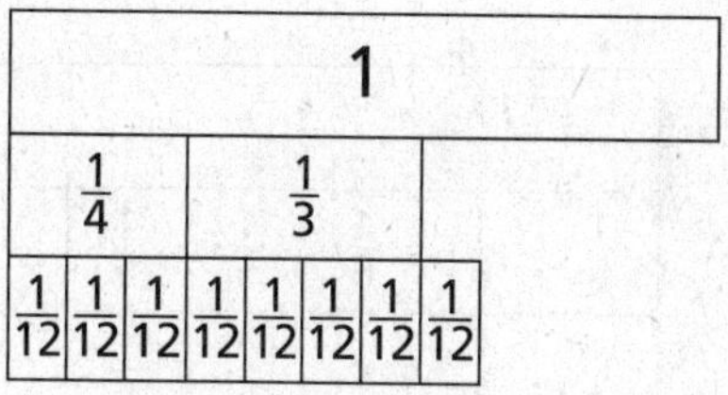

Ⓑ 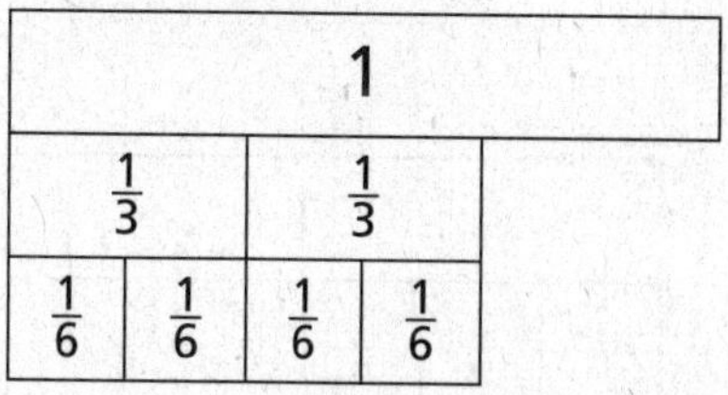

Ⓒ 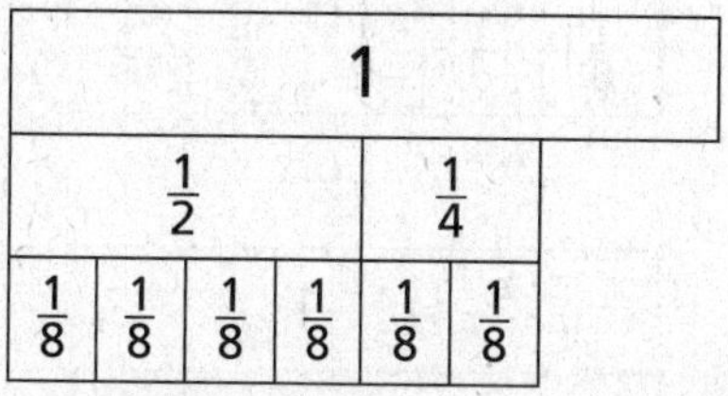

Ⓓ 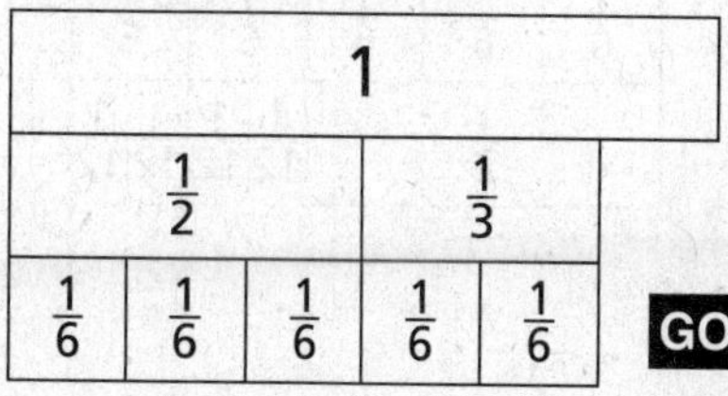

GO ON

26. Which division expression is represented by the model?

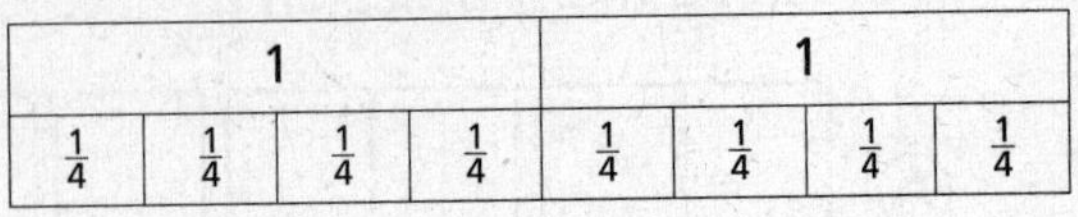

Ⓐ $2 \div \frac{1}{16}$

Ⓑ $2 \div \frac{1}{4}$

Ⓒ $8 \div \frac{1}{2}$

Ⓓ $8 \div \frac{1}{8}$

27. Which shows how to use objects to model $\frac{5}{6} - \frac{1}{2}$?

Ⓐ 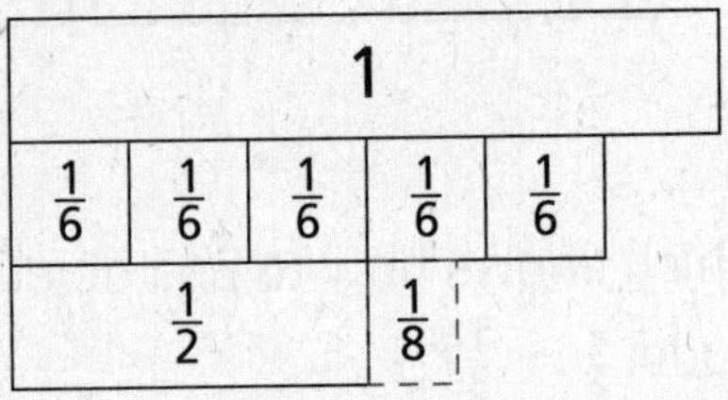

Ⓑ 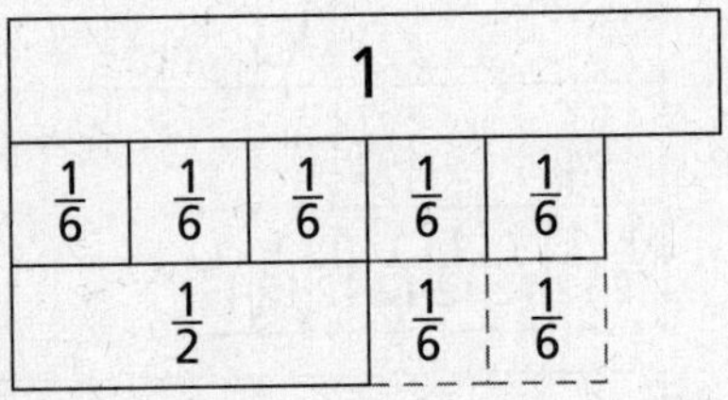

Ⓒ 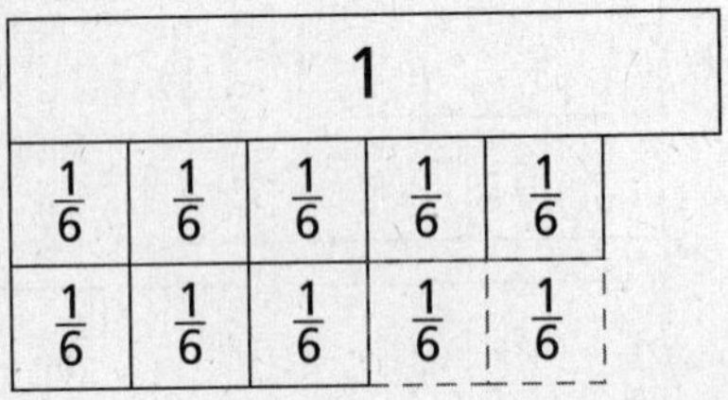

Ⓓ 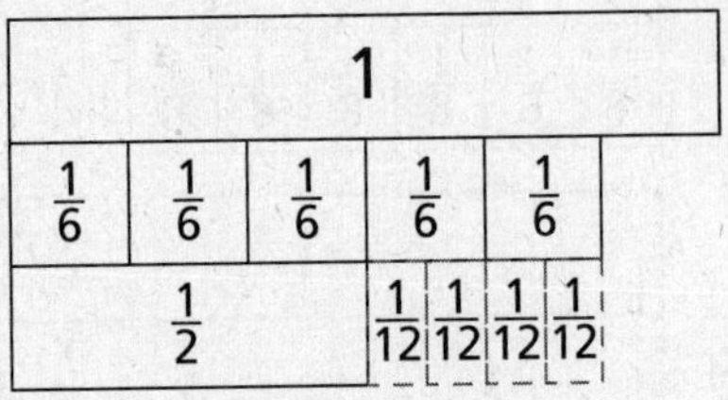

28. Oliver has 6 pounds of sliced turkey. Which model represents the number of sandwiches he can make if he uses $\frac{1}{3}$ pound of turkey in each sandwich?

Ⓐ 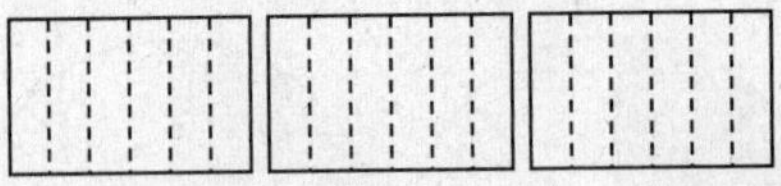

Ⓑ 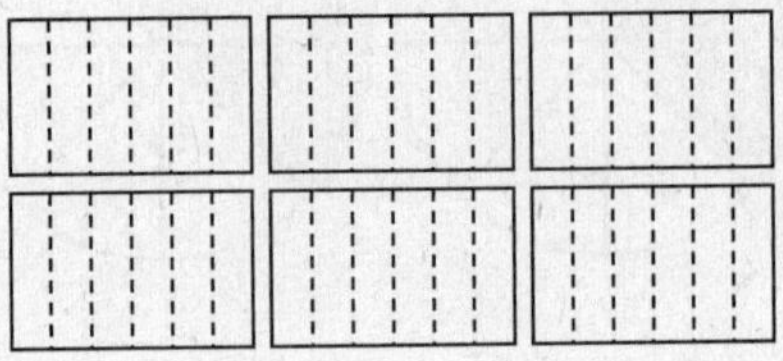

Ⓒ 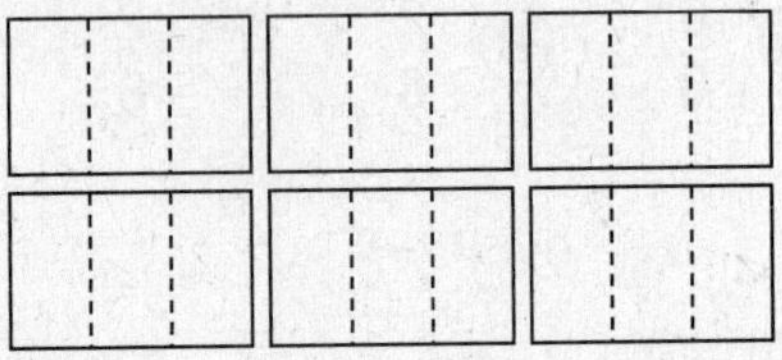

Ⓓ 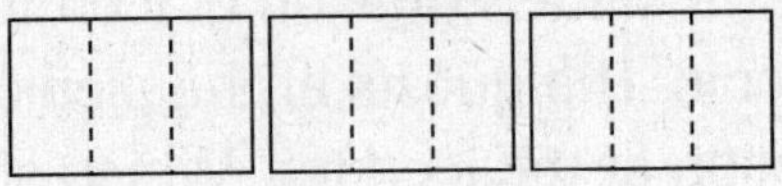

29. José mixes $1\frac{1}{3}$ cups of grapes and $2\frac{1}{2}$ cups of strawberries. How many cups of fruit does he have in all?

Ⓐ $3\frac{2}{3}$ cups

Ⓑ $3\frac{3}{4}$ cups

Ⓒ $1\frac{3}{4}$ cups

Ⓓ $3\frac{5}{6}$ cups

30. Serena decorated $\frac{1}{3}$ of her pennant with red stars and $\frac{3}{8}$ of the pennant with silver stars. What fraction of Serena's pennant is decorated with stars?

Ⓐ $\frac{8}{24}$ Ⓑ $\frac{12}{24}$ Ⓒ $\frac{17}{24}$ Ⓓ $\frac{3}{24}$

STOP

Name ______________________________

Fill in the bubble for the correct answer.

1. Which statement about 63 is true?

Ⓐ It is prime.

Ⓑ It is neither prime nor composite.

Ⓒ It is composite and prime.

Ⓓ It is composite.

2. Linda writes the expression $12 + (2 \times 5)$ to represent the number of books she packed. Which story matches the expression she wrote?

Ⓐ Linda packed a box with 12 books. Then she packed 2 boxes with 5 books in each box.

Ⓑ Linda packed a box with 12 books. Then she packed the box with 2 books and 5 more.

Ⓒ Linda packed a box with 12 books. Then she packed a box with 2 books and another box with 5 books.

Ⓓ Linda packed 5 boxes with 2 books in each box. Then she packed 5 boxes with 12 books in each box.

3. Devon simplified a numerical expression. The correct answer is 6. Which could be the expression?

Ⓐ $(12 - 8) \times 9$

Ⓑ $9 + (12 - 8)$

Ⓒ $12 \div (9 - 8)$

Ⓓ $(8 \times 9) \div 12$

4. A recipe calls for 2 cups of whole wheat flour and 1 cup of white flour. Simplify the expression $4 \times (2 + 1)$ to find the number of cups of flour Lenny needs to make four times the recipe. How many cups of flour does Lenny need in all?

Record your answer and fill in the bubbles on the grid. Be sure to use the correct place value.

			.		
⓪	⓪	⓪		⓪	⓪
①	①	①		①	①
②	②	②		②	②
③	③	③		③	③
④	④	④		④	④
⑤	⑤	⑤		⑤	⑤
⑥	⑥	⑥		⑥	⑥
⑦	⑦	⑦		⑦	⑦
⑧	⑧	⑧		⑧	⑧
⑨	⑨	⑨		⑨	⑨

GO ON

Name ________________________________

5. Gina's bookshelf has 3 shelves with 9 nonfiction books on each shelf and 2 shelves with 11 fiction books on each shelf. Which expression shows the number of books on Gina's bookshelf?

Ⓐ $(3 + 9) \times (2 + 11)$

Ⓑ $(3 \times 9) + (2 \times 11)$

Ⓒ $3 \times (9 \times 2) + 11$

Ⓓ $3 \times (9 + 2) + 11$

6. Matt had \$20. Then he worked 7 hours for \$8 each hour. Which expression matches the words?

Ⓐ 7 × (\$12 + \$8)

Ⓑ (7 × \$20) − \$8

Ⓒ (\$20 − \$8) × 7

Ⓓ \$20 + (7 × \$8)

7. Which is a prime number?

Ⓐ 32

Ⓑ 38

Ⓒ 37

Ⓓ 33

8. A jewelry designer has 120 beads. In one day, she uses 3 packets of 12 beads and 4 packets of 10 beads. Which expression represents the number of beads left at the end of the day?

Ⓐ $120 - [(3 \times 12) + (4 \times 10)]$

Ⓑ $[120 - (3 \times 12)] + (4 \times 10)$

Ⓒ $120 - [(3 + 4) \times (12 + 10)]$

Ⓓ $120 - (3 \times 12 + [4 \times 10])$

9. What is the value of the expression?

$$4 \times [(25 \times 1) + (12 \times 2)]$$

Ⓐ 148 Ⓒ 28

Ⓑ 196 Ⓓ 49

10. Tami wrote these factor pairs for a number:

1 and 20, 2 and 10, and 4 and 5

For which number did Tami write the factor pairs?

Ⓐ 20 Ⓒ 29

Ⓑ 11 Ⓓ 17

GO ON

11. Which words match the expression?

$(4 \times 6) \div 3$

Ⓐ Ella has 4 boxes of granola bars. Then she buys 6 more granola bars. She shares all the granola bars equally among 3 friends.

Ⓑ Ella has 3 boxes with 6 granola bars in each box. She shares all the granola bars equally among 3 friends.

Ⓒ Ella has 6 granola bars. She divides each granola bar into 3 equal pieces. She shares all of the pieces equally among 4 friends.

Ⓓ Ella has 4 boxes with 6 granola bars in each box. She shares the granola bars equally among 3 friends.

12. Which statement about the number 11 is true?

Ⓐ It is composite.

Ⓑ It is prime.

Ⓒ It is neither prime nor composite.

Ⓓ It is divisible by 3.

13. Payal needs to simplify $6 \times (12 - 8) + 7$. What should be her first step?

Ⓐ Multiply 6 by 12.

Ⓑ Multiply 6 by 7.

Ⓒ Add 8 to 7.

Ⓓ Subtract 8 from 12.

14. Which of the following numbers is **NOT** a factor of 56?

Ⓐ 8

Ⓑ 4

Ⓒ 6

Ⓓ 7

15. What is the value of the expression?

$[(20 \times 4) + (8 \times 6)] \times 2$

Ⓐ 256

Ⓑ 176

Ⓒ 296

Ⓓ 100

GO ON

16. Reba had \$27 to spend at the state fair. She spent \$4 on lunch and \$15 on rides.

Which expression matches the words?

Ⓐ \$27 − (\$15 − \$4)

Ⓑ \$27 − (\$15 + \$4)

Ⓒ (\$15 + \$4) − \$27

Ⓓ (\$15 − \$4) + \$27

17. A farmer planted 24 green apple trees and three times as many red apple trees. The trees are in 12 equal rows.

Which expression represents the number of apple trees in each row of the orchard?

Ⓐ $24 + [(3 \times 24)] \div 12$

Ⓑ $[24 \times (3 + 24)] \div 12$

Ⓒ $[24 + (3 \times 24)] \div 12$

Ⓓ $(24 \times 3) \div 12$

18. Which expression has a value of 4?

Ⓐ $16 - [(13 + 7) - (12 + 4)]$

Ⓑ $[(16 - 13) + 7] - (12 + 4)$

Ⓒ $16 \div [(13 + 7) - (12 + 4)]$

Ⓓ $16 \div [(13 - 7) + (12 - 4)]$

19. Which is a composite number?

Ⓐ 52

Ⓑ 17

Ⓒ 2

Ⓓ 89

20. A baker baked 250 cupcakes. He sold 4 boxes of 12 chocolate cupcakes, and 20 boxes of 6 vanilla cupcakes. Which expression shows how many of the cupcakes were left?

Ⓐ $[250 + 4 \times 12] - (20 \times 6)$

Ⓑ $250 - [4 \times (12 \times 20 \times 6)]$

Ⓒ $250 + [(4 \times 12) \times (20 \times 6)]$

Ⓓ $250 - [(4 \times 12) + (20 \times 6)]$

STOP

Fill in the bubble for the correct answer.

1. Sanya buys a pack of pencils and a pencil sharpener for $8. The pencil sharpener costs 3 times as much as the pack of pencils. How much does the pack of pencils cost?

Ⓐ $6

Ⓑ $2

Ⓒ $4

Ⓓ $1

2. A librarian placed 9 books from his cart on a library bookshelf. He then had 18 books left on the cart.

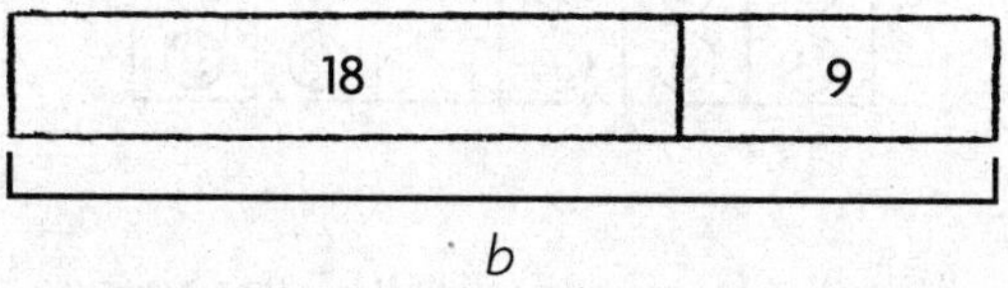

How many books did the librarian have on the cart before he shelved any books?

Ⓐ 27

Ⓑ 9

Ⓒ 21

Ⓓ 17

3. A farm stand displays 3 baskets with 12 peaches in each basket and 2 baskets with 15 plums in each basket. A customer buys 8 pieces of fruit. Which equation shows how to find the number of pieces of fruit, *p*, left in the baskets?

Ⓐ $3 + 12 \times 2 + 15 - 8 = p$

Ⓑ $12 - 3 + 15 - 2 \times 8 = p$

Ⓒ $3 \times 12 + 2 \times 15 + 8 = p$

Ⓓ $3 \times 12 + 2 \times 15 - 8 = p$

4. A group of 72 students is divided into 9 equal groups for a field trip. There must be 1 adult chaperone for every 4 students. How many chaperones are needed for each group?

Ⓐ 4 Ⓒ 8

Ⓑ 2 Ⓓ 12

5. What is the value of *m* in the equation?

$$2 + 2 \times 4 = 9 + m$$

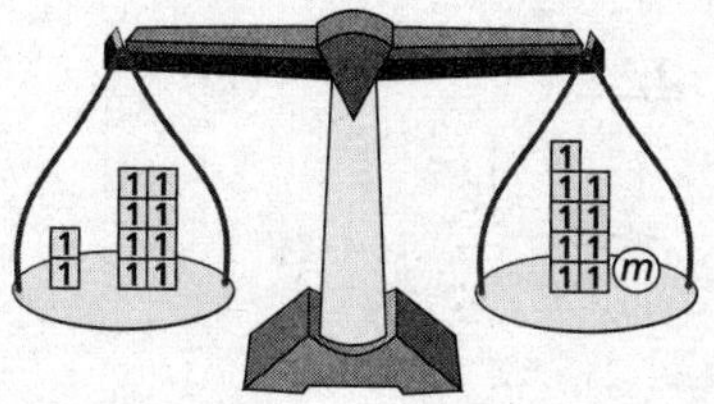

Ⓐ 3 Ⓑ 7 Ⓒ 1 Ⓓ 10

GO ON

Name ______________________________

6. A garden has 3 rows of tomato plants. Each row has 13 plants.

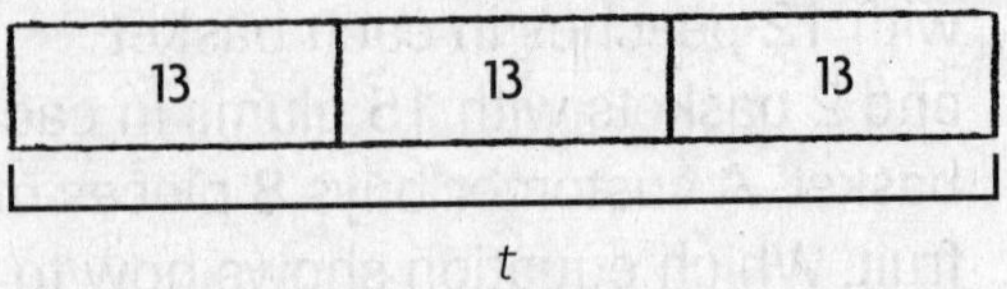

Which equation can be used to solve for *t*, the total number of tomato plants?

Ⓐ $t \div 3 = 13$ Ⓒ $13 - t = 3$

Ⓑ $13 \div t = 3$ Ⓓ $3t = 13$

7. What is the value of *v* in the equation?

$$21 - v = 8 \times 2$$

Ⓐ 15 Ⓒ 5

Ⓑ 37 Ⓓ 13

8. What value of *r* makes the equation true?

$$11 + 2 \times 6 = 45 - r$$

Ⓐ 46 Ⓒ 12

Ⓑ 22 Ⓓ 1

9. The desks in Joe's classroom are arranged in 7 rows. Each row contains 5 desks. The equation that describes the number of desks, *d*, in the classroom is $d \div 7 = 5$. How many desks are in Joe's classroom?

Record your answer and fill in the bubbles on the grid. Be sure to use the correct place value.

			.		
⓪	⓪	⓪		⓪	⓪
①	①	①		①	①
②	②	②		②	②
③	③	③		③	③
④	④	④		④	④
⑤	⑤	⑤		⑤	⑤
⑥	⑥	⑥		⑥	⑥
⑦	⑦	⑦		⑦	⑦
⑧	⑧	⑧		⑧	⑧
⑨	⑨	⑨		⑨	⑨

10. Natalie keeps her doll collection in a display case. She places 15 international dolls on 5 shelves with the same number on each shelf. She also places 2 antique dolls on each shelf. Which equation can be used to find the number of dolls, *d*, on each shelf?

Ⓐ $d \div 5 + 2 = 15$

Ⓑ $d \times 5 + 2 = 15$

Ⓒ $15 \times 5 + 2 = d$

Ⓓ $15 \div 5 + 2 = d$

GO ON

11. What value of c makes the equation true?

$$5 + c + 3 = 3 + 10 + 4$$

Ⓐ 9　　Ⓒ 5

Ⓑ 4　　Ⓓ 6

12. Thomas divides 48 large paper clips equally among 4 containers. Then he divides 12 small paper clips equally among the same 4 containers. How many paper clips are in each container?

Ⓐ 30　　Ⓒ 4

Ⓑ 15　　Ⓓ 20

13. A baker uses 4 cups of sugar for each of 3 cakes and 2 cups of sugar for each of 5 pies. Then she uses 6 cups of sugar to make frosting.

Which equation shows how to find s, the number of cups of sugar used in all?

Ⓐ $4 \times 2 + 3 \times 5 + 6 = s$

Ⓑ $4 \times 3 + 2 \times 5 - 6 = s$

Ⓒ $4 \times 3 + 2 \times 5 + 6 = s$

Ⓓ $4 - 3 + 5 - 2 + 6 = s$

14. What is the value of w in the equation?

$$6w + 5 = 41$$

Ⓐ 11

Ⓑ 30

Ⓒ 52

Ⓓ 6

15. Cleo's bicycle weighs 19 pounds. When she puts her backpack in the bike basket the total weight of the bike is 27 pounds.

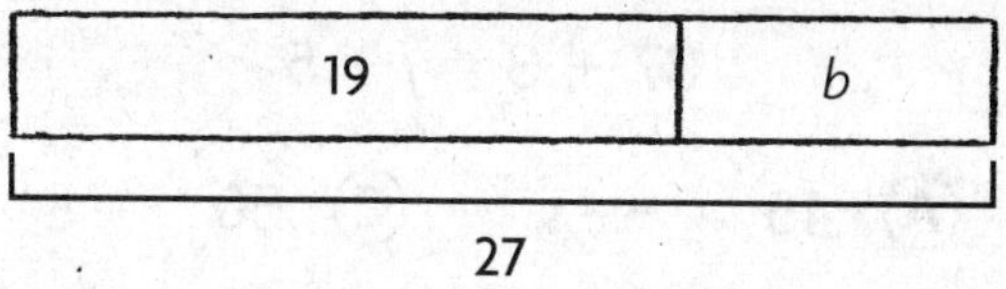

Which equation can be used to find b, the weight of the backpack?

Ⓐ $b - 19 = 27$

Ⓑ $19 - b = 27$

Ⓒ $19 + b = 27$

Ⓓ $b + 33 = 27$

GO ON

16. Lori buys 6 packages of 8 red pens each and 4 packages of 12 blue pens each. She donated 24 of the pens.

Which equation shows how to find p, the number of pens Lori has left?

Ⓐ $6 \times 8 + 4 \times 12 - 24 = p$

Ⓑ $24 - 8 - 6 + 12 - 4 = p$

Ⓒ $6 \times 4 + 8 \times 12 - 24 = p$

Ⓓ $6 \times 8 + 4 \times 12 + 24 = p$

17. What is the value of j in the equation?

$$37 + 3 = j - 5$$

Ⓐ 45 Ⓒ 50

Ⓑ 32 Ⓓ 35

18. Eliza's sister earns \$126 for 6 hours of work. The equation $6h = 126$ can be used to find h, the amount she earns in one hour.

How much does Eliza's sister earn in one hour?

Ⓐ \$12 Ⓒ \$21

Ⓑ \$20 Ⓓ \$132

19. Nellie biked 4 times as far as Ned. Together, Nellie and Ned biked 15 miles. The equation $4n + n = 15$ can be used to find n, the number of miles Ned biked.

How many miles did Ned bike?

Ⓐ 4

Ⓑ 3

Ⓒ 5

Ⓓ 11

20. There are 6 steps leading up to a museum. Each step is 8 inches high.

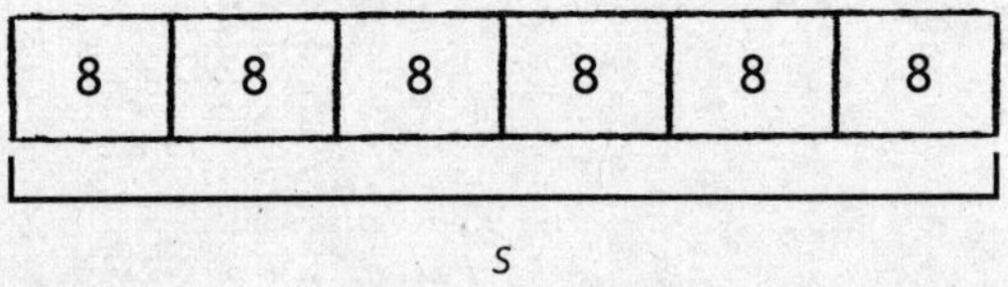

Which equation can be used to find the total height of the steps?

Ⓐ $6 + s = 8$

Ⓑ $8 \div s = 6$

Ⓒ $8 - s = 6$

Ⓓ $6 \times 8 = s$

STOP

Fill in the bubble for the correct answer.

1. Justin stores his sports equipment in a cube-shaped box.

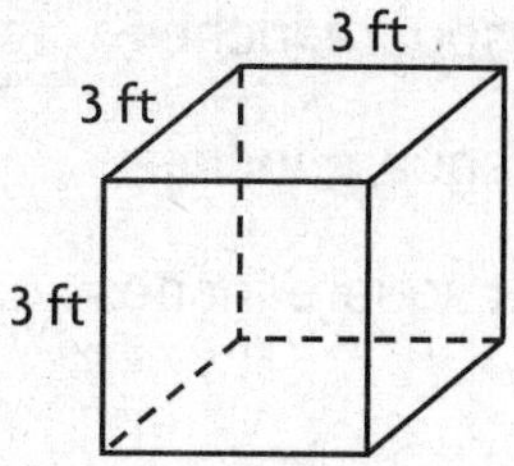

Which equation can he use to find the volume of the box?

Ⓐ $V = 3 \times 3$

Ⓑ $V = 3 + 3 + 3$

Ⓒ $V = 3 \times 3 \times 3$

Ⓓ $V = 9 + 3$

2. A tailor wants to find the perimeter of a piece of fabric.

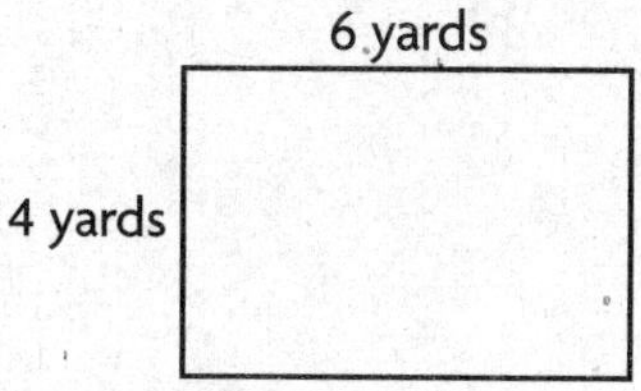

Which equation can he use to find the perimeter?

Ⓐ $P = 6 + 4 + 6 + 4$

Ⓑ $P = 6 \times 4$

Ⓒ $P = 6 + 4$

Ⓓ $P = 2 \times 10 + 2 \times 6$

3. Jasmine built a display box. She wants to line the bottom of the box with foil. What is the area of the surface she wants to cover?

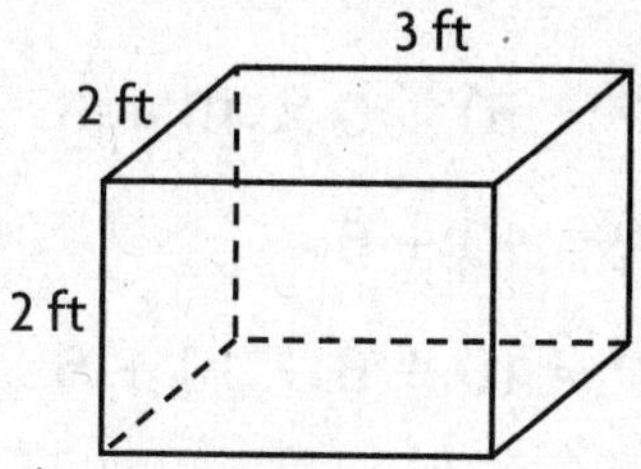

Ⓐ 4 square feet

Ⓑ 6 square feet

Ⓒ 12 square feet

Ⓓ 7 square feet

4. Which equation can be used to find the volume of the prism?

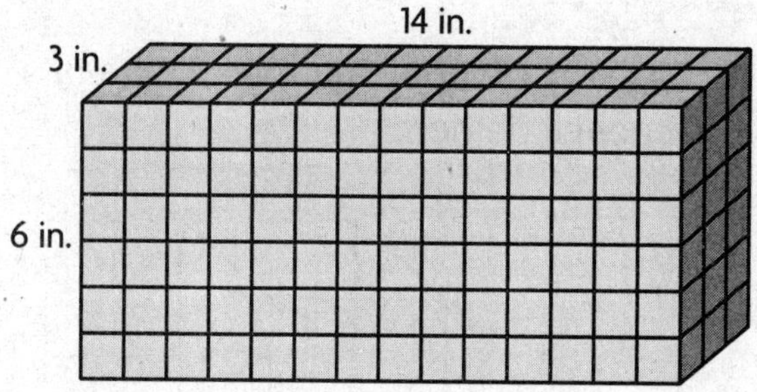

Ⓐ $V = 14 + 3 + 6$

Ⓑ $V = (2 \times 14) + (2 \times 3)$

Ⓒ $V = 42 + 6$

Ⓓ $V = 42 \times 6$

GO ON

5. Maria's mother wants to build a fence around a rectangular-shaped vegetable garden. The garden is 10 feet long and 6 feet wide. Which equation can she use to find the perimeter?

Ⓐ $P = 10 \times 6$

Ⓑ $P = 10 + 6 \times 10 + 6$

Ⓒ $P = 10 + 6$

Ⓓ $P = 10 + 6 + 10 + 6$

6. Greg is building a wooden box. The box is 4 feet long and 3 feet wide. He wants the volume of the box to be 60 cubic feet. To what height should Greg build the box?

Ⓐ 5 feet Ⓒ 9 feet

Ⓑ 30 feet Ⓓ 32 feet

7. Javier is determining the volume of a pencil holder.

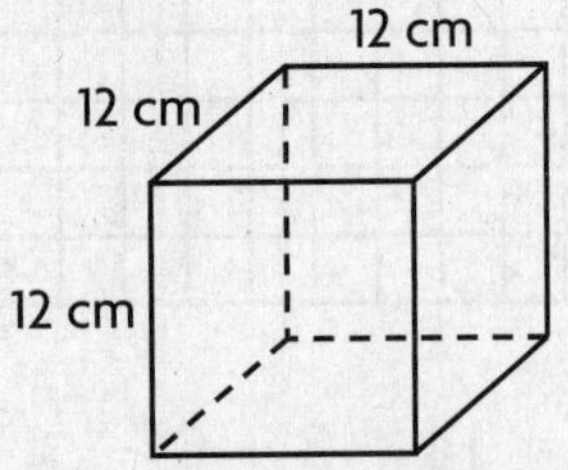

Which equation can Javier use to find the volume of his pencil holder?

Ⓐ $V = 12 + 12 + 12$

Ⓑ $V = 144 \times 12$

Ⓒ $V = 12 \times 12 + 12$

Ⓓ $V = 144 + 12$

8. What is the area of a rectangle that measures 12 inches by 9 inches?

Ⓐ 108 square inches

Ⓑ 42 square inches

Ⓒ 17 square inches

Ⓓ 972 square inches

9. Eric has a shoebox. Which equation can he use to find the volume of the shoebox?

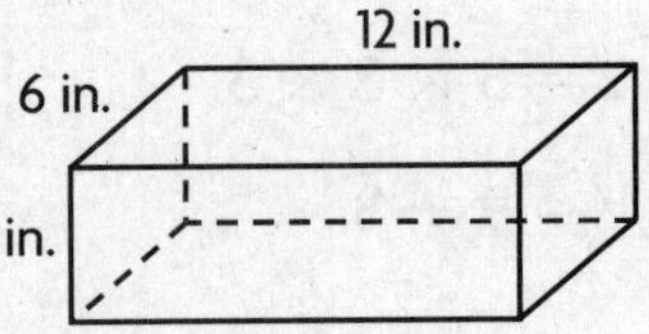

Ⓐ $V = 12 \times 6$

Ⓑ $V = 12 + 6 + 4$

Ⓒ $V = 72 \times 4$

Ⓓ $V = 36 + 4$

10. What is the perimeter of the rectangle?

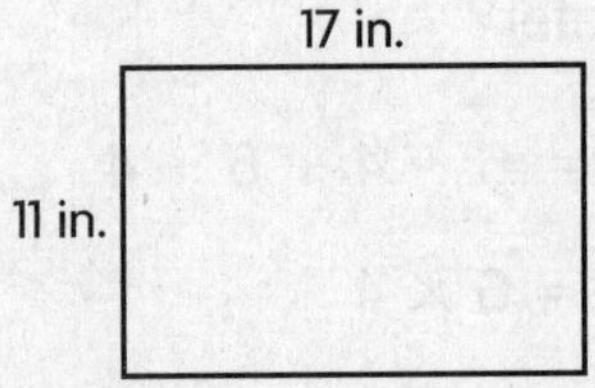

Ⓐ 187 inches Ⓒ 56 inches

Ⓑ 215 inches Ⓓ 28 inches

GO ON

11. Ann makes a quilt that is 8 feet long and 5 feet wide. What is the perimeter of the quilt?

Ⓐ 13 feet
Ⓑ 26 feet
Ⓒ 30 feet
Ⓓ 40 feet

12. Lisa uses centimeter cubes to build a rectangular prism.

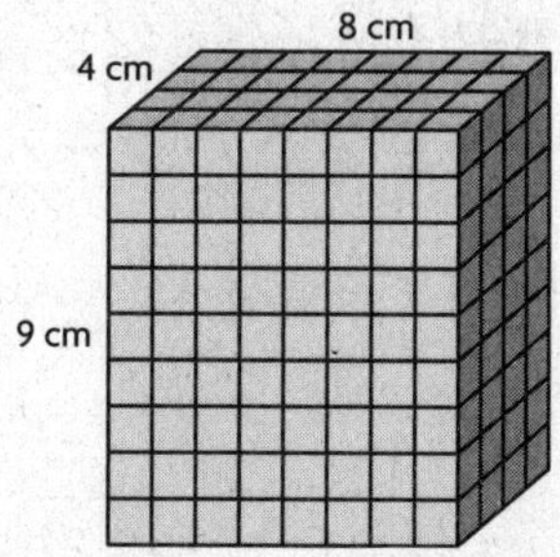

Which equation can Lisa use to find the volume of the rectangular prism?

Ⓐ $V = 8 + 4 + 9$
Ⓑ $V = 8 \times 4 \times 9$
Ⓒ $V = 8 \times 9$
Ⓓ $V = 2 \times 8 + 2 \times 4$

13. What is the area of the rectangle?

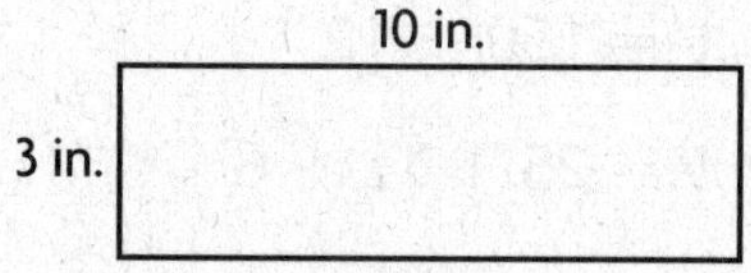

Ⓐ 13 square inches
Ⓑ 26 square inches
Ⓒ 60 square inches
Ⓓ 30 square inches

14. Earl wants to sew lace trim around the edges of a rectangular pillow that measures 12 inches by 6 inches. Which equation can Earl use to find the amount of lace trim he needs?

Ⓐ $P = 12 + 6$
Ⓑ $P = 12 \times 6$
Ⓒ $P = 12 + 6 + 12 + 6$
Ⓓ $P = 12 \times 6 + 12 \times 6$

15. A jeweler has a display counter that is 7 feet long and 4 feet wide. If she uses square tiles, each with a side length of 1 foot, what is the area she needs to cover with tile?

Record your answer and fill in the bubbles on the grid. Be sure to use the correct place value.

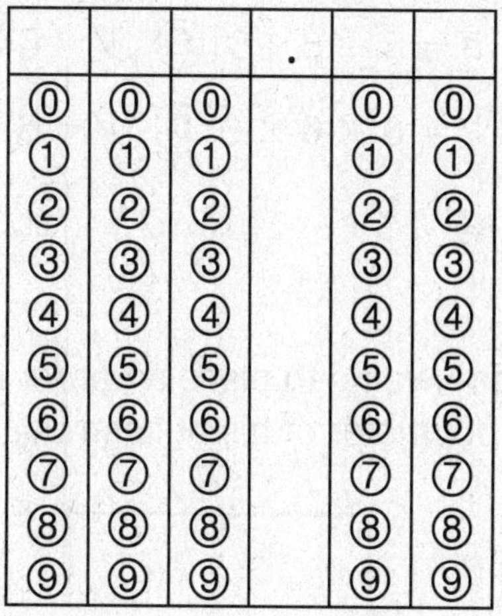

GO ON

16. Jayna saves her coins in a box.

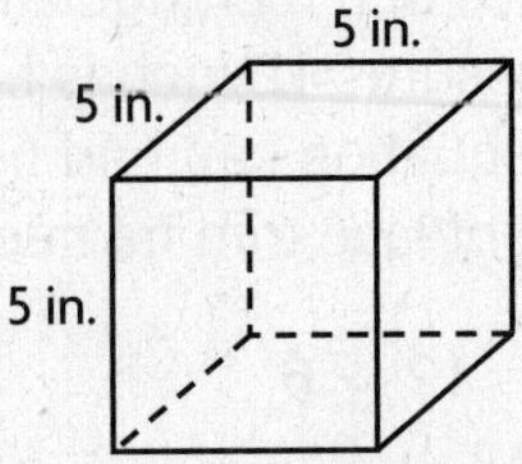

Which equation can Jayna use to find the volume of the box?

Ⓐ $V = 5 \times 5$ Ⓒ $V = 5 + 5 + 5$

Ⓑ $V = 25 + 5$ Ⓓ $V = 25 \times 5$

17. Which equation can be used to find the volume of the cube?

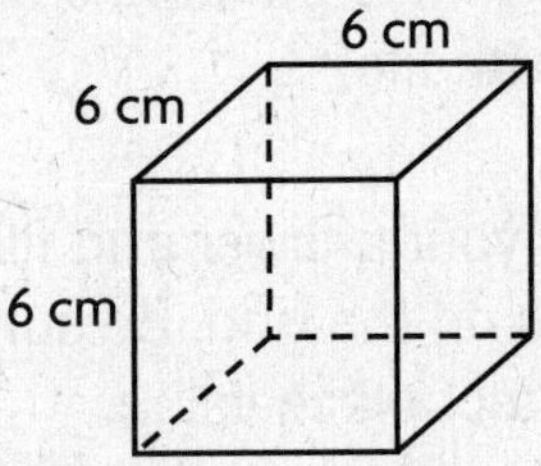

Ⓐ $V = 6 + 6 + 6$ Ⓒ $V = 6 \times 3$

Ⓑ $V = 6 \times 6 \times 6$ Ⓓ $V = 6 \times 6$

18. Jordan wants to place a border around the perimeter of his bulletin board.

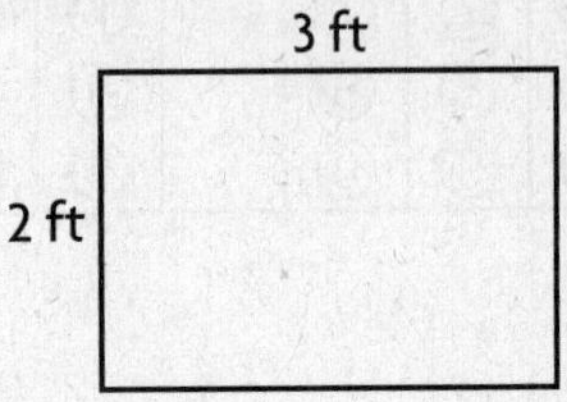

How much border does Jordan need?

Ⓐ 6 feet Ⓒ 10 feet

Ⓑ 12 feet Ⓓ 5 feet

19. Ruth packs clothes into a box.

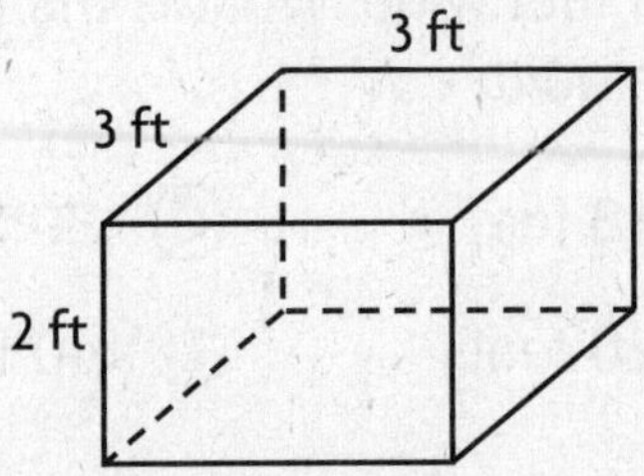

Which formula can Ruth use to find the volume of the box?

Ⓐ $V = 3 + 3 + 2$

Ⓑ $V = 3 \times 3 \times 2$

Ⓒ $V = 3 \times 3$

Ⓓ $V = 3 + 3 \times 2$

20. Kate has a box for keepsakes.

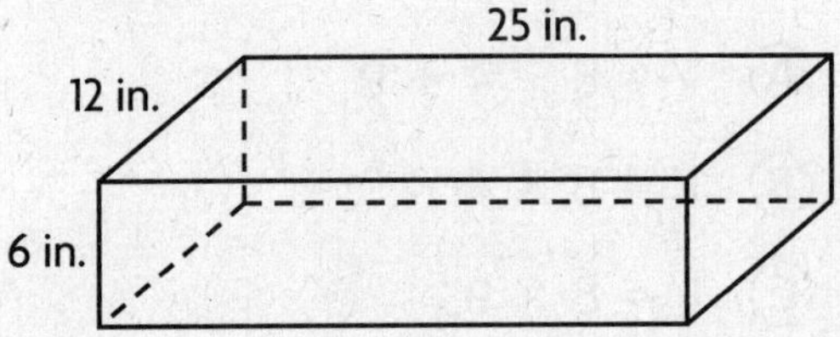

Which equation can Kate use to find the volume of the box?

Ⓐ $V = 25 \times 12 \times 6$

Ⓑ $V = (12 \times 25) + (12 \times 6)$

Ⓒ $V = 150 + 12$

Ⓓ $V = 25 + 12 + 6$

STOP

Name ______________________________

Fill in the bubble for the correct answer.

1. The rule $t = 5r$ shows that each ride at the state fair requires 5 tickets. Which number pairs can be used to show the pattern on a graph?

   Ⓐ (2, 7) (3, 8) (4, 9) (5, 10)
   Ⓑ (2, 10) (3, 15) (4, 20) (5, 25)
   Ⓒ (2, 5) (3, 5) (4, 5) (5, 5)
   Ⓓ (2, 10) (3, 11) (4, 12) (5, 13)

Use the graph for 2–3.

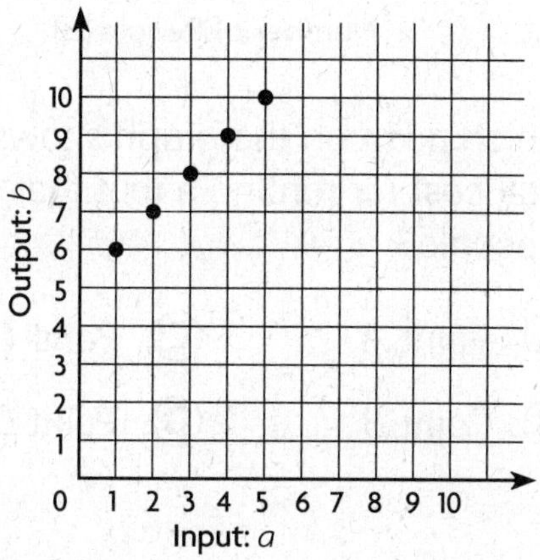

2. Which rule describes the pattern in the graph?

   Ⓐ $b = 5a$
   Ⓑ $a = b + 5$
   Ⓒ $a = 5b$
   Ⓓ $b = a + 5$

3. Which number pair extends the pattern on the graph?

   Ⓐ (11, 5)
   Ⓑ (6, 12)
   Ⓒ (6, 11)
   Ⓓ (6, 18)

4. Paul uses a number pattern to graph a point on a grid. He graphs the number pair (3, 5). Which statement about the point is true?

   Ⓐ 3 is the distance of the point from 0 on the vertical number line.
   Ⓑ 3 is the distance of the point from 0 on the horizontal number line.
   Ⓒ 5 is the distance of the point from 0 on the horizontal number line.
   Ⓓ 5 is the input value from the pattern.

5. The table uses the rule $y = x + 7$.

Input	x	1	2	3
Output	y	■	■	■

Which set of numbers correctly completes the output values in the table?

   Ⓐ 8, 9, 10
   Ⓑ 7, 14, 21
   Ⓒ 8, 10, 12
   Ⓓ 6, 5, 4

GO ON

6. Which rule describes the pattern in the table?

Input	v	7	8	9	10
Output	w	21	24	27	30

Ⓐ $w = v + 3$

Ⓑ $v = w + 3$

Ⓒ $v = 3w$

Ⓓ $w = 3v$

7. The rule $s = w + 2$ shows that in a board game the score, s, for guessing the correct title of a movie is the number of words, w, in the title plus 2. Which number pair shows the score for a title with 5 words?

Ⓐ (2, 5)

Ⓑ (5, 10)

Ⓒ (5, 7)

Ⓓ (2, 7)

8. The rule $b = 7s$ shows that each shirt, s, needs 7 buttons. How many buttons, b, are needed for 3 shirts?

Ⓐ 10 Ⓒ 40

Ⓑ 21 Ⓓ 28

9. The total cost for renting a tent depends on the size of the tent plus a fee for the tent. The rule is $c = 3 + p$, where c is the cost and p is the number of people the tent sleeps.

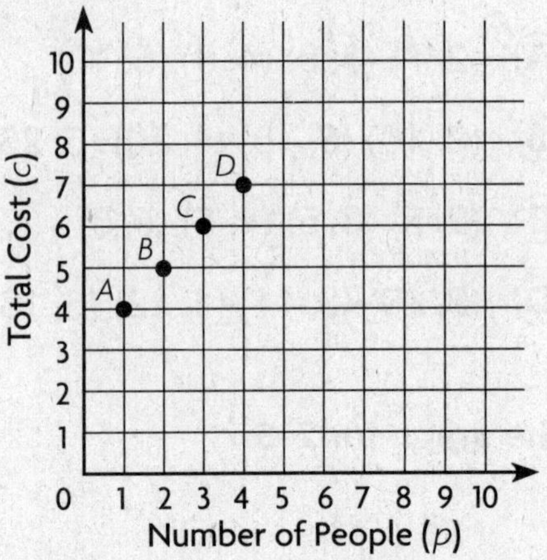

Which point on the graph shows the total cost for renting a tent that sleeps 3 people?

Ⓐ Point A Ⓒ Point C

Ⓑ Point B Ⓓ Point D

10. Millie uses the pattern rule $l = 6b$ to generate the first three terms in the pattern.

Beetles	b	1	2	3	4
Legs	l	6	12	18	■

What is the value of the missing number?

Ⓐ 24 Ⓒ 22

Ⓑ 32 Ⓓ 16

GO ON

11. Which rule describes the pattern in the table?

Input	*c*	3	4	5	6
Output	*d*	11	12	13	14

Ⓐ $d = c + 9$ Ⓒ $d = 3c$

Ⓑ $d = c + 8$ Ⓓ $d = 8c$

12. The table uses the rule $b = 5a$.

Input	*a*	2	4	6	8
Output	*b*	■	■	■	■

Which set of numbers correctly completes the output values in the table?

Ⓐ 7, 9, 11, 13

Ⓑ 10, 15, 25, 30

Ⓒ 10, 20, 30, 40

Ⓓ 10, 25, 30, 45

13. The rule for an input/output table is $g = f + 2$. What is the output if the input is 10?

Ⓐ 8 Ⓒ 20

Ⓑ 12 Ⓓ 18

14. Ben uses the rule $k = j + 10$ to show a pattern in the graph. He uses *k* to represent the output and *j* to represent the input.

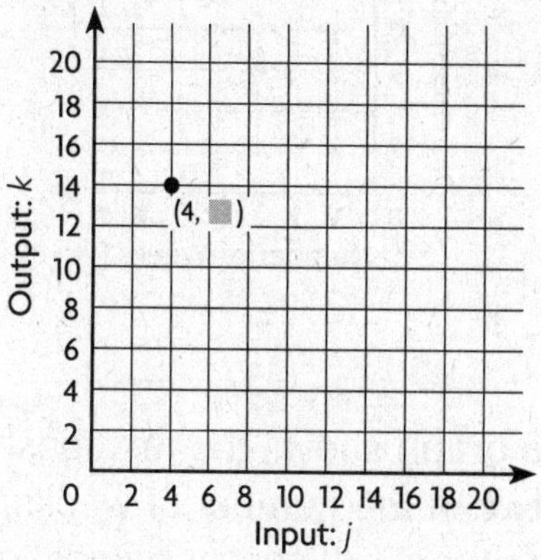

If the input is 4, what is the other number in the number pair?

Record your answer and fill in the bubbles on the grid. Be sure to use the correct place value.

			.		
⓪	⓪	⓪		⓪	⓪
①	①	①		①	①
②	②	②		②	②
③	③	③		③	③
④	④	④		④	④
⑤	⑤	⑤		⑤	⑤
⑥	⑥	⑥		⑥	⑥
⑦	⑦	⑦		⑦	⑦
⑧	⑧	⑧		⑧	⑧
⑨	⑨	⑨		⑨	⑨

15. The rule $b = 8m$ shows that each member, *m*, of the library may borrow 8 books, *b*, per visit. Which number pair shows the maximum number of books 4 members can check out in a single visit?

Ⓐ (8, 32) Ⓒ (4, 12)

Ⓑ (8, 16) Ⓓ (4, 32)

GO ON

Use the graph for 16–17.

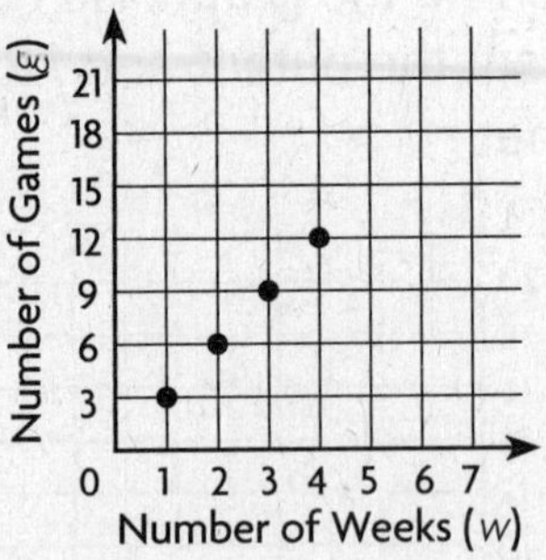

16. The graph shows the relationship between the number of weeks, w, and the number of soccer games, g, played. Which rule describes the pattern on the graph?

Ⓐ $g = w + 3$
Ⓑ $g = 2w$
Ⓒ $g = 3w$
Ⓓ $w = 3g$

17. Which number pair extends the pattern on the graph?

Ⓐ (5, 10)
Ⓑ (15, 5)
Ⓒ (6, 15)
Ⓓ (5, 15)

18. Jasmine uses the rule $s = h + 4$ to complete a table and make a graph. Which number pair would be on the graph?

Ⓐ (4, 22)
Ⓑ (8, 12)
Ⓒ (16, 32)
Ⓓ (2, 4)

19. Ron uses the rule $t = f + 3$ to determine the number of triangles in each figure in a pattern.

Figure	f	1	2	3	4	5
Triangles	t	4	5	6	7	■

What is the value of the missing number?

Ⓐ 12
Ⓑ 15
Ⓒ 10
Ⓓ 8

20. Cal uses the rule $m = 2n$ to show a pattern in the graph. He uses m to represent the output and n to represent the input.

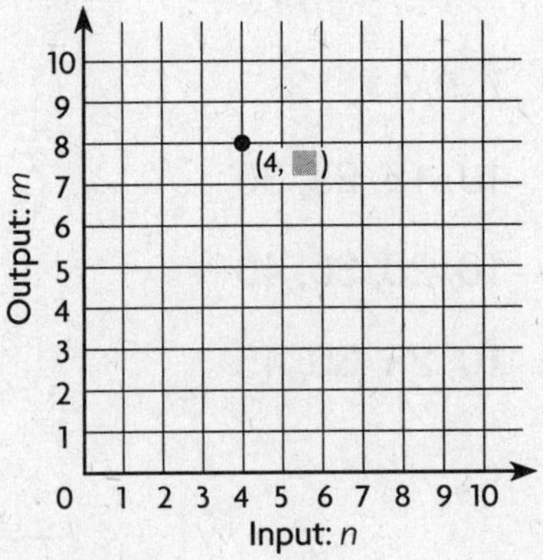

If the input is 4, what is the other number in the number pair?

Ⓐ 8
Ⓑ 4
Ⓒ 6
Ⓓ 2

STOP

Fill in the bubble for the correct answer.

1. Lisette simplified a numerical expression. The correct answer is 8. Which could be the expression?

Ⓐ $(10 \times 4) \div (2 + 3)$

Ⓑ $(10 \times 4) \div 2 + 3$

Ⓒ $3 + (10 \times 4) \div 2$

Ⓓ $(10 \times 2) + (3 \times 4)$

2. Ina wants to find the volume of a tissue box.

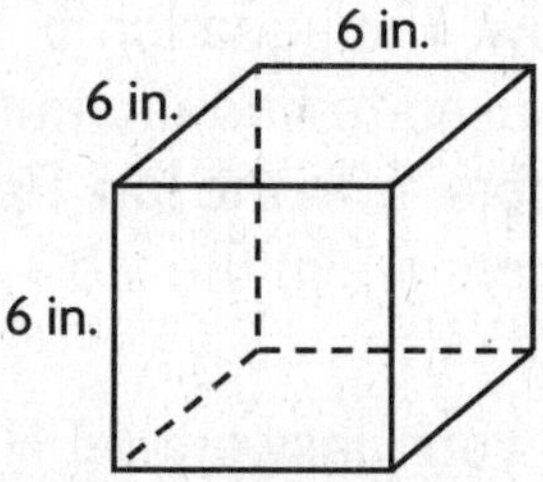

Which equation can she use to find the volume of the tissue box?

Ⓐ $V = 6 + 6 + 6$

Ⓑ $V = 36 + 6$

Ⓒ $V = 6 \times 6 \times 6$

Ⓓ $V = 6 \times 6$

3. What is the value of y in the equation?

$$3 \times 12 = y - 14$$

Ⓐ 22 Ⓒ 1

Ⓑ 5 Ⓓ 50

4. Marcos wants to find the volume of a gift box he bought.

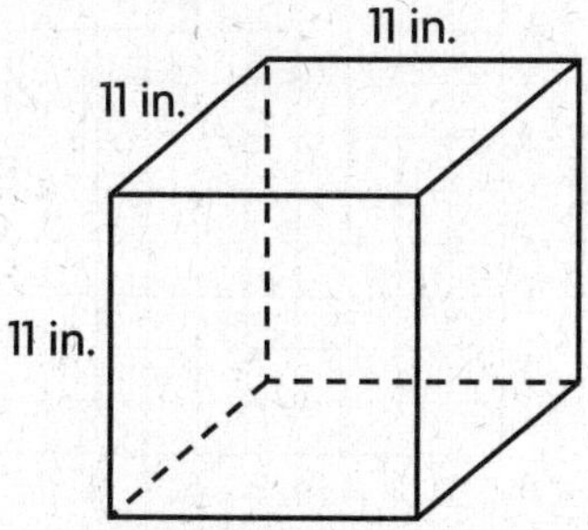

Which equation can he use to find the volume of the gift box?

Ⓐ $V = 11 + 11 + 11$

Ⓑ $V = 121 \times 11$

Ⓒ $V = 121 + 11$

Ⓓ $V = 11 \times 11 + 11$

5. Maria displays 6 boxes in a row. Each box has the same length. The total length of the boxes is 96 inches.

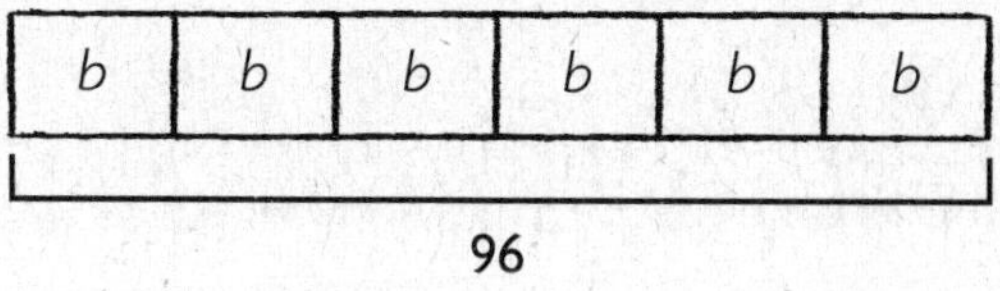

Which equation can be used to find b, the length of one box?

Ⓐ $6 + b = 96$ Ⓒ $6b = 96$

Ⓑ $96 - b = 6$ Ⓓ $6 \div b = 96$

GO ON

Name ______________________________

Use the graph for 6–7.

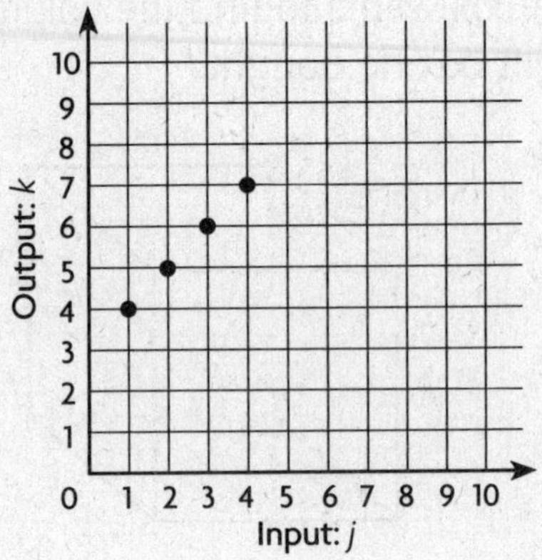

6. Which rule describes the pattern on the graph?

Ⓐ $k = j + 3$ Ⓒ $j = 3k$

Ⓑ $j = k + 3$ Ⓓ $k = 3j$

7. Which number pair extends the pattern on the graph?

Ⓐ (6, 8) Ⓒ (5, 8)

Ⓑ (8, 5) Ⓓ (7, 9)

8. Which is a prime number?

Ⓐ 57 Ⓒ 69

Ⓑ 89 Ⓓ 51

9. Chad's room is shaped like a rectangle and measures 12 feet long by 8 feet wide. He wants to put a wallpaper border around the room. How much border does he need?

Ⓐ 24 feet

Ⓑ 20 feet

Ⓒ 32 feet

Ⓓ Not here

10. In the computer lab there are 12 rows of computers with 11 computers in each row. The equation $c \div 12 = 11$ can be used to find the number of computers, c, in the lab. How many computers are in the lab?

Record your answer and fill in the bubbles on the grid. Be sure to use the correct place value.

			.		
⓪	⓪	⓪		⓪	⓪
①	①	①		①	①
②	②	②		②	②
③	③	③		③	③
④	④	④		④	④
⑤	⑤	⑤		⑤	⑤
⑥	⑥	⑥		⑥	⑥
⑦	⑦	⑦		⑦	⑦
⑧	⑧	⑧		⑧	⑧
⑨	⑨	⑨		⑨	⑨

GO ON

11. Jane buys 5 packages of 8 apples and 7 packages of 4 apples. She uses 23 of the apples to make applesauce.

Which equation shows how to find the number of apples, *a*, Jane has left?

Ⓐ $5 \times 8 + 7 \times 4 + 23 = a$

Ⓑ $5 + 8 \times 7 + 4 - 23 = a$

Ⓒ $5 \times 8 + 7 \times 4 - 23 = a$

Ⓓ $5 \times 7 + 8 \times 4 - 23 = a$

12. What is the value of the expression?

$$4 \times [(8 \times 2) - (5 + 6)]$$

Record your answer and fill in the bubbles on the grid. Be sure to use the correct place value.

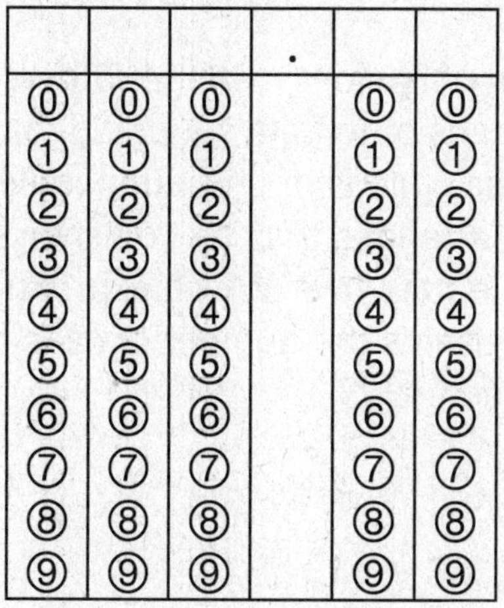

13. Tyquan wants to determine the volume of a storage box.

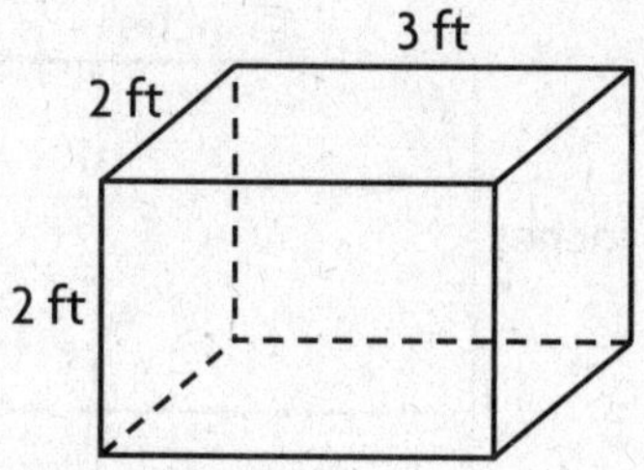

Which equation can he use to find the volume of the box?

Ⓐ $V = 3 \times 2 \times 2$

Ⓑ $V = 3 + 2 + 2$

Ⓒ $V = (2 \times 3) + (2 \times 2)$

Ⓓ $V = 3 \times 2$

14. Carlos made a table.

Input	*x*	5	6	7	8
Output	*y*	20	24	28	32

Which rule describes the pattern in the table?

Ⓐ $y = x + 4$

Ⓑ $y = 4x$

Ⓒ $x = y + 4$

Ⓓ $x = 4y$

GO ON

15. An artist buys a rectangular piece of canvas on to which to paint.

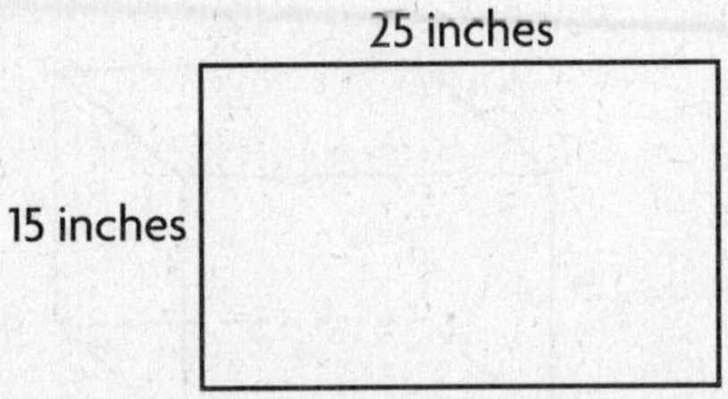

Which equation can she use to find the perimeter of the canvas?

Ⓐ $P = 25 + 15 + 25 + 15$

Ⓑ $P = 2 \times 25 + 15$

Ⓒ $P = 25 + 15$

Ⓓ $P = 25 \times 15$

16. Which value of *v* makes the equation true?

$$5 + v + 6 = 14 + 4 + 2$$

Ⓐ 20 Ⓒ 11

Ⓑ 2 Ⓓ 9

17. The table uses the rule $b = a + 6$.

Input	*a*	1	2	3
Output	*b*	■	■	■

Which set of numbers correctly completes the output values in the table?

Ⓐ 7, 8, 9 Ⓒ 9, 12, 15

Ⓑ 5, 4, 3 Ⓓ 6, 12, 18

18. Tony uses the rule $f = 3g$ to show a pattern in the graph. He uses f to represent the output and *g* to represent the input.

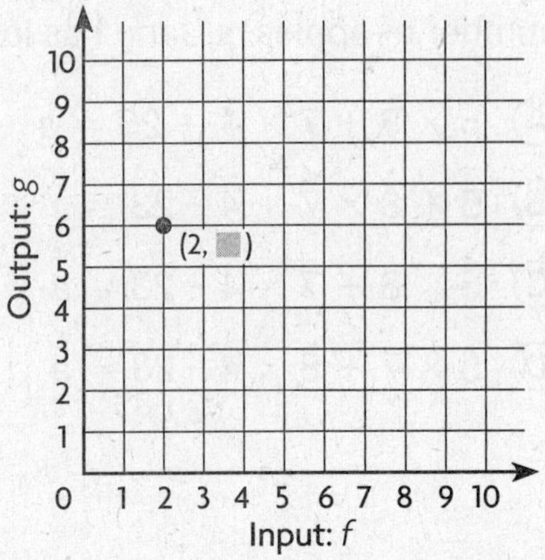

If the input is 2, what is the other number in the pair?

Ⓐ 2 Ⓒ 6

Ⓑ 3 Ⓓ 5

19. A grocery store manager orders 32 cans of tomato soup and four times as many cans of chicken noodle soup. She arranges the cans on shelves in 8 equal rows. Which expression represents the number of cans of soup in each row?

Ⓐ $[32 \times (4 \times 32)] \div 8$

Ⓑ $[32 + (4 \times 32)] \div 8$

Ⓒ $[32 \times (4 + 32)] \div 8$

Ⓓ $[32 + (4 \times 32) \div 8]$

GO ON

20. Which number has a factor of 7?

Ⓐ 48

Ⓑ 58

Ⓒ 24

Ⓓ 63

21. What is the value of d in the equation?

$$d - 19 = 6 + 3 \times 8$$

Ⓐ 91

Ⓑ 49

Ⓒ 30

Ⓓ 11

22. A potter uses 2 blocks of clay for each of 3 small pots and 3 blocks of clay for each of 4 medium pots. Then he uses 5 blocks of clay to make one large pot.

Which equation shows how to find the total number of blocks of clay, c, used?

Ⓐ $2 + 3 \times 3 + 4 \times 5 = c$

Ⓑ $2 \times 3 + 3 \times 4 \times 5 = c$

Ⓒ $2 \times 3 + 3 \times 4 + 5 = c$

Ⓓ $2 \times 3 + 3 \times 4 - 5 = c$

23. The inside of an inflatable kiddie pool is 5 feet long, 4 feet wide, and 2 feet deep. Which equation can be used to find the volume of the pool?

Ⓐ $v = 5 \times 4 \times 2$

Ⓑ $v = 5 + 4$

Ⓒ $v = 5 + 4 + 2$

Ⓓ $v = 5 \times 4$

24. Which of the following equations can be used to find the volume of the rectangular prism?

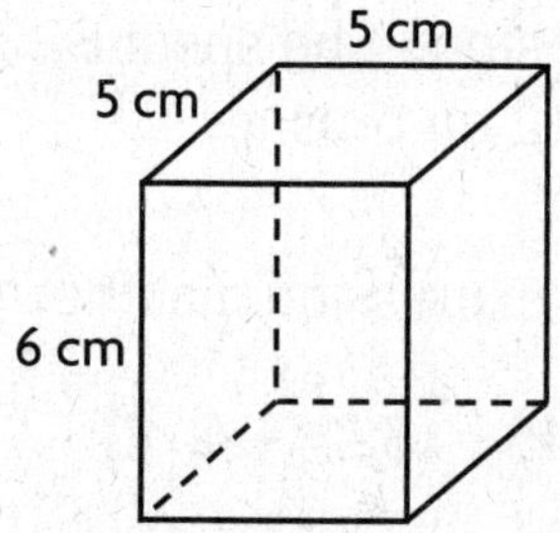

Ⓐ $V = 5 + 5 + 6$

Ⓑ $V = (2 \times 5) + (2 \times 5)$

Ⓒ $V = 25 \times 6$

Ⓓ $V = 30 + 5$

GO ON

25. What is the volume of the rectangular prism?

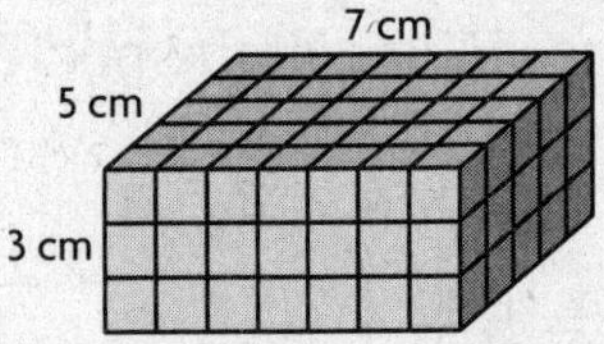

Ⓐ 150 cubic centimeters

Ⓑ 15 cubic centimeters

Ⓒ 24 cubic centimeters

Ⓓ 105 cubic centimeters

26. Becca had \$45 to spend at the art supply store. She spent \$23 on paints and \$12 on brushes.

Which expression matches the words?

Ⓐ \$45 – (\$23 + \$12)

Ⓑ \$45 – (\$23 – \$12)

Ⓒ (\$23 + \$12) – \$45

Ⓓ \$45 + (\$23 – \$12)

27. What is the perimeter of the square?

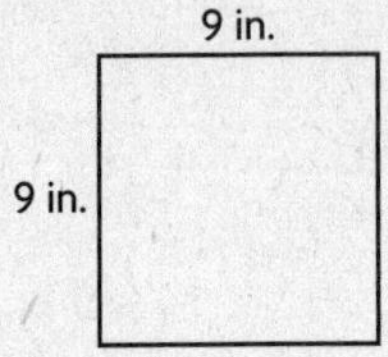

Ⓐ 18 inches Ⓒ 36 inches

Ⓑ 81 inches Ⓓ 45 inches

28. Which value of x makes the equation true?

$$11 + 7 + 8 = 13 + x + 9$$

Ⓐ 8 Ⓒ 7

Ⓑ 4 Ⓓ 10

29. The rule $s = 8t$ shows that each tent needs 8 stakes to hold it in place. How many stakes, s, are needed for 5 tents, t?

Ⓐ 13 Ⓒ 26

Ⓑ 32 Ⓓ 40

30. What is the area of the rectangle?

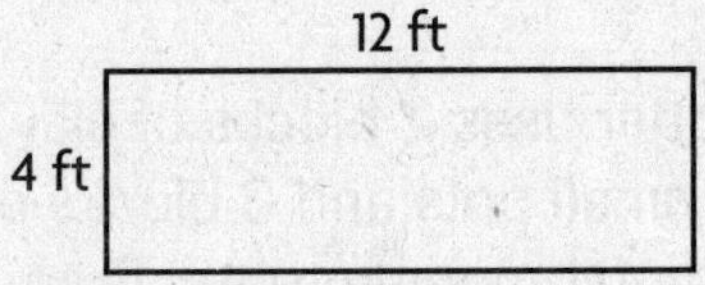

Ⓐ 48 square feet

Ⓑ 16 square feet

Ⓒ 24 square feet

Ⓓ 32 square feet

STOP

Name ______________________________

Fill in the bubble for the correct answer.

1. Which quadrilateral has exactly one pair of parallel sides?

Ⓐ Trapezoid
Ⓑ Parallelogram
Ⓒ Rectangle
Ⓓ Rhombus

2. A triangle has angles measuring 45°, 45°, and 90° and two congruent sides. Which describes the triangle?

Ⓐ Scalene acute
Ⓑ Scalene right
Ⓒ Equilateral acute
Ⓓ Isosceles right

3. Which figure belongs in the section of the Venn diagram labeled Rhombuses?

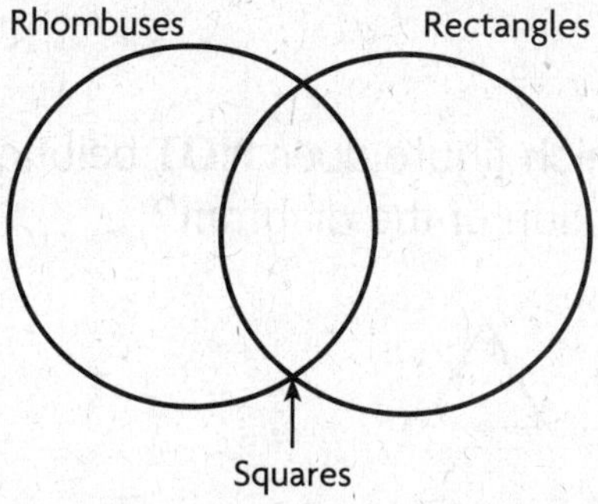

Ⓐ 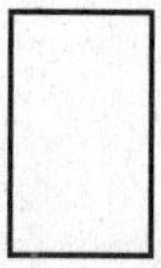
Ⓑ 
Ⓒ 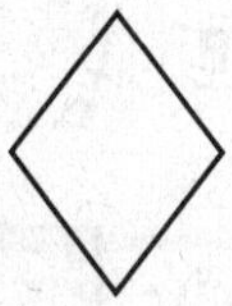
Ⓓ 

4. Which lists ways to classify the figure?

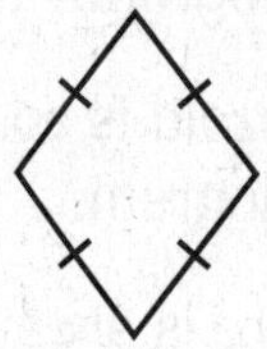

Ⓐ Quadrilateral, parallelogram, trapezoid
Ⓑ Quadrilateral, rhombus, rectangle
Ⓒ Quadrilateral, rhombus, square
Ⓓ Quadrilateral, parallelogram, rhombus

5. Which is a name for the polygon?

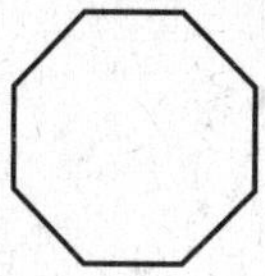

Ⓐ Decagon
Ⓑ Octagon
Ⓒ Pentagon
Ⓓ Quadrilateral

GO ON

6. Which statement is **NOT** true?

Ⓐ A rhombus is always a parallelogram.

Ⓑ A trapezoid is sometimes a parallelogram.

Ⓒ A square is always a rhombus.

Ⓓ A parallelogram is sometimes a rectangle.

7. Lisa drew a polygon with 7 sides, 7 angles, and 7 vertices. What type of polygon did Lisa draw?

Ⓐ Heptagon

Ⓑ Hexagon

Ⓒ Nonagon

Ⓓ Triangle

8. Which is a name for the polygon?

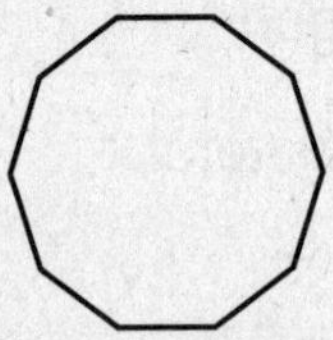

Ⓐ Quadrilateral

Ⓑ Octagon

Ⓒ Decagon

Ⓓ Triangle

Use the Venn diagram for 9–10.

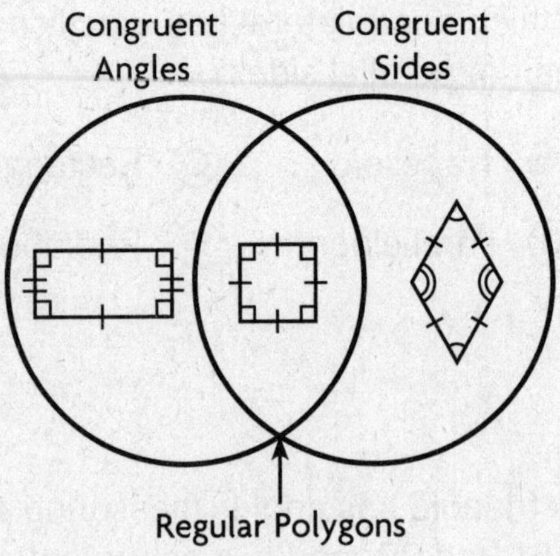

9. Which figure belongs in the section of the diagram labeled Regular Polygons?

Ⓐ 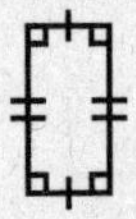

Ⓑ 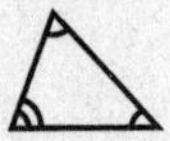

Ⓒ 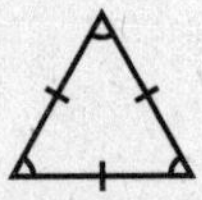

Ⓓ 

10. Which figure does **NOT** belong in any section of the diagram?

Ⓐ 

Ⓑ 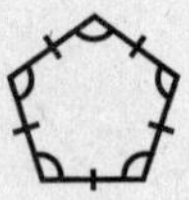

Ⓒ 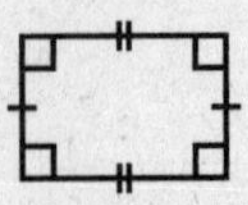

Ⓓ 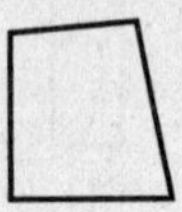

GO ON

Name ____

11. Which triangle is scalene and obtuse?

Ⓐ 

Ⓒ 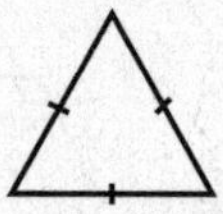

Ⓑ 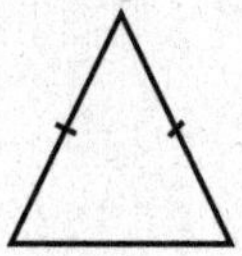

Ⓓ 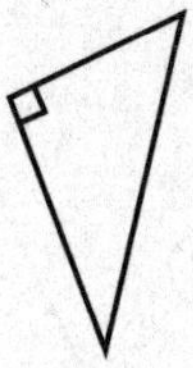

12. In art class, Kanji drew a nonagon. Which figure is Kanji's?

Ⓐ 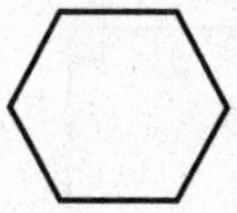

Ⓒ 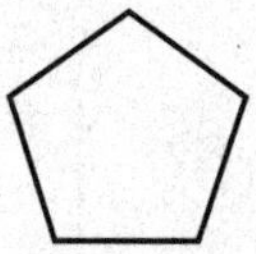

Ⓑ 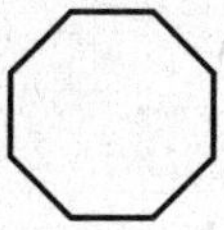

Ⓓ 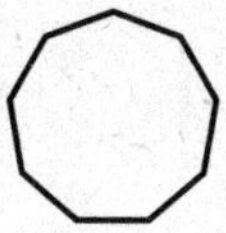

13. Which best describes the triangle?

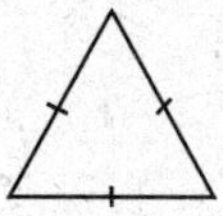

Ⓐ Scalene right

Ⓑ Equilateral acute

Ⓒ Isosceles obtuse

Ⓓ Isosceles right

14. Maria has triangle *ABC*. She folds side *AB* to side *BC* and they match evenly. She folds side *BC* to side *CA* and they match evenly. She folds side *CA* to side *AB* and they match evenly. Which describes Maria's triangle?

Ⓐ Isosceles

Ⓑ Scalene

Ⓒ Equilateral

Ⓓ Right

15. Greg made a table to classify different kinds of triangles.

Triangle by Length of Sides			
Triangle by Angle Measure		**Scalene**	**Isosceles**
	Acute		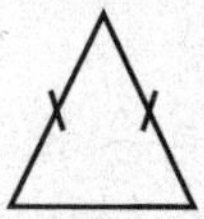
	Obtuse	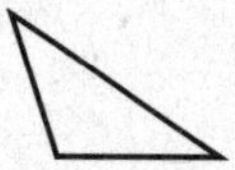	?

Which triangle completes the table?

Ⓐ 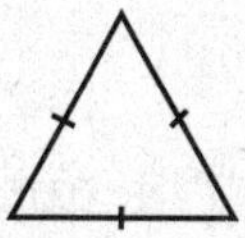

Ⓒ 

Ⓑ 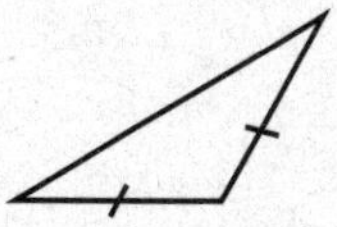

Ⓓ 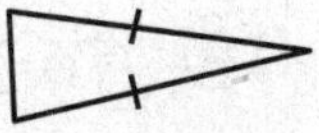

GO ON

16. What is the measure, in degrees, of the largest angle in a right triangle?

Record your answer and fill in the bubbles on the grid. Be sure to use the correct place value.

			.		
0	0	0		0	0
1	1	1		1	1
2	2	2		2	2
3	3	3		3	3
4	4	4		4	4
5	5	5		5	5
6	6	6		6	6
7	7	7		7	7
8	8	8		8	8
9	9	9		9	9

17. Which kind of triangle does not have any congruent sides?

Ⓐ Equilateral

Ⓑ Acute

Ⓒ Scalene

Ⓓ Right

18. Which statement must be true about a parallelogram that has 4 right angles?

Ⓐ It is a square.

Ⓑ It is a rectangle.

Ⓒ It is a trapezoid.

Ⓓ It is a rhombus.

19. Which polygon is regular?

Ⓐ 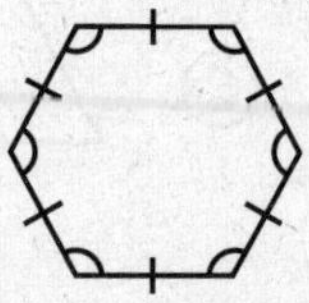

Ⓑ 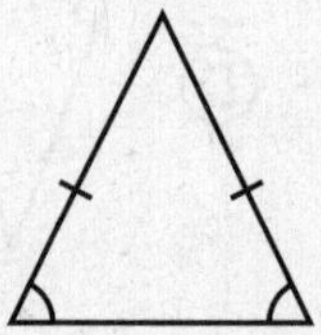

Ⓒ 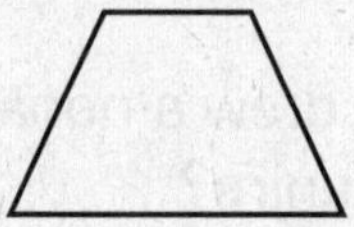

Ⓓ 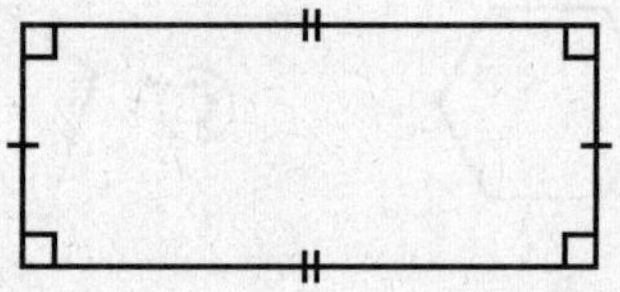

20. Which triangle has exactly two congruent sides?

Ⓐ 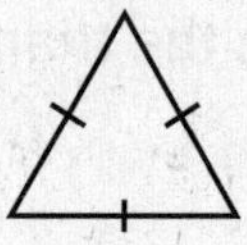

Ⓑ 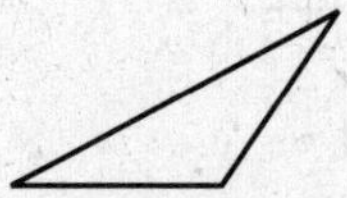

Ⓒ 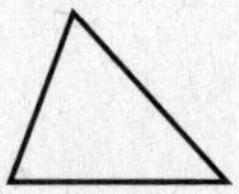

Ⓓ 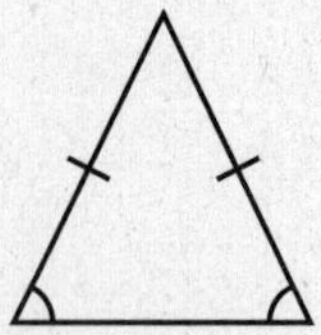

STOP

Fill in the bubble for the correct answer.

1. Derek used unit cubes to build a rectangular prism. He used 28 cubes to make the bottom layer and made the prism 3 layers high. What is the volume of Derek's prism?

Ⓐ 84 cubic units
Ⓑ 252 cubic units
Ⓒ 31 cubic units
Ⓓ 16 cubic units

Use the table for 2–3.

Volume of a Rectangular Prism After Each Level is Added to the Base				
Height (in layers)	1	2	3	4
Volume (in cubic units)	8	16	■	■

2. When the rectangular prism has a volume of 16 cubic units, how many cubic units are in each layer?

Ⓐ 32 Ⓒ 16
Ⓑ 8 Ⓓ 2

3. What is the volume of the rectangular prism when it has a height of 4 layers?

Ⓐ 16 cubic units
Ⓑ 54 cubic units
Ⓒ 18 cubic units
Ⓓ 32 cubic units

4. Bettina's toolbox is shaped like a rectangular prism with a length of 28 inches, a width of 10 inches, and a height of 8 inches. What is the volume of the toolbox?

Ⓐ 264 cubic inches
Ⓑ 2,240 cubic inches
Ⓒ 288 cubic inches
Ⓓ 2,640 cubic inches

5. How many cubes were used to make the figure?

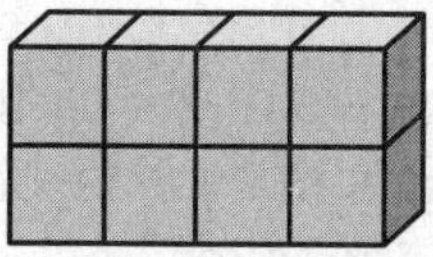

Ⓐ 4
Ⓑ 2
Ⓒ 8
Ⓓ 16

GO ON

Name ______________________________

6. What is the volume of the rectangular prism?

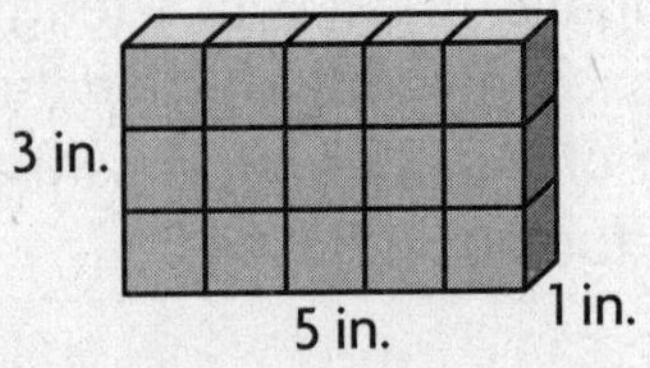

Ⓐ 9 cubic inches

Ⓑ 30 cubic inches

Ⓒ 16 cubic inches

Ⓓ 15 cubic inches

7. A printer company is shipping ink cartridges. If a shipping container holds 5 layers of ink cartridges, with 6 cartridges in each layer, and each ink cartridge takes up 1 cubic unit of space, what is the volume of the shipping container?

Ⓐ 30 cubic units

Ⓑ 180 cubic units

Ⓒ 20 cubic units

Ⓓ 11 cubic units

8. Franca wants to make a rectangular prism out of 50 cubes that have side lengths of one inch. She wants the prism to be 1 inch tall. Which of the following shows a dimension combination Franca should **NOT** use?

Ⓐ $(2 \times 25) \times 1$ Ⓒ $(25 \times 1) \times 1$

Ⓑ $(5 \times 10) \times 1$ Ⓓ $(1 \times 50) \times 1$

9. Ivan bought a box to store his trading cards. He wrote an equation that shows the volume of his box. Which equation did Ivan write?

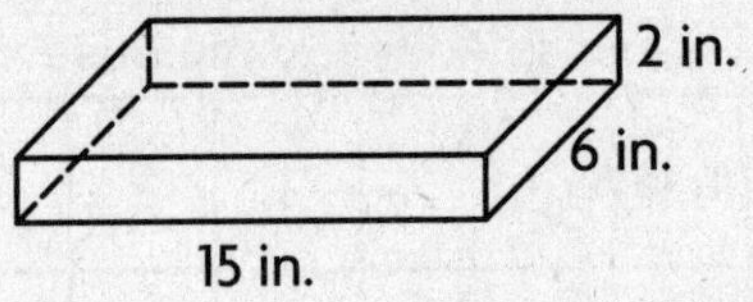

Ⓐ $15 + 6 + 2 = 23$ cubic units

Ⓑ $15 \times 6 + 2 = 92$ cubic units

Ⓒ $15 \times 6 \times 2 = 180$ cubic units

Ⓓ $15 \times 6 = 90$ cubic units

10. Cassie built two solid figures.

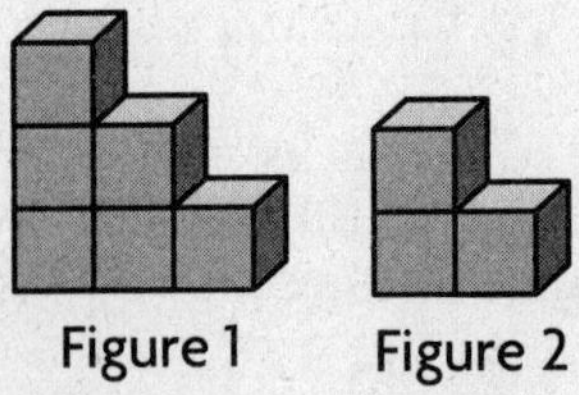

How many more unit cubes did Cassie use in Figure 1 than in Figure 2?

Ⓐ 6 Ⓑ 3 Ⓒ 12 Ⓓ 9

GO ON

11. The volume of the rectangular prism is 480 cubic centimeters. What is the unknown measurement?

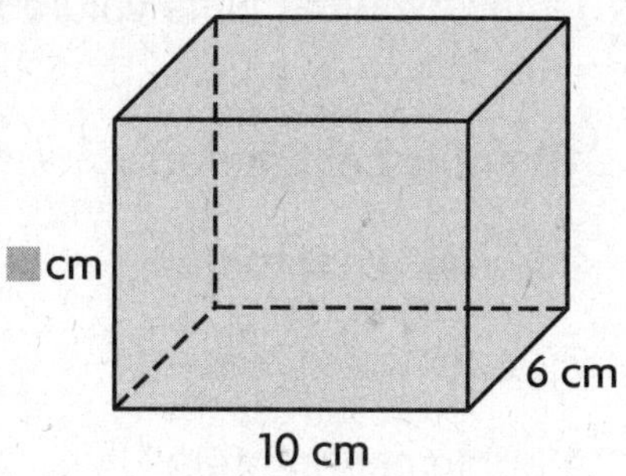

$V = 480$ cu cm

Ⓐ 24 centimeters

Ⓑ 10 centimeters

Ⓒ 48 centimeters

Ⓓ 8 centimeters

12. How many unit cubes were used to make the solid figure?

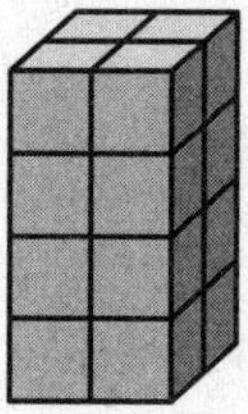

Record your answer and fill in the bubbles on the grid. Be sure to use the correct place value.

			.		
⓪	⓪	⓪		⓪	⓪
①	①	①		①	①
②	②	②		②	②
③	③	③		③	③
④	④	④		④	④
⑤	⑤	⑤		⑤	⑤
⑥	⑥	⑥		⑥	⑥
⑦	⑦	⑦		⑦	⑦
⑧	⑧	⑧		⑧	⑧
⑨	⑨	⑨		⑨	⑨

13. What is the volume of the rectangular prism?

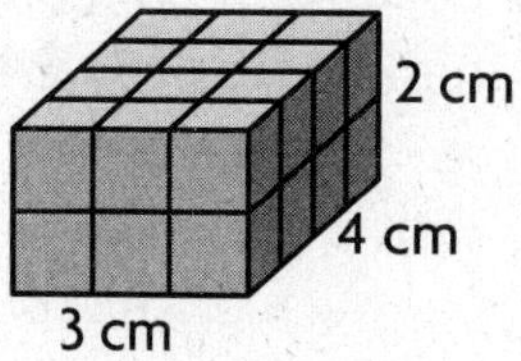

Ⓐ 24 cubic centimeters

Ⓑ 27 cubic centimeters

Ⓒ 12 cubic centimeters

Ⓓ 10 cubic centimeters

14. Ana wants to make a rectangular prism using 1-inch cubes. She plans to use exactly 48 cubes. How many different bases can she make if her rectangular prisms are all 4 inches tall?

Ⓐ 1 Ⓑ 12 Ⓒ 8 Ⓓ 3

15. What is the volume of the rectangular prism?

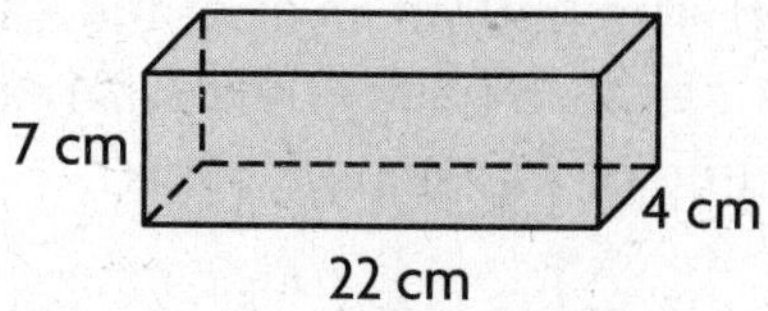

Ⓐ 88 cubic centimeters

Ⓑ 616 cubic centimeters

Ⓒ 316 cubic centimeters

Ⓓ 154 cubic centimeters

GO ON

16. Hector wants to make a rectangular prism that is 6 inches tall. How many different bases can he make if each prism is made of exactly 24 one-inch cubes?

Ⓐ 6
Ⓑ 2
Ⓒ 24
Ⓓ 8

17. The base of a raised garden bed is 6 feet by 4 feet. The height of the garden bed is 2 feet. How many cubic feet of soil are needed to fill the garden bed?

Ⓐ 13 cubic feet
Ⓑ 24 cubic feet
Ⓒ 9 cubic feet
Ⓓ 48 cubic feet

18. A shipping box is filled with pastry boxes. Each pastry box measures 1 cubic foot. The shipping box is 3 feet high. The bottom layer of the shipping box can fit 6 pastry boxes. What is the volume of the shipping box?

Ⓐ 24 cubic feet
Ⓑ 18 cubic feet
Ⓒ 9 cubic feet
Ⓓ 10 cubic feet

19. Kinte built a rectangular prism with centimeter cubes. The base of his prism contains 6 cubes. If the prism has 12 layers, what is its volume?

Ⓐ 18 cubic centimeters
Ⓑ 96 cubic centimeters
Ⓒ 72 cubic centimeters
Ⓓ 4 cubic centimeters

20. Raven wants to determine the volume of her art supply box. Which equation should Raven write to find the volume?

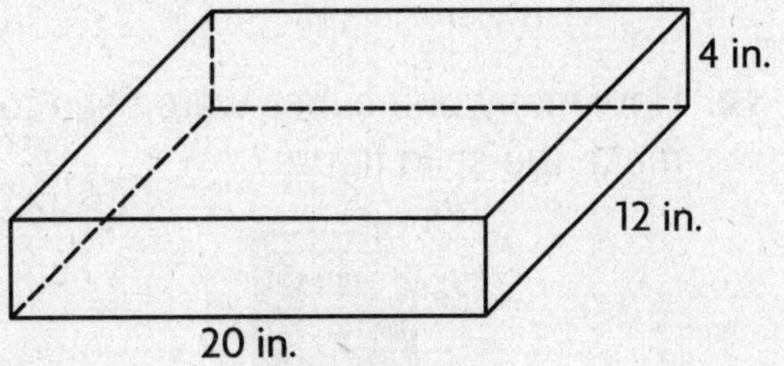

Ⓐ $240 \times 4 = 960$ cubic inches
Ⓑ $20 \times 12 + 4 = 244$ cubic inches
Ⓒ $20 + 12 + 4 = 36$ cubic inches
Ⓓ $240 + 4 = 244$ cubic inches

STOP

Fill in the bubble for the correct answer.

1. Carmen's puppy weighs 9 pounds. Her kitten weighs 74 ounces. How many more ounces does her puppy weigh than her kitten?

Ⓐ 16 ounces

Ⓑ 70 ounces

Ⓒ 38 ounces

Ⓓ 144 ounces

2. Russ has 20 meters of yarn. How many decimeters of yarn does Russ have?

Ⓐ 20 decimeters

Ⓑ 2 decimeters

Ⓒ 200 decimeters

Ⓓ 2,000 decimeters

3. Jason wants to measure the lengths of different leaves. Which unit would be best for measuring the lengths of the leaves?

Ⓐ Foot

Ⓑ Centimeter

Ⓒ Kilometer

Ⓓ Yard

4. Lola poured 18 cups of water into a large pot to cook pasta. Ruth poured more water into her pot than Lola. Which could be the amount of water Ruth poured?

Ⓐ 5 quarts

Ⓑ 100 fluid ounces

Ⓒ 8 pints

Ⓓ 1 gallon

5. Mel selects three lengths of yarn for an art project. The first piece is 9 inches long, the second piece is 2 feet long, and the third piece is 1 yard long. How many inches of yarn does Mel have in all?

Ⓐ 12 inches

Ⓑ 108 inches

Ⓒ 69 inches

Ⓓ 36 inches

GO ON

6. Sharon has 56 centimeters of cord to make a beaded key ring. How many millimeters of cord does Sharon have?

Ⓐ 5,600 millimeters

Ⓑ 560 millimeters

Ⓒ 5.6 millimeters

Ⓓ 56,000 millimeters

7. Adele helped her brother wax a 7-foot long surfboard. How many inches long is the surfboard they waxed?

Ⓐ 144 inches

Ⓑ 49 inches

Ⓒ 84 inches

Ⓓ 19 inches

8. The Crandell family's van can tow a maximum of 2 tons. A storage pod that weighs 1,500 pounds is attached to the van. How many more pounds can the van tow in addition to the pod?

Ⓐ 2,500 pounds

Ⓑ 5,000 pounds

Ⓒ 3,500 pounds

Ⓓ 500 pounds

9. Yasmin wants to find the mass of a quarter. Which tool should she use to measure the mass?

Ⓐ Metric ruler

Ⓑ Medical scale

Ⓒ Pan balance

Ⓓ Large scale

10. Kai lives 3 kilometers from school, Brea lives 30,000 meters from school, and Cal lives 30,000 centimeters from school. Which statement about these distances is true?

Ⓐ Kai lives the farthest from school.

Ⓑ Brea lives the closest to school.

Ⓒ Cal lives farther from school than Kai.

Ⓓ Brea lives the farthest from school.

GO ON

11. A box containing 8 identical bags of peanuts weighs 3 pounds. How many ounces does each bag of peanuts weigh?

Ⓐ 16 ounces

Ⓑ 48 ounces

Ⓒ 6 ounces

Ⓓ 3 ounces

12. Miriam used gallons as a unit of measure. Which of the following objects is she most likely to have been measuring?

Ⓐ Capacity of a bath tub

Ⓑ Capacity of a mug

Ⓒ Length of a pool

Ⓓ Weight of a bag of apples

13. On Monday, Marcy walked 528 yards. If she walks the same distance each day, how many days will it take for Marcy to walk a total of 3 miles?

Ⓐ 3 days

Ⓑ 30 days

Ⓒ 10 days

Ⓓ 7 days

14. Marc determines that his family uses 8 pints of milk each week. How many fluid ounces of milk is this?

Ⓐ 64 fluid ounces

Ⓑ 32 fluid ounces

Ⓒ 16 fluid ounces

Ⓓ 128 fluid ounces

15. A truck is carrying 10,000 pounds of supplies. How many tons of supplies is the truck carrying?

Ⓐ 20,000 tons

Ⓑ 5 tons

Ⓒ 5,000 tons

Ⓓ 20 tons

GO ON

16. Patrick used 1,000 milliliters of milk to make one batch of pudding. How many liters of milk does Patrick need to make 3 batches of pudding?

Ⓐ 3 liters

Ⓑ 30 liters

Ⓒ 3,000 liters

Ⓓ 300 liters

17. Dean walked 3 miles. Sally walked farther than Dean. Which could be the distance Sally walked?

Ⓐ 14,855 feet

Ⓑ 5,380 yards

Ⓒ 5,008 yards

Ⓓ 15,280 feet

18. Evan wants to measure the distance across a field. Which tool should he use to measure the distance?

Ⓐ Measuring cup

Ⓑ Spring scale

Ⓒ Ruler

Ⓓ Trundle wheel

19. Trevor needs to buy an aquarium that can hold 2 dekaliters of water. Which of the following containers is **NOT** large enough to hold that amount of water?

Ⓐ An aquarium that holds 20 liters

Ⓑ An aquarium that holds 200 deciliters

Ⓒ An aquarium that holds 20,000 centiliters

Ⓓ An aquarium that holds 2,000 milliliters

20. Gina makes 6 kilograms of snack mix for a party. She puts the snack mix into small bags for guests. If Gina fills each bag with 100 grams of snack mix, how many bags can she fill?

Record your answer and fill in the bubbles on the grid. Be sure to use the correct place value.

			.		
⓪	⓪	⓪		⓪	⓪
①	①	①		①	①
②	②	②		②	②
③	③	③		③	③
④	④	④		④	④
⑤	⑤	⑤		⑤	⑤
⑥	⑥	⑥		⑥	⑥
⑦	⑦	⑦		⑦	⑦
⑧	⑧	⑧		⑧	⑧
⑨	⑨	⑨		⑨	⑨

STOP

Name ________________________________

Fill in the bubble for the correct answer.

1. Elyse records the weight of her kitten over time. She wants to graph the data on a coordinate grid.

Kitten's Weight				
Age (in months)	1	2	3	4
Weight (in ounces)	12	32	48	64

Which set of ordered pairs will she graph?

Ⓐ (1, 2), (3, 4), (12, 32), (48, 64)

Ⓑ (12, 1), (32, 2), (48, 3), (64, 4)

Ⓒ (1, 12), (2, 32), (3, 48), (4, 64)

Ⓓ (1, 32), (2, 12), (3, 64), (4, 48)

2. The rule for a pattern is $y = 3x$. Which point in the coordinate plane does **NOT** represent the pattern rule?

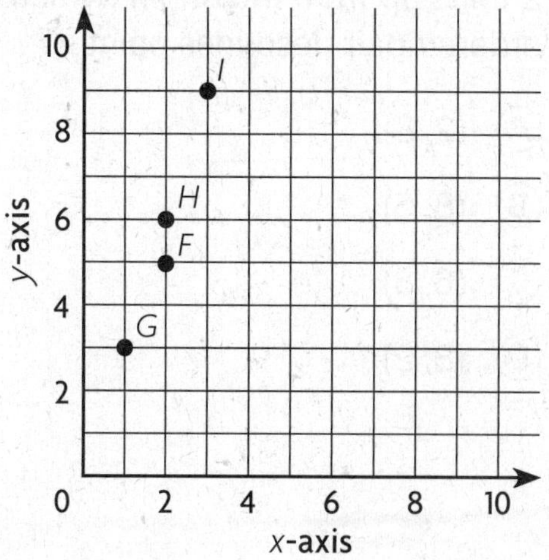

Ⓐ *F* Ⓒ *H*

Ⓑ *G* Ⓓ *I*

3. Point *C* is 7 units to the right and 3 units up from the origin. Which ordered pair describes point *C*?

Ⓐ (3, 7) Ⓒ (7, 3)

Ⓑ (0, 7) Ⓓ (3, 0)

Use the table for 4–5.

Sandwiches				
Sandwiches	1	2	3	4
Cheese (slices)	3	6	9	

4. The *x*-coordinate represents the number of sandwiches and the *y*-coordinate represents the number of cheese slices. Which ordered pair represents the point showing the number of cheese slices in 4 sandwiches?

Ⓐ (1, 4) Ⓒ (4, 4)

Ⓑ (4, 12) Ⓓ (4, 16)

5. Andrew plots the pattern from the input/output table on a coordinate grid. The *x*-coordinate represents the number of sandwiches, 5. Which ordered pair shows the pattern?

Ⓐ (15, 5) Ⓒ (3, 5)

Ⓑ (5, 8) Ⓓ (5, 15)

GO ON

Name ______________________________

Use the table for 6–7.

Figures with Circles				
Figure Number, f	1	2	3	4
Number of Circles, c	5	6	7	8

6. The rule for the pattern in the table is $c = f + 4$, where c represents the output, the number of circles, and f represents the input, the figure number. Which ordered pair will be on the graph?

Ⓐ (8, 6) Ⓒ (10, 6)
Ⓑ (6, 10) Ⓓ (6, 2)

7. The rule for the pattern in the table is $c = f + 4$. If f represents the x-coordinate and c represents the y-coordinate, which ordered pair represents the point for Figure 3 on a coordinate grid?

Ⓐ (3, 3) Ⓒ (3, 7)
Ⓑ (7, 3) Ⓓ (3, 1)

8. Point L is 5 units to the right and 8 units up from the origin. Which ordered pair describes point L?

Ⓐ (8, 5) Ⓒ (3, 8)
Ⓑ (5, 0) Ⓓ (5, 8)

9. Jan plots a point on the coordinate grid that is 3 units to the right and 5 units up from the origin. Which point on the coordinate grid did she plot?

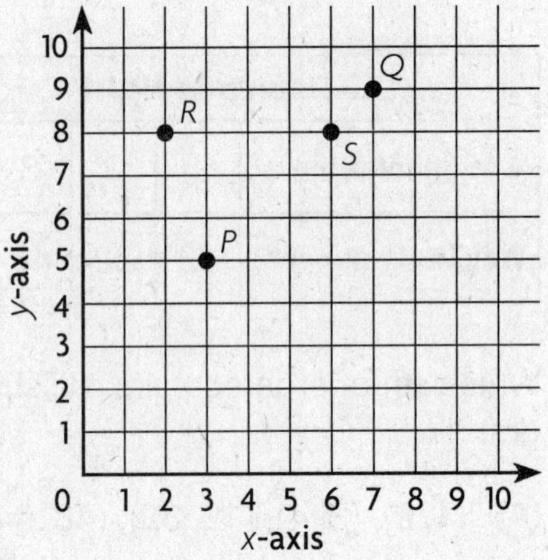

Ⓐ P
Ⓑ Q
Ⓒ R
Ⓓ S

10. Point Z is 8 units to the right and 2 units up from the origin. Which ordered pair describes point Z?

Ⓐ (2, 8)
Ⓑ (8, 6)
Ⓒ (6, 8)
Ⓓ (8, 2)

GO ON

11. In an ordered pair the *x*-coordinate represents the input and the *y*-coordinate represents the output. Which ordered pair follows the pattern rule *multiply input by 4*?

Ⓐ (1, 5)

Ⓑ (4, 1)

Ⓒ (2, 8)

Ⓓ (4, 8)

12. The input/output table shows the amount of money Brittney's mother spends on gas.

Money Spent on Gas					
Weeks	1	2	3	4	5
Amount Spent	\$25	\$50	\$75	\$100	■

If the *x*-coordinate is the number of weeks and the *y*-coordinate is the amount spent, which ordered pair represents the point showing the amount Brittney's mother spent on gas in 5 weeks?

Ⓐ (150, 5)

Ⓑ (5, 150)

Ⓒ (125, 5)

Ⓓ (5, 125)

Use the table for 13–14.

Coin Trade				
Number of Dimes	1	2	3	4
Number of Nickels	2	4	6	8

13. Clara trades 2 nickels for 1 dime. She records the data in an input/output table then graphs the data from the table. Which ordered pairs will be on the graph?

Ⓐ (1, 2), (3, 4), (2, 4), (6, 8)

Ⓑ (1, 2), (2, 4), (3, 6), (4, 8)

Ⓒ (1, 4), (2, 2), (3, 8), (4, 6)

Ⓓ (2, 1), (4, 2), (6, 3), (8, 4)

14. Clara trades 2 nickels for each dime she has. She records the data in an input/output table reflecting the rule $y = 2x$, where y represents the number of nickels and x represents the number of dimes. How many nickels does Clara trade for 5 dimes?

Ⓐ 5 Ⓑ 12 Ⓒ 20 Ⓓ 10

15. A triangle has 3 angles. In an ordered pair, the *x*-coordinate represents the number of triangles, and the *y*-coordinate represents the total number of angles. If the *x*-coordinate is 8, what is the *y*-coordinate?

Ⓐ 24 Ⓑ 5 Ⓒ 11 Ⓓ 8

GO ON

16. Dean plots a point to represent the ordered pair (2, 1). Which describes how to locate this point?

Ⓐ Move 2 units up from the origin and 1 unit to the right.

Ⓑ Move 2 units to the right and 1 unit up from the origin.

Ⓒ Move 2 units to the right and 1 more unit to the right.

Ⓓ Move 1 unit up from the origin and 2 units to the left.

17. The rule for a pattern is $f = g + 1$. If g is the x-coordinate and f is the y-coordinate, which point in the coordinate plane does **NOT** follow the pattern rule?

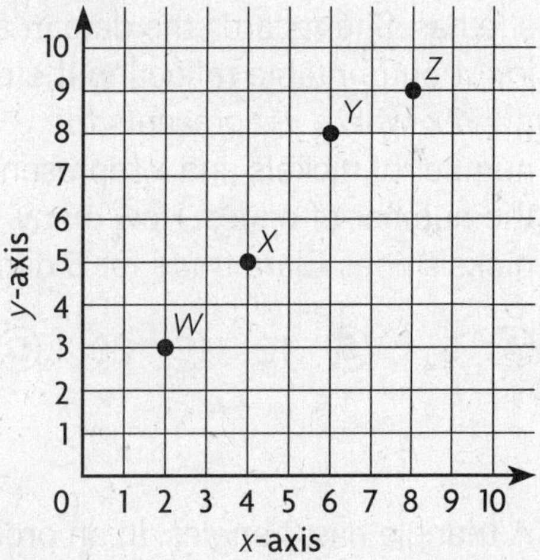

Ⓐ W Ⓒ Y

Ⓑ X Ⓓ Z

18. Pablo graphs the data from the table.

Making Muffins				
Muffins (in batches)	1	2	3	4
Flour (in cups)	2	4	6	8

Which ordered pair represents the point showing the amount of flour needed for 2 batches of muffins?

Ⓐ (1, 2) Ⓒ (4, 2)

Ⓑ (2, 2) Ⓓ (2, 4)

19. A pentagon has 5 sides. In an ordered pair, the x-coordinate represents the number of pentagons, and the y-coordinate represents the total number of sides. If the x-coordinate is 9, what is the y-coordinate?

Record your answer and fill in the bubbles on the grid. Be sure to use the correct place value.

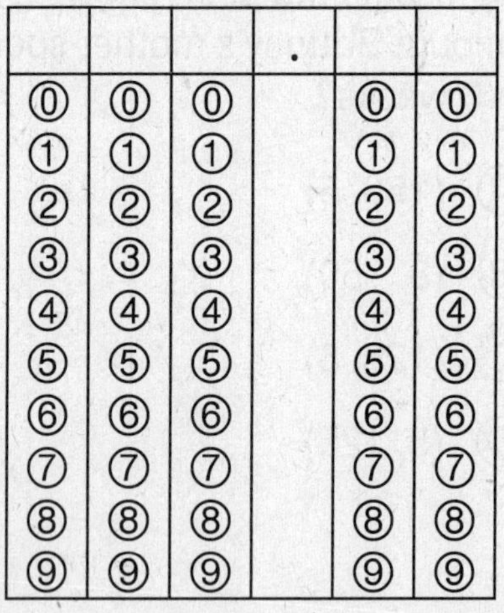

STOP

Name ______________________________

Fill in the bubble for the correct answer.

1. Which lists ways to classify the figure?

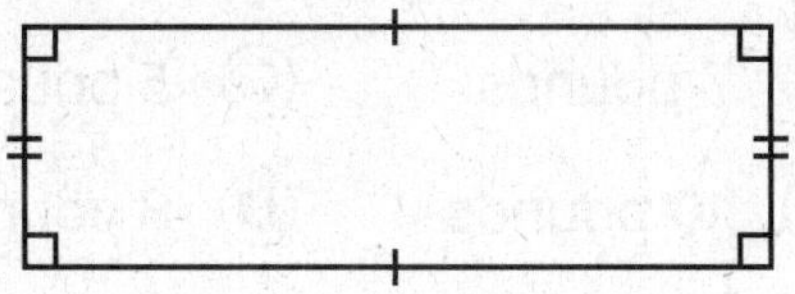

Ⓐ Quadrilateral, rhombus

Ⓑ Quadrilateral, parallelogram, rectangle

Ⓒ Quadrilateral, rhombus, rectangle

Ⓓ Quadrilateral, trapezoid

2. Helen stores her writing supplies in a box. She writes an equation to find the volume of the box. Which equation does Helen write?

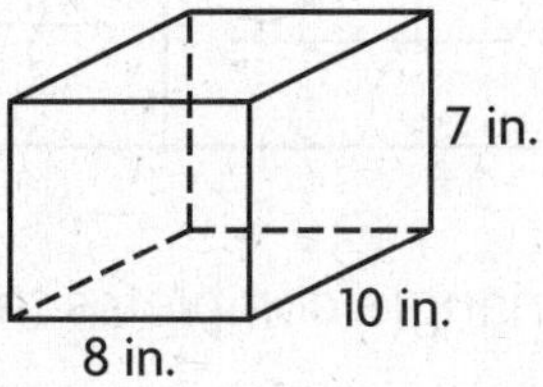

Ⓐ $10 \times 8 + 7 = 87$ cubic inches

Ⓑ $10 \times 8 = 80$ cubic inches

Ⓒ $10 + 8 + 7 = 25$ cubic inches

Ⓓ $10 \times 8 \times 7 = 560$ cubic inches

3. Yasmine wants to measure the perimeter of the school playground. Which tool should she use?

Ⓐ Trundle wheel

Ⓑ Spring scale

Ⓒ Measuring cup

Ⓓ Pan balance

Use the graph for 4–5.

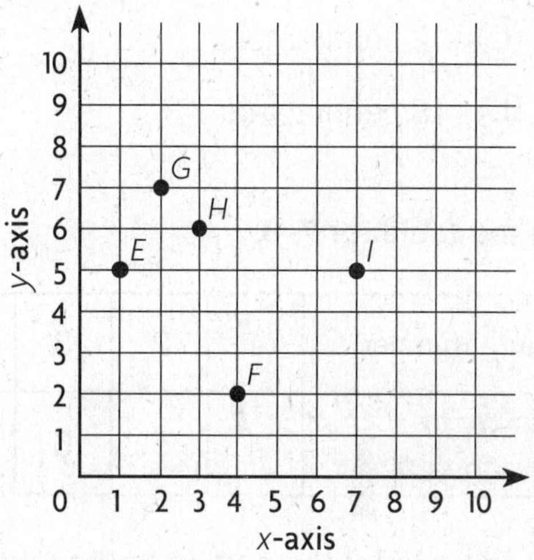

4. What ordered pair represents point *G*?

Ⓐ (7, 2) Ⓒ (2, 7)

Ⓑ (0, 7) Ⓓ (7, 5)

5. Jarah wants to draw a star on the point in the coordinate grid represented by the ordered pair (1, 5). What point is at (1, 5)?

Ⓐ *E* Ⓑ *F* Ⓒ *H* Ⓓ *I*

GO ON

Name ____________________

6. The volume of the rectangular prism is 360 cubic centimeters. What is the unknown measurement?

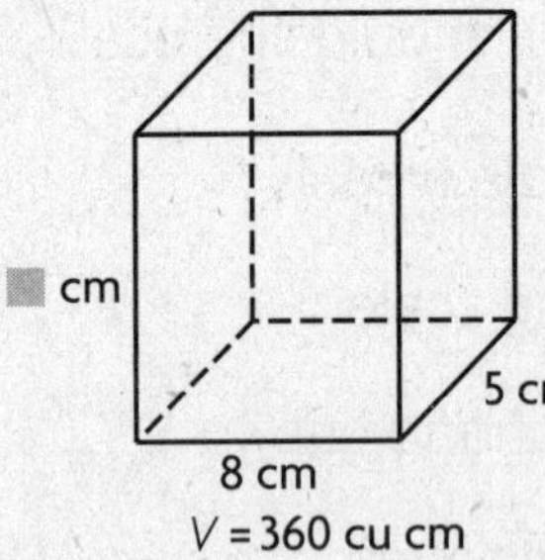

Ⓐ 36 centimeters

Ⓑ 9 centimeters

Ⓒ 12 centimeters

Ⓓ 18 centimeters

Use the table for 7–8.

Figure Number, *f*	1	2	3	4
Number of Hexagons, *h*	4	5	6	7

7. The rule for the pattern in the table is $h = f + 3$, where h represents the number of hexagons and f represents the figure number. If the figure number is 7, how many hexagons are there?

Ⓐ 8 Ⓑ 4 Ⓒ 9 Ⓓ 10

8. Velita graphs the data from the table on a coordinate grid. What ordered pair names the point that represents Figure 4?

Ⓐ (4, 7) Ⓒ (1, 4)

Ⓑ (4, 3) Ⓓ (4, 4)

9. Nigella uses 80 ounces of tomatoes to make spaghetti sauce. How many pounds of tomatoes does she use?

Ⓐ 7 pounds Ⓒ 5 pounds

Ⓑ 10 pounds Ⓓ 8 pounds

10. Carl makes a table to classify different kinds of triangles.

		Triangle by Length of Sides	
		Scalene	**Isosceles**
Triangle by Angle Measure	**Acute**	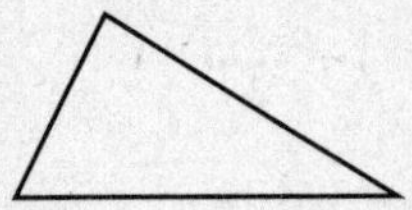	?
	Obtuse	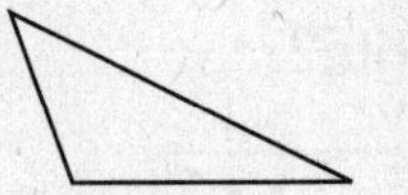	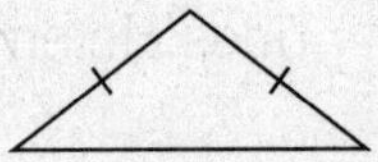

Which triangle completes the table?

Ⓐ 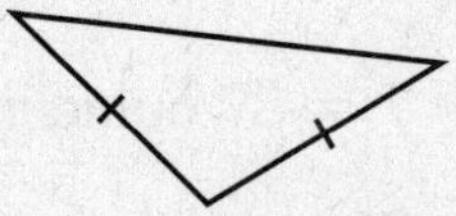

Ⓑ 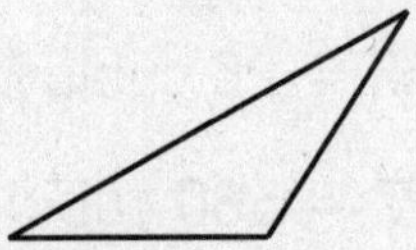

Ⓒ 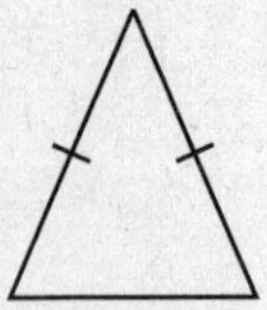

Ⓓ 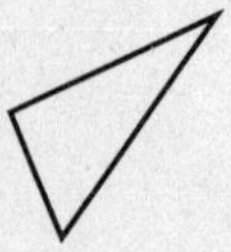

GO ON

11. A grasshopper weighs 300 milligrams. How many centigrams does the grasshopper weigh?

Ⓐ 30 centigrams

Ⓑ 3,000 centigrams

Ⓒ 3 centigrams

Ⓓ 0.3 centigrams

12. Desiré wants to make a rectangular prism using 1-inch cubes. She plans to use exactly 36 cubes. How many different bases can she make if her rectangular prisms are all 3 inches tall?

Ⓐ 7　　Ⓒ 4

Ⓑ 3　　Ⓓ 12

13. Which is a name for the polygon?

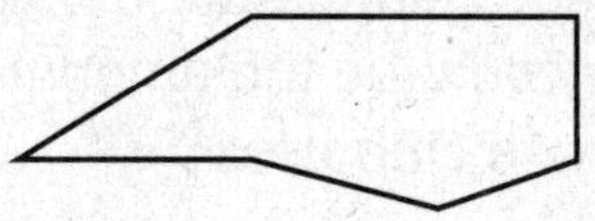

Ⓐ Hexagon　　Ⓒ Nonagon

Ⓑ Quadrilateral　　Ⓓ Not here

14. Which unit would be best for measuring the distance between two towns?

Ⓐ Inch　　Ⓒ Foot

Ⓑ Yard　　Ⓓ Mile

Use the table for 15–16.

Books Tyrone Mails to Relatives				
Number of Books, b	1	2	3	4
Number of Stamps, s	3	6	9	12

15. Tyrone mails copies of the same book to relatives. For each book he mails, Tyrone uses 3 stamps. He records the information in a table then graphs the data. Which ordered pairs will be on Tyrone's graph?

Ⓐ (1, 2), (3, 4), (3, 6), (9, 12)

Ⓑ (1, 3), (2, 12), (3, 6), (4, 9)

Ⓒ (3, 1), (6, 2), (9, 3), (12, 4)

Ⓓ (1, 3), (2, 6), (3, 9), (4, 12)

16. The pattern in the table follows the rule $s = 3b$, where s represents the number of stamps, and b represents the number of books. How many stamps does Tyrone need to mail 9 books?

Ⓐ 15

Ⓑ 6

Ⓒ 27

Ⓓ 30

GO ON

17. Tim's dad serves 1 cup of apple cider to each of 32 guests. How many quarts of apple cider does Tim's dad serve?

Ⓐ 8 quarts
Ⓑ 12 quarts
Ⓒ 4 quarts
Ⓓ 16 quarts

18. Evan wants to determine the volume of this box. Which equation should Evan write to find the volume?

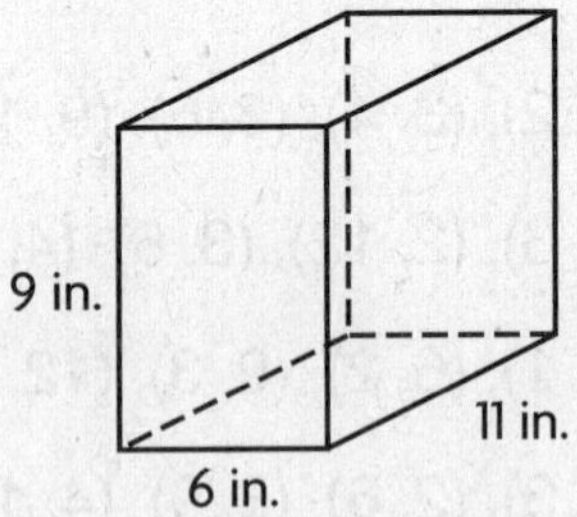

Ⓐ $11 \times 6 + 9 = 75$ cubic inches

Ⓑ $66 + 9 = 75$ cubic inches

Ⓒ $66 \times 9 = 594$ cubic inches

Ⓓ $11 + 6 + 9 = 26$ cubic inches

19. A triangle has angles measuring 90°, 50°, and 40° and no congruent sides. Which descibes the triangle?

Ⓐ Scalene right

Ⓑ Isosceles right

Ⓒ Equilateral acute

Ⓓ Scalene acute

20. John records the growth of a sunflower in a table. He wants to make a graph from the data in the table.

Sunflower Height				
Age (in weeks)	1	2	3	4
Height (in centimeters)	20	45	75	95

Which ordered pairs will be on John's graph?

Ⓐ (1, 3), (2, 4), (20, 75), (45, 95)

Ⓑ (1, 20), (2, 45), (3, 75), (4, 95)

Ⓒ (1, 45), (2, 20), (3, 95), (4, 75)

Ⓓ (1, 2), (3, 4), (20, 45), (75, 95)

21. The drama club uses 5 yards of fabric to decorate stage sets. The dance club uses more fabric than the drama club. Which could be the amount of fabric the dance club uses?

Ⓐ 4 feet

Ⓑ 185 inches

Ⓒ 150 inches

Ⓓ 9 feet

GO ON

22. Hiro helps his mother stir 15 dekagrams of rye flour into a dough mixture. How many decigrams of rye flour do they stir in?

Ⓐ 1.5 decigrams

Ⓑ 150 decigrams

Ⓒ 1,500 decigrams

Ⓓ 0.15 decigrams

23. Adam has triangle *NOP*. He folds side *NO* to side *OP* and they match evenly. He folds side *OP* to side *PN* and they do not match evenly. Which describes Adam's triangle?

Ⓐ Scalene

Ⓑ Acute

Ⓒ Equilateral

Ⓓ Isosceles

24. How many unit cubes were used to make the solid figure?

Ⓐ 9

Ⓑ 3

Ⓒ 18

Ⓓ 6

25. An octagon has eight sides. Richard plots a pattern showing the number of octagons and the total number of sides. In a set of ordered pairs in the pattern, the *x*-coordinate represents the number of octagons, and the *y*-coordinate represents the total number of sides. If the *x*-coordinate is 7, what is the *y*-coordinate?

Record your answer and fill in the bubbles on the grid. Be sure to use the correct place value.

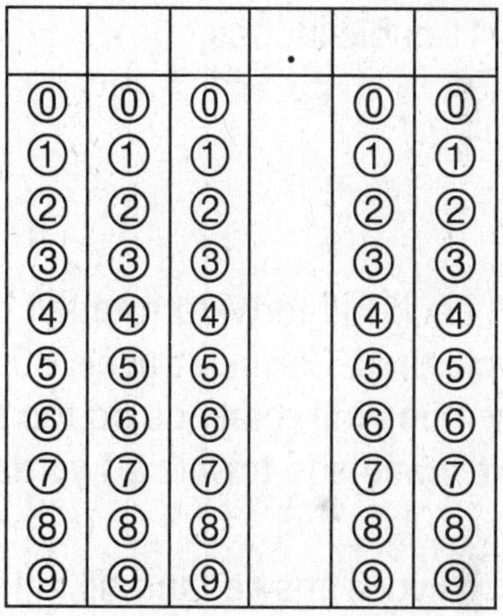

26. On a biking tour Xi bikes 4 miles each hour with his family.

Time (hr)	1	2	3	4
Distance biked (m)	4	8	12	■

Which ordered pair represents the number of miles Xi bikes in 4 hours?

Ⓐ (4, 4)

Ⓑ (4, 12)

Ⓒ (4, 1)

Ⓓ (4, 16)

GO ON

27. What is the volume of the rectangular prism?

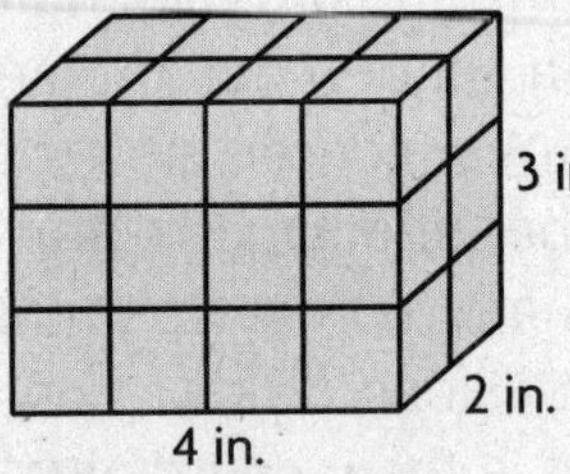

Ⓐ 22 cubic inches

Ⓑ 12 cubic inches

Ⓒ 24 cubic inches

Ⓓ 11 cubic inches

28. With each full forward rotation of her bicycle tires, Carmen travels 60 inches. How many full rotations do the tires make when she travels 30 yards?

Record your answer and fill in the bubbles on the grid. Be sure to use the correct place value.

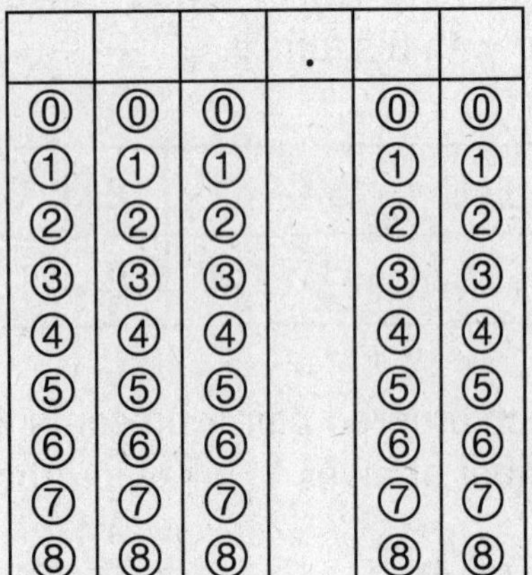

Use the Venn diagram for 29–30.

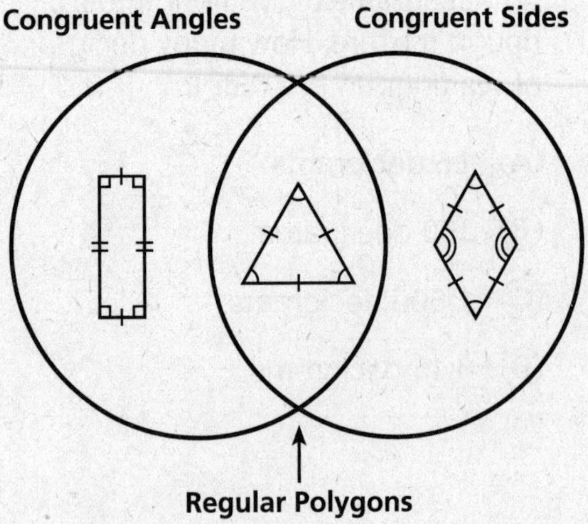

29. Which figure belongs in the section of the Venn diagram labeled 'Congruent Angles?'

Ⓐ 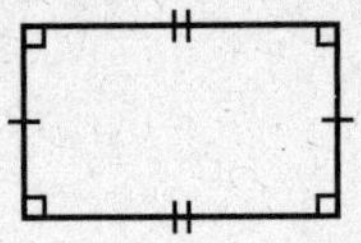

Ⓒ 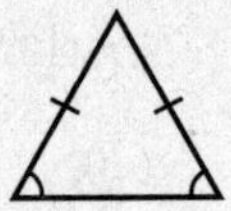

Ⓑ 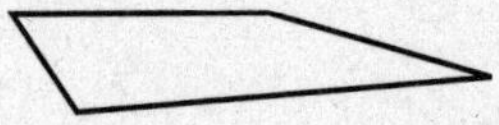

Ⓓ 

30. Which figure does **NOT** belong in any section of the diagram?

Ⓐ 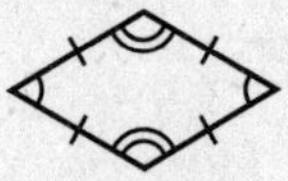

Ⓒ 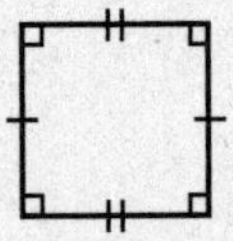

Ⓑ 

Ⓓ 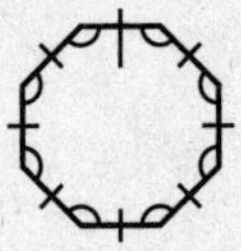

STOP

Name ______________________________

Fill in the bubble for the correct answer.

1. A track and field coach records the events his track team members are competing in.

Track and Field Events			
relay	sprint	relay	hurdles
hurdles	sprint	relay	relay
hurdles	relay	sprint	hurdles
relay	hurdle	sprint	relay

The coach makes a frequency table of the data. What is the frequency of team members in the relay race?

Ⓐ 7 Ⓒ 4

Ⓑ 3 Ⓓ 16

2. Dacia tracked the weather for two months. She recorded the data in a frequency table.

Weather in April and May	
Type of Weather	**Frequency**
Cloudy	14
Rainy	18
Sunny	29

How many more days were either sunny or cloudy than were rainy?

Ⓐ 42 Ⓒ 25

Ⓑ 16 Ⓓ 11

Use the frequency table for 3–4.

Students vote for their favorite outdoor activity. The frequency table shows the results.

Students' Favorite Outdoor Activity	
Type of Activity	**Frequency**
Biking	21
Canoeing	9
Hiking	13
Walking	4

3. How many more students voted for biking than for hiking?

Ⓐ 9 Ⓒ 21

Ⓑ 8 Ⓓ 12

4. How many students voted in all?

Ⓐ 43 Ⓒ 38

Ⓑ 30 Ⓓ 47

5. Syd makes a frequency table to record the types of photos she took on vacation. She wants to display the data in a bar graph.

Vacation Photos Taken				
Subject	**Animals**	**Monuments**	**People**	**Scenery**
Number	9	5	12	7

How many bars will the graph have?

Ⓐ 5 Ⓒ 4

Ⓑ 9 Ⓓ 7

GO ON

Use the bar graph for 6–8.

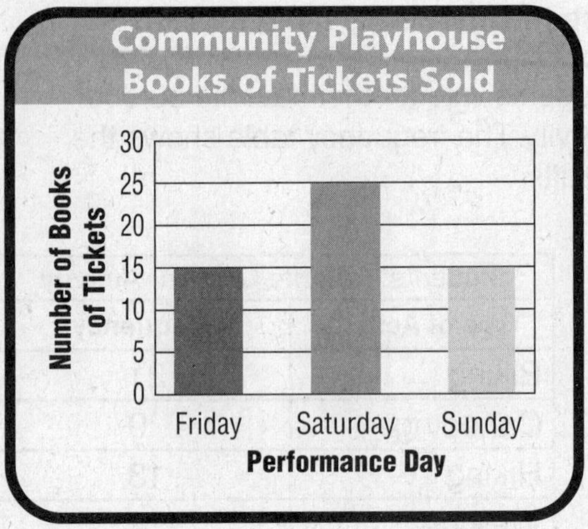

6. How many more books of tickets were sold for the performances on Saturday and Sunday than for the performance on Friday?

Ⓐ 40 Ⓒ 15

Ⓑ 55 Ⓓ 25

7. Six fewer books of tickets were sold for the performance on Sunday than for the performance on Monday. How many books of tickets were sold for the Monday performance?

Ⓐ 21 Ⓒ 15

Ⓑ 9 Ⓓ 13

8. Suppose a bar is added to the graph to show that the number of books of tickets sold for Tuesday is greater than those sold for Sunday but less than those sold for Saturday. Which could be a number where the bar would stop?

Ⓐ 9 Ⓒ 14

Ⓑ 17 Ⓓ 26

Use the tables for 9–10.

Favorite Type of Museums			
history	art	art	science
science	science	art	art
science	history	media	science
history	media	science	media
art	art	history	science

Favorite Type of Museums

Type of Museum	Frequency
Art	6
History	4
Media	3
Science	?

9. What number should be used to complete the frequency table for the students who chose science museums?

Ⓐ 3 Ⓒ 1

Ⓑ 7 Ⓓ 5

10. How many more students chose art museums than history museums as their favorite?

Ⓐ 4 Ⓒ 10

Ⓑ 6 Ⓓ 2

GO ON

11. A park ranger records the types of animals she sees one morning.

Animals Seen			
deer	deer	elk	deer
deer	elk	deer	bear
elk	deer	bear	deer

Which frequency table represents the data?

Ⓐ

Animals Seen	
Type of Animal	**Frequency**
Bear	2
Deer	3
Elk	7

Ⓑ

Animals Seen	
Type of Animal	**Frequency**
Bear	3
Deer	7
Elk	2

Ⓒ

Animals Seen	
Type of Animal	**Frequency**
Bear	2
Deer	7
Elk	3

Ⓓ

Animals Seen	
Type of Animal	**Frequency**
Bear	2
Deer	12
Elk	7

Use the bar graph for 12–14.

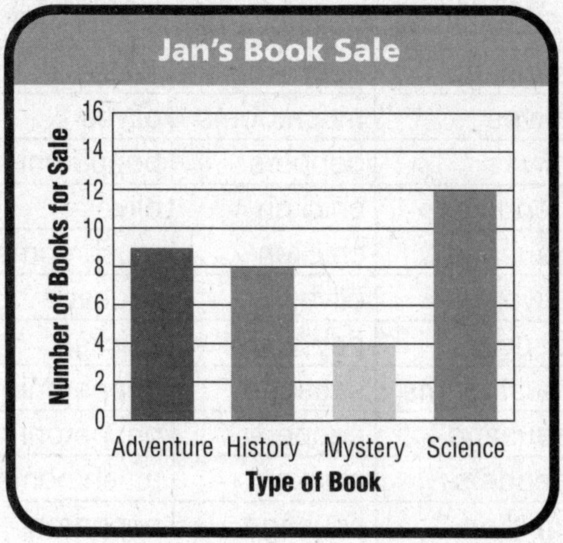

12. Jan has 3 fewer biographies than history books for sale. How many biographies does she have for sale?

Ⓐ 11 Ⓒ 8
Ⓑ 3 Ⓓ 5

13. Jan plans to sell each book for $5. How much more money would Jan make from selling all her science books than from selling all her mystery books?

Ⓐ $20 Ⓒ $15
Ⓑ $40 Ⓓ $56

14. Suppose the bar graph showed that Jan sold more classic novels than science books. Which could be a number where the bar for classic novels would stop?

Ⓐ 12 Ⓒ 6
Ⓑ 14 Ⓓ 10

GO ON

Use the tables for 15–16.

Pizza Toppings Ordered		
sausage	pepperoni	sausage
olives	mushrooms	olives
olives	peppers	pepperoni
peppers	chicken	olives
sausage	chicken	mushrooms
olives	olives	sausage
peppers	pepperoni	chicken
mushrooms	sausage	pepperoni
sausage	peppers	pepperoni
peppers	chicken	mushrooms
chicken	sausage	pepperoni
pepperoni	olives	olives
olives	sausage	peppers

Pizza Toppings Ordered	
Type of Topping	Frequency
chicken	5
mushrooms	4
olives	?
pepperoni	7
peppers	6
sausage	8

15. Which number completes the frequency table for the number of times olives were selected?

Ⓐ 8 Ⓒ 9

Ⓑ 3 Ⓓ 12

16. If toppings cost $2 each, how much extra would be charged for all the orders of peppers and sausage?

Ⓐ $28 Ⓒ $34

Ⓑ $14 Ⓓ $30

Use the bar graph for 17–18.

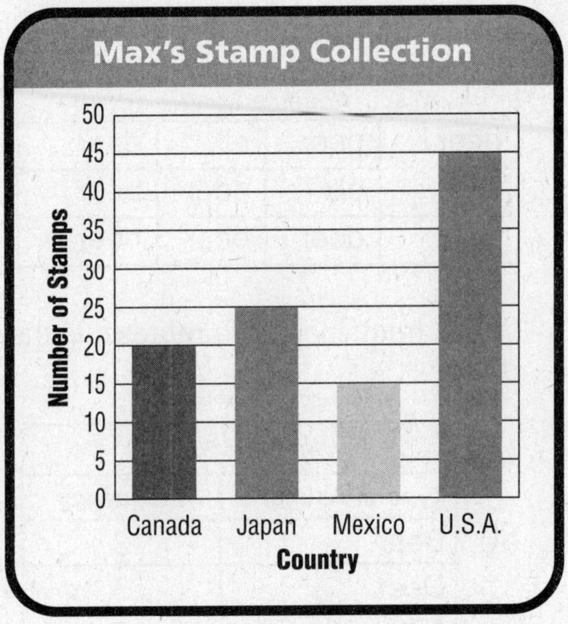

17. How many more stamps does Max have from Japan than from Mexico?

Ⓐ 15 Ⓒ 30

Ⓑ 10 Ⓓ 20

18. Max sells 32 of his U.S.A. stamps. How many stamps does Max have left in his collection?

Record your answer and fill in the bubbles on the grid. Be sure to use the correct place value.

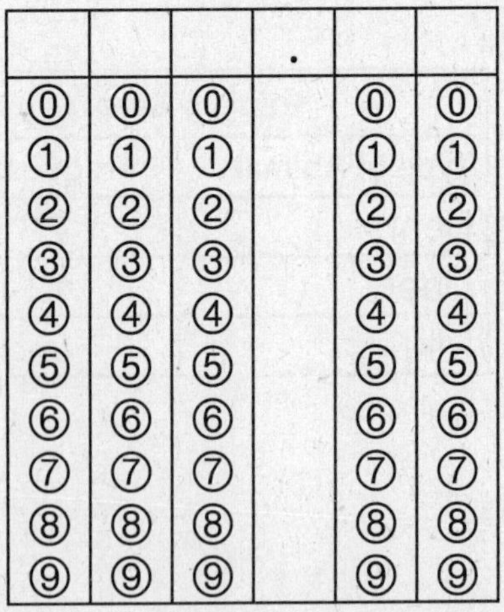

STOP

Fill in the bubble for the correct answer.

Use the stem-and-leaf plot for 1–2.

Jenny records the heights of her family members. The heights, in inches, are 50, 53, 45, 52, 68, 56, 47, 69, and 60. The stem-and-leaf plot shows some of the data.

Heights of Jenny's Family Members (inches)

Stem	Leaf
4	5 7
5	?
6	0 8 9

1. What are the leaves for stem 5?

Ⓐ 2, 3, 7
Ⓑ 0, 2, 3, 5
Ⓒ 0, 2, 3, 6
Ⓓ 2, 3, 5

2. What is the range of the heights?

Ⓐ 24
Ⓑ 45
Ⓒ 13
Ⓓ 26

Use the table for 3–4.

Travel Time						
Distance from School (mi)	1	6	3	11	3	9
Travel Time (min)	6	12	10	30	9	18

3. Which is the best scale to use for both the *x*-axis and the *y*-axis on a scatter plot of the data?

Ⓐ 1 Ⓑ 10 Ⓒ 30 Ⓓ 3

4. Which ordered pair would **NOT** represent a point on a scatter plot of the data?

Ⓐ (6, 12) Ⓒ (3, 18)
Ⓑ (3, 9) Ⓓ (11, 30)

5. The table shows the amount of time it took hikers to travel the entire length of a hiking trail.

Time to Complete Trail (hours)						
2	$1\frac{3}{4}$	$2\frac{1}{4}$	$1\frac{1}{2}$	2	1	$1\frac{1}{2}$
$2\frac{1}{2}$	2	$1\frac{3}{4}$	$2\frac{1}{2}$	$2\frac{1}{4}$	2	3

A park ranger wants to make a dot plot of the data. How many dots should he place to show hiking times greater than 2 hours?

Ⓐ 1 Ⓑ 5 Ⓒ 2 Ⓓ 3

GO ON

Use the dot plot for 6–7.

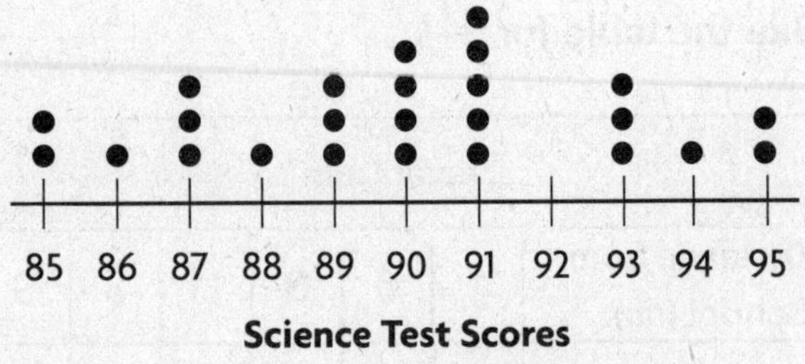

6. What is the range of test scores?

Ⓐ 5 Ⓑ 15 Ⓒ 10 Ⓓ 3

7. How many more students received a score of 90 or less than received a score greater than 90?

Ⓐ 11 Ⓑ 6 Ⓒ 14 Ⓓ 3

8. A museum director records the number of people who visited the museum on 9 different days and the amount of money that was donated on each day.

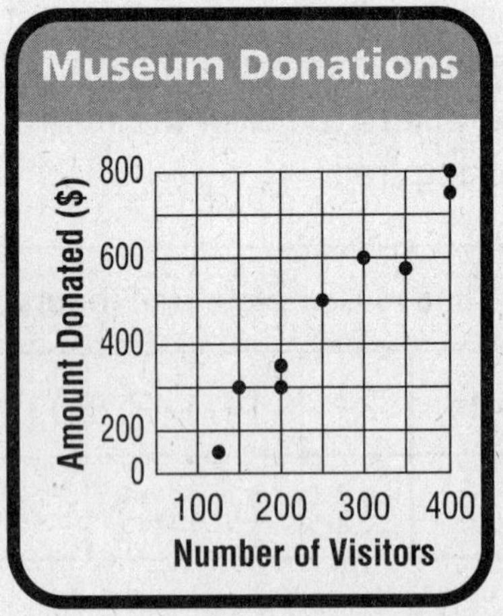

She displays the data on a scatter plot. About how much money was donated per day when 200 people visited the museum?

Ⓐ about \$600 Ⓒ about \$300

Ⓑ about \$100 Ⓓ about \$800

Use the scatter plot for 9–10.

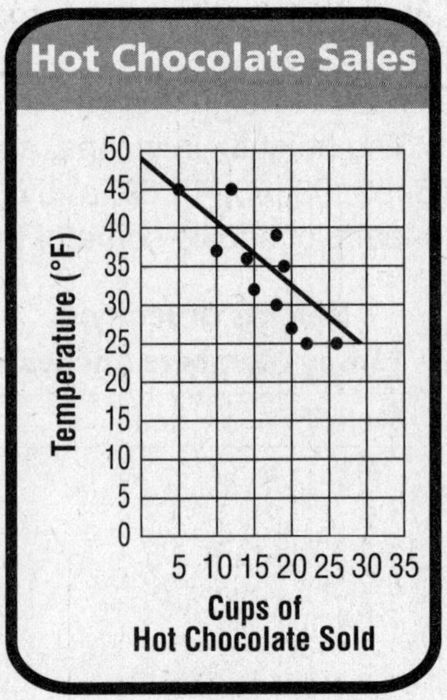

9. Which statement about the data shown in the scatter plot is true?

Ⓐ As the temperature increases, hot chocolate sales increase.

Ⓑ As the temperature decreases, hot chocolate sales increase.

Ⓒ As the temperature increases, hot chocolate sales stay the same.

Ⓓ As the temperature decreases, hot chocolate sales decrease.

10. When the temperature hit 45°F, 5 cups of hot chocolate were sold. Which ordered pair shows this data on the scatter plot?

Ⓐ (45, 50) Ⓒ (45, 5)

Ⓑ (5, 45) Ⓓ (5, 40)

GO ON

Use the dot plot for 11–12.

Darnell measured leaves as part of a science project. To the nearest centimeter, the length of each leaf is 12, 13, 12, 12, 15, 13, 14, 15, 12, 12, 15, 14, 13, 14, and 11. The dot plot shows some of the data.

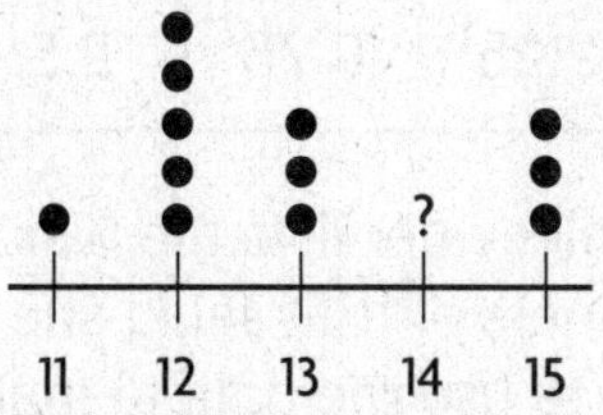

Length of Leaves (cm)

11. How many dots should Darnell mark above 14?

Ⓐ 3
Ⓑ 1
Ⓒ 0
Ⓓ 5

12. How many more leaves measured 12 centimeters long than measured 15 centimeters long?

Record your answer and fill in the bubbles on the grid. Be sure to use the correct place value.

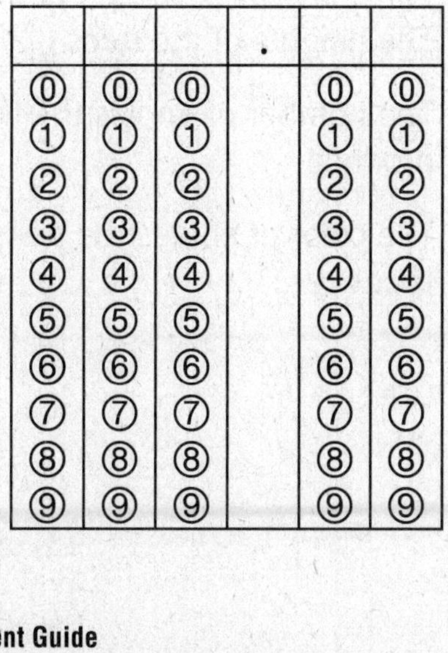

Use the stem-and-leaf plot for 13–14.

The distances Clea biked weekly, in miles, are 49, 31, 36, 41, 28, 44, 23, 34, 32, 33, and 25. The stem-and-leaf plot shows some of the data.

Distances Clea Biked Weekly (miles)

Stem	Leaf
2	?
3	1 2 3 4 6
4	1 4 9

13. What are the leaves for stem 2?

Ⓐ 1, 2, 3, 4, 6
Ⓑ 3, 5, 8
Ⓒ 2, 3, 5, 6
Ⓓ 2, 3, 5, 8

14. Clea finds the total number of miles she biked in the weeks she biked more than 40 miles. Next month she plans to bike twice as many miles as that total. How many miles does Clea plan to bike next month?

Ⓐ 180 miles
Ⓑ 134 miles
Ⓒ 90 miles
Ⓓ 268 miles

GO ON

15. The dot plot shows the different amounts of wheat flour a baker mixes into each loaf of bread.

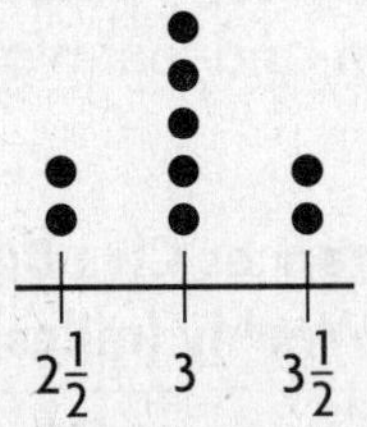

Wheat Flour (cups)

What is the total amount of wheat flour the baker would use to make all of the loaves of bread?

Ⓐ 9 cups Ⓒ 21 cups

Ⓑ 24 cups Ⓓ 27 cups

Use the stem-and-leaf plot for 16–17.

Number of Books Read by Students

Stem	Leaf
1	3 4 4 6 9
2	1 1 2 3 4 6 7 8 8
3	0 2 2 4 5 7
4	1 2 3

16. How many more students read fewer than 25 books than read more than 35 books?

Ⓐ 6 Ⓑ 10 Ⓒ 4 Ⓓ 14

17. Students who read more than 25 and fewer than 35 books were given a book certificate worth $5. Students who read 35 books or more were given a book certificate worth $10. What is the total value of the book certificates given to students?

Ⓐ $13 Ⓑ $65 Ⓒ $10 Ⓓ $90

18. Pre-packaged fruit salad is sold in different weights at a deli.

Weight of Fruit Salads Sold (lb)				
2.5	1.25	1.75	1.25	1.75
1.75	2.25	0.75	2.5	1

The deli owner lists the weights of the containers of fruit salad she sells. She wants to use the data to make a dot plot. How many dots should she use to represent the number of 1.75-pound containers of fruit salad sold?

Ⓐ 8 Ⓒ 5

Ⓑ 3 Ⓓ 10

19. A farmer wants to show the relationship between the ages of his apple trees and the number of apples they produce. He collects the data to make a scatter plot. He puts tree ages in years on one axis. Which data should he put on the other axis?

Ⓐ The price of the apples

Ⓑ The heights of the trees

Ⓒ The number of apples the trees produce

Ⓓ The color of apples the trees produce

STOP

Fill in the bubble for the correct answer.

Use the bar graph for 1–2.

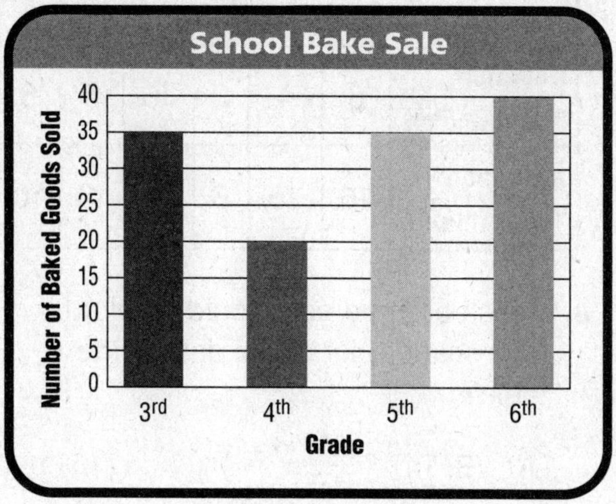

1. Ten fewer baked goods were sold by 2nd grade students than by 3rd grade students. How many baked goods were sold by 2nd grade students?

Ⓐ 35

Ⓑ 25

Ⓒ 45

Ⓓ 10

2. Each item at the bake sale sold for $2. How much more money was made by the 6th grade students than by the 4th grade students?

Ⓐ $80

Ⓑ $20

Ⓒ $40

Ⓓ $10

Use the scatter plot for for 3–4.

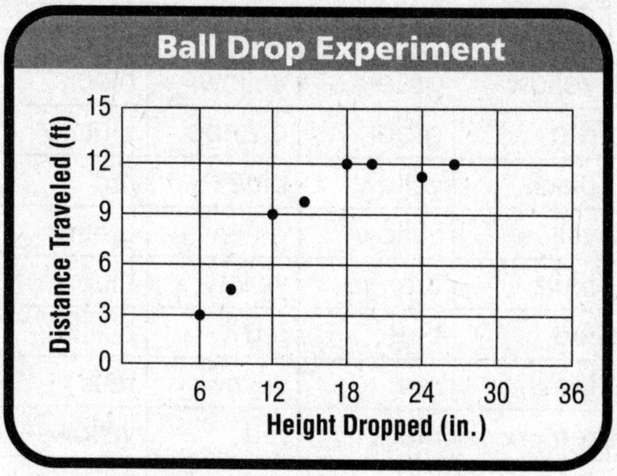

3. Which ordered pair appears to represent a point on the scatter plot?

Ⓐ (3, 6) Ⓒ (6, 3)

Ⓑ (10, 15) Ⓓ (12, 21)

4. Which best describes the scatter plot?

Ⓐ The farther the ball travels, the shorter the distance it was dropped from.

Ⓑ The shorter the distance the ball travels, the greater the height it was dropped from.

Ⓒ The greater the height the ball is dropped from, the farther it travels.

Ⓓ The height the ball is dropped from does not affect the distance it travels.

GO ON

Use the tables for 5–7.

Yarn Colors Used to Knit Socks

blue	red	blue	red
yellow	green	yellow	black
red	green	orange	blue
black	yellow	blue	red
yellow	yellow	green	green
blue	orange	yellow	blue
red	blue	red	black
green	red	yellow	red
red	black	red	yellow

Yarn Colors Used to Knit Socks

Color of Yarn	Frequency
Blue	7
Black	4
Green	?
Orange	2
Red	10
Yellow	8

5. What is the frequency of green yarn being used to knit socks?

Ⓐ 7 Ⓑ 5 Ⓒ 6 Ⓓ 4

6. What is the frequency of red yarn or blue yarn being used to knit socks?

Ⓐ 7 Ⓑ 2 Ⓒ 17 Ⓓ 9

7. Each pair of socks sells for $5. How much more money can be made from selling all the blue socks than from selling all the orange socks?

Ⓐ $45 Ⓑ $10 Ⓒ $20 Ⓓ $25

Use the table for 8–9.

Water Consumed While Biking

Distance Biked (miles)	8	4	2	10	8	6
Amount of Water (cups)	16	10	6	20	14	10

8. Which ordered pair would be plotted on a scatter plot of the data in the table?

Ⓐ (8, 14)

Ⓑ (4, 4)

Ⓒ (14, 10)

Ⓓ (8, 2)

9. Which is the best scale for both the *x*-axis and the *y*-axis in a scatter plot of the data?

Ⓐ 2

Ⓑ 10

Ⓒ 7

Ⓓ 20

GO ON

Name ____

Use the bar graph for 10–11.

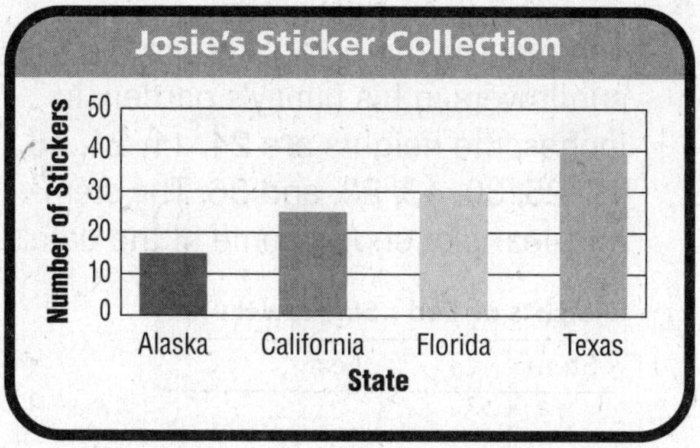

10. How many more stickers does Josie have from Florida than from Alaska?

Ⓐ 20

Ⓑ 5

Ⓒ 15

Ⓓ 10

11. Josie gives her sister half of her stickers from Texas and 15 of her stickers from California. How many stickers from Texas and California does Josie have left?

Ⓐ 45

Ⓑ 80

Ⓒ 20

Ⓓ 30

Use the dot plot for 12–13.

Tracy recorded the weights of bags of marbles. To the nearest ounce, the weight of each bag of marbles is 16, 15, 13, 15, 15, 13, 13, 15, 14, and 16. The dot plot shows some of the data.

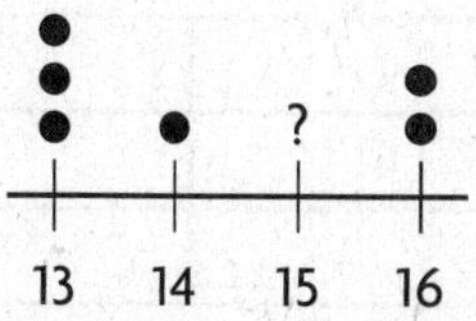

12. How many dots should Tracy place above 15?

Ⓐ 0 Ⓑ 4 Ⓒ 2 Ⓓ 3

13. What is the range of the weights?

Ⓐ 16 ounces Ⓒ 10 ounces

Ⓑ 3 ounces Ⓓ 13 ounces

14. A music teacher recorded his students' favorite instruments. He makes a frequency table of the data.

Students' Favorite Instrument

violin	drums	trumpet	drums
trumpet	trumpet	violin	violin
drums	violin	trumpet	drums
violin	trumpet	violin	violin

What is the frequency of students who chose the violin as their favorite instrument?

Ⓐ 7 Ⓑ 1 Ⓒ 5 Ⓓ Not here

GO ON

Use the frequency table for 15–16.

Visitors voted for their favorite zoo animal.

Visitors' Favorite Zoo Animals	
Animal	**Frequency**
Giraffe	11
Gorilla	18
Lion	9
Zebra	27

15. How many more visitors voted for zebras than for lions?

Ⓐ 16 Ⓒ 18

Ⓑ 9 Ⓓ 36

16. How many visitors did **NOT** choose the gorilla as their favorite animal?

Record your answer and fill in the bubbles on the grid. Be sure to use the correct place value.

			.		
0	0	0		0	0
1	1	1		1	1
2	2	2		2	2
3	3	3		3	3
4	4	4		4	4
5	5	5		5	5
6	6	6		6	6
7	7	7		7	7
8	8	8		8	8
9	9	9		9	9

Use the stem-and-leaf plot for 17–18.

Ted records the heights of the sunflowers in his family's garden. In inches, the heights are 24, 11, 21, 18, 15, 25, 30, 13, 23, and 36. The stem-and-leaf plot shows some of the data.

Heights of Ted's Sunflowers (in.)

Stem	Leaf
1	?
2	1 3 4 5
3	0 6

17. What leaves should Ted write for stem 1?

Ⓐ 1, 3, 5, 8

Ⓑ 1, 3, 8

Ⓒ 1, 2, 3, 5, 8

Ⓓ 2, 3, 5, 8

18. Ted spends $2 on a plant stake for each sunflower that is taller than 25 inches. How much money does Ted spend on plant stakes?

Ⓐ $6

Ⓑ $4

Ⓒ $2

Ⓓ $8

GO ON

19. Students voted for their favorite lunch and recorded the data in a frequency table.

Students' Favorite Lunches	
Type of Lunch	**Frequency**
Sandwich	6
Hamburger	5
Pizza	13
Tacos	7

How many more students chose pizza than chose hamburgers as their favorite lunch?

Ⓐ 8 Ⓑ 13 Ⓒ 18 Ⓓ 4

Use the stem-and-leaf plot for 20–21.

Points Scored by Players

Stem	Leaf
3	0 1 3 3 5
4	1 2 4 4 4 5 6 9
5	0 1 2 3 8
6	2 4 7

20. How many more players scored 35 or fewer points than scored more than 60 points?

Ⓐ 5 Ⓑ 7 Ⓒ 2 Ⓓ 8

21. The team donated $100 to a charity for each point above 60 points scored by a single player in a season. How much did the team donate to the charity in all?

Ⓐ $300 Ⓒ $19,300

Ⓑ $1,300 Ⓓ $600

Use the tables for 22–23.

Students' Favorite Gym Activities			
softball	kickball	free play	kickball
basketball	kickball	free play	softball
free play	softball	kickball	kickball
kickball	free play	kickball	basketball
kickball	kickball	softball	kickball
kickball	free play	kickball	kickball

Students' Favorite Gym Activities	
Activity	**Frequency**
Basketball	2
Free Play	?
Kickball	13
Softball	4

22. Which number completes the frequency table for the number of times free play was selected?

Ⓐ 5

Ⓑ 10

Ⓒ 4

Ⓓ 2

23. How many more times was kickball chosen than softball?

Ⓐ 13

Ⓑ 4

Ⓒ 17

Ⓓ 9

GO ON

Name ______________________________________

24. An artist mixes blue dye in several cups to make different colors of dye. The dot plot shows the amounts of blue dye used in each cup.

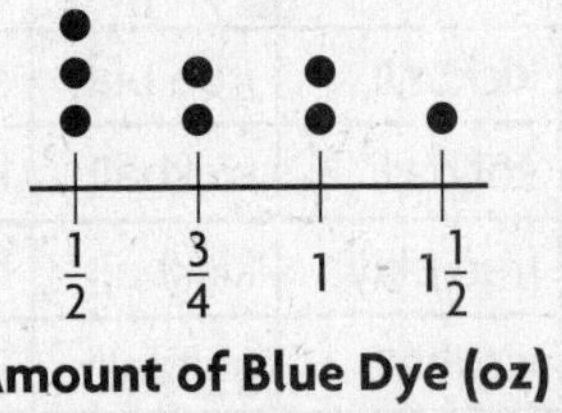

How many ounces of blue dye are used in all?

Ⓐ $6\frac{1}{2}$ ounces

Ⓑ 4 ounces

Ⓒ $3\frac{3}{4}$ ounces

Ⓓ 5 ounces

25. A bookseller prices used books for sale. He lists the prices in a table and wants to use the data to make a dot plot.

Used Book Prices				
\$5.50	\$5.25	\$4.75	\$5.25	\$5.25
\$5.75	\$5.50	\$5.75	\$5.50	\$5.00

How many dots should he use to represent books that have a price of less than \$5.50?

Ⓐ 10

Ⓑ 3

Ⓒ 5

Ⓓ 6

26. The bar graph shows the number of visitors to an aquarium gift shop over 5 days.

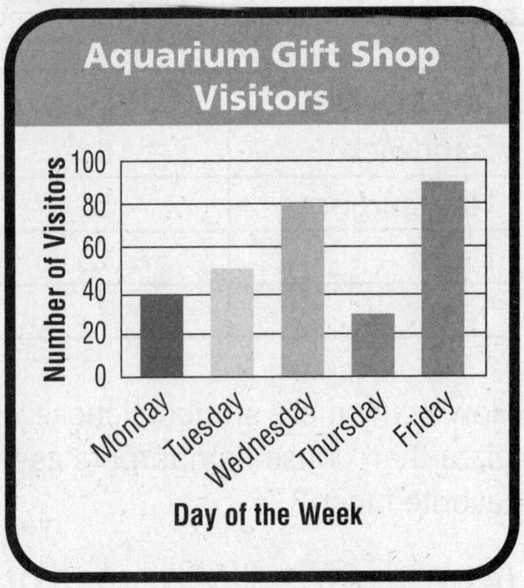

How many more people visited the aquarium gift shop on Monday and Wednesday than on Tuesday and Thursday?

Record your answer and fill in the bubbles on the grid. Be sure to use the correct place value.

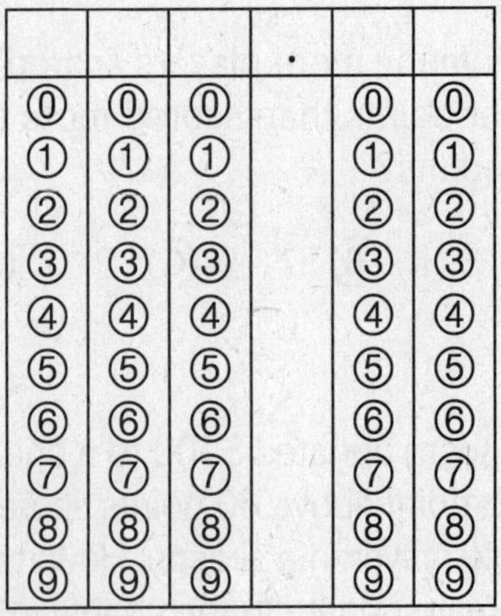

STOP

Fill in the bubble for the correct answer.

1. Daria's gross monthly income is $1,200. Her total monthly payroll taxes are $175. What is Daria's net monthly income?

Ⓐ $1,375
Ⓑ $700
Ⓒ $1,025
Ⓓ $500

2. Each month, Gita earns $22 doing yard work. Her monthly allowance is $30. She makes a monthly budget and sees that her monthly expenses are $65. How much does Gita need to earn from tutoring to balance her budget?

Ⓐ $8 Ⓒ $5
Ⓑ $13 Ⓓ $3

3. Ms. Ortega earns $850 a week. She pays $52.64 in federal income taxes, $37.09 in state income taxes, and $12.90 in other taxes. How much does Ms. Ortega pay in taxes?

Ⓐ $49.99
Ⓑ $12.63
Ⓒ $102.63
Ⓓ $747.37

4. Ms. West's new garage has a value of $7,000. The property tax rate in her town is $20.11 per year for every $1,000 of property value. The property tax is paid yearly. How much tax will Ms. West pay on her new garage in one year?

Ⓐ $104.77 Ⓒ $1,407.70
Ⓑ $14.07 Ⓓ $140.77

5. Valerie wants to use a personal identification number (PIN) to make her purchase more secure. Which method of payment can Valerie use?

Ⓐ Credit card Ⓒ Check
Ⓑ Cash Ⓓ Debit card

6. Alicia makes a monthly budget. Her monthly allowance is $25. She makes $35 each month walking her neighbor's dog. Her monthly expenses are $80. How much does she need to earn from selling her old textbooks to balance her budget?

Ⓐ $15 Ⓒ $60
Ⓑ $80 Ⓓ $20

GO ON

7. Elise earned $790 dollars this week. Her federal income taxes were $92.25. Her pay after taxes was $655.60. How much did she pay in state income taxes if she paid only federal and state income taxes?

Ⓐ $15.95 Ⓒ $697.75

Ⓑ $42.15 Ⓓ Not here

Use the chart for 8–9.

Cliff's Financial Record: Month of May

Date	Description	Received ($)	Expenses ($)	Available Funds ($)
	Balance: end of April			0
2	babysitting	25.50		25.50
3	sell toys	7.50		33.00
4	DVD		5.25	27.75
5	game room		4.05	23.70

8. Which expression shows how to find the amount of money Cliff has in available funds after he buys a DVD?

Ⓐ $33 + $5.25 Ⓒ $33 − $4.05

Ⓑ $33 + $25.25 Ⓓ $33 − $5.25

9. Cliff received $10 in allowance on May 6 and spent $2.50 on bus fare on May 7. What amount of money did Cliff have in available funds at the end of the day on May 7?

Ⓐ $12.50 Ⓒ $31.20

Ⓑ $62.64 Ⓓ $7.50

10. Mr. Tonka wants to purchase a bike from an online store. If he purchases the bike using a check, the cost is $210 plus a $25 shipping fee. If Mr. Tonka purchases the bike with a credit card, he will make 5 payments of $42 plus a $1.50 fee for every payment and a $25 shipping fee. How much will Mr. Tonka save if he purchases the bike using a check?

Ⓐ $7.50

Ⓑ $242.50

Ⓒ $235

Ⓓ $1.50

11. The Jefferson family's monthly income is $2,800. They budget $1,375 for rent, $530 for food, $250 for clothing, $275 for transportation expenses, $300 for savings, and $150 for entertainment. Which of the following changes can be made to balance the Jefferson family's budget?

Ⓐ Increase the rent to $3,455.

Ⓑ Decrease the rent to $1,335.

Ⓒ Decrease the clothing expense to $170.

Ⓓ Decrease the clothing expense to $190.

GO ON

12. Which statement about a property tax of $1,550, on a home with a value of $100,000, is true?

Ⓐ The property tax rate is $10.50 for every thousand dollars in value.

Ⓑ The property tax rate is $155 for every thousand dollars in value.

Ⓒ The property tax rate is $25 for every thousand dollars in value.

Ⓓ The property tax rate is $15.50 for every thousand dollars in value.

13. Doug wants to purchase a new camera online for $95.

FOCUS SHARP CAMERA
$95
Pay by check: $95 + shipping
Pay by credit card: 4 payments of $24 + $3 fee per payment
SHIPPING: $20 or FREE shipping with credit card payments

Which equation shows *T*, the total cost of the camera, if Doug pays by credit card?

Ⓐ $T = 4 \times (\$24 + \$3)$

Ⓑ $T = \$95 + \$24 + \$3$

Ⓒ $T = \$95 + \$20$

Ⓓ $T = 4 \times \$24 + 4 \times \$3 + \$20$

14. The pay stub shows Rita's weekly net income and payroll taxes.

1001

Employee: Rita Moran	Total earnings		
	Federal income tax	$64.00	
	State income tax	$33.17	
	Other taxes	$9.03	
Pay period:		Total taxes	$106.20
June 3 - 7		Final Pay	$423.75

Detach and retain for your records.

What is Rita's weekly gross income?

Ⓐ $529.95 Ⓒ $487.75

Ⓑ $465.95 Ⓓ $317.55

15. Theo's June budget is not balanced. By how much must he reduce expenses to balance his budget?

Theo's June Budget	
Income	**Expenses**
Allowance: $50	New Headphones: $64
Washing cars: $27	Transportation: $50
Sell Used Books: $15	Savings: $25

Ⓐ $92

Ⓑ $40

Ⓒ $47

Ⓓ $8

GO ON

16. Kaia is buying new hiking boots for her camping trip. The boots cost $65 plus tax. Kaia gives the cashier $100 and receives $29.80 in change. How much sales tax does Kaia pay on her purchase?

Ⓐ $70.20
Ⓑ $100
Ⓒ $5.20
Ⓓ $65

17. Bryant earns $16 per hour after taxes and works 35 hours each week. This week his expenses were $624. How many more hours would he have to work to balance his budget?

Ⓐ 1 hour
Ⓑ 3 hours
Ⓒ 2 hours
Ⓓ 4 hours

18. Donna wants to purchase an item that costs $375. She has $250 in her bank account, so she used her credit card to pay for the item. How much more money would Donna have needed in her bank account to make the purchase with a debit card instead of a credit card?

Ⓐ $250
Ⓑ $625
Ⓒ $125
Ⓓ $75

19. What is payroll tax?

Ⓐ Money an employer withholds from an employee's earnings

Ⓑ Money paid to a city, town, state government or the U.S. government

Ⓒ Money added to the cost of items or services

Ⓓ Money earned over a period of time

20. A family's monthly income is $2,500. Their monthly expenses are shown.

Monthly Expenses	
Rent	$1,050
Utilities	$184
Food	$550
Education	$250
Entertainment and Travel	$125

What is the maximum amount, in dollars, that the family can save each month after all expenses are paid?

Record your answer and fill in the bubbles on the grid. Be sure to use the correct place value.

			.		
⓪	⓪	⓪		⓪	⓪
①	①	①		①	①
②	②	②		②	②
③	③	③		③	③
④	④	④		④	④
⑤	⑤	⑤		⑤	⑤
⑥	⑥	⑥		⑥	⑥
⑦	⑦	⑦		⑦	⑦
⑧	⑧	⑧		⑧	⑧
⑨	⑨	⑨		⑨	⑨

GO ON

Use the table for 21–22.

Olivia's September Budget	
Income	**Expenses**
Allowance: $44	Monthly club dues: $8
Babysitting: $20	Savings: $25
	School supplies: $38

21. Which of the following changes can be made to balance Olivia's budget?

Ⓐ Increase the amount saved to $30.

Ⓑ Decrease the allowance amount to $37.

Ⓒ Increase the babysitting income to $27.

Ⓓ Decrease the amount saved to $20.

22. Olivia's income is the same in October as it was in September. She does not purchase any school supplies but spends $14 on a school trip. By which amount can Olivia increase her savings and still have a balanced budget in October?

Ⓐ $17 Ⓑ $42 Ⓒ $34 Ⓓ $24

23. Mr. Muncy pays $125 in payroll taxes each week. The federal income tax is 0.80 of the weekly payroll taxes. How much does Mr. Muncy pay in federal income tax each week?

Ⓐ $25 Ⓒ $225

Ⓑ $105.80 Ⓓ $100

24. Toby works at a book store. Last week his gross income was $105.74. This week his gross income is $117.52. The total of his payroll taxes for the two weeks is $28.37. How can you find his net income for the two weeks?

Ⓐ Find the sum of the gross incomes. Then add the payroll taxes.

Ⓑ Find the sum of the gross incomes. Then subtract the payroll taxes.

Ⓒ Add the payroll taxes to the gross income for each week. Then add the sums.

Ⓓ Subtract the payroll taxes from the gross income for each week. Then add the totals.

25. Lia buys a personal music player online using electronic payments. She makes 3 payments of $21 plus a $2 processing fee for each payment. What is the total amount, in dollars, that Lia pays?

Record your answer and fill in the bubbles on the grid. Be sure to use the correct place value.

			.		
⓪	⓪	⓪		⓪	⓪
①	①	①		①	①
②	②	②		②	②
③	③	③		③	③
④	④	④		④	④
⑤	⑤	⑤		⑤	⑤
⑥	⑥	⑥		⑥	⑥
⑦	⑦	⑦		⑦	⑦
⑧	⑧	⑧		⑧	⑧
⑨	⑨	⑨		⑨	⑨

GO ON

26. Mr. Kumar buys a set of books online that cost $75. He uses an electronic payment method to pay for the books, making 3 payments of $25, plus a $2 processing fee for each payment. How much more money does Mr. Kumar pay for the books using this electronic payment method?

Ⓐ $81 Ⓒ $5
Ⓑ $6 Ⓓ $2

27. Ms. Martinez works at a state park. Her gross income is $680 a week. The pay stub shows Ms. Martinez's weekly payroll taxes.

1003

Employee: Maria Martinez	Total earnings		$680.00
	Federal income tax	$47.00	
	State income tax	$18.24	
Pay period:	Other taxes	$5.29	
	Total taxes		$70.53
June 24-28	Final Pay		

Detach and retain for your records.

What is Ms. Martinez's weekly net income?

Ⓐ $750.53
Ⓑ $609.47
Ⓒ $633.00
Ⓓ $703.47

28. The sales tax is $0.03 for every dollar. Abbie buys $90 worth of items. What is the total cost of her purchase?

Ⓐ $90.03 Ⓒ $1.03
Ⓑ $2.70 Ⓓ $92.70

Use the chart for 29–30.

Mary's Financial Record: Month of November

Date	Description	Received ($)	Expenses ($)	Available Funds ($)
	Balance: end of October			0
3	birthday check	35		35
7	paper route	10		45
10	T-shirt		13.75	31.25
10	skate rental		5.18	26.07
10	allowance	?		42.57

29. Which expression shows how to find the amount of money Mary has in available funds after she buys a T-shirt?

Ⓐ $45 − $5.18
Ⓑ $31.25 − $13.75
Ⓒ $45 − $13.75
Ⓓ $13.75 − $5.18

30. How much money does Mary receive in allowance?

Ⓐ $16.50 Ⓒ $18.93
Ⓑ $42.57 Ⓓ $24.50

STOP

Student's Name ______________________ Date ____________

Prerequisite Skills Inventory

Item	TEKS*	Common Error	Soar to Success Math
1	4.8.B	May not understand how to convert measurements from a larger unit to a smaller unit within the metric system	44.32
2	4.6.B	May not understand how to identify lines of symmetry	40.19
3	4.5.D	May not understand how to find the area of a rectangle	48.27
4	4.3.G	May not understand how to relate fractions to decimals	9.31, 9.38
5	4.4.A	May not understand how to subtract decimals to hundredths	22.37
6	4.4.D	May not understand how to multiply a 4-digit number by a 1-digit number	12.59
7	4.10.B	May not understand how to calculate profit	21.35, 22.35
8	4.3.A	May not understand how to use unit fractions	20.19
9	4.8.A	May not understand how to estimate relative measurements in the customary system	43.07, 46.37
10	4.3.E	May not understand how to add fractions with equal denominators	14.54
11	4.2.D	May not understand how to round whole numbers	15.19, 15.20
12	4.3.F	May not understand how to use benchmarks to estimate the reasonableness of a sum of fractions	20.24
13	4.7.E	May not understand how to calculate the measure of angles from given information	38.36, 14.49
14	4.10.A	May not understand how to distinguish fixed from variable expenses	21.37
15	4.5.A	May not understand how to use a strip diagram to solve multi-step problems	14.48, 14.49
16	4.2.C	May not understand how to compare whole numbers	7.34, 7.35
17	4.3.C	May not understand how to find equivalent fractions	9.36, 20.38
18	4.4.F	May not understand how to divide a 4-digit number by a 1-digit number	13.36
19	4.4.A	May not understand how to add whole numbers	10.43
20	4.4.G	May not understand how to round numbers to estimate products	12.59

***TEKS**—Texas Essential Knowledge and Skills; **RtI**—Response to Intervention

Student's Name ______________________ Date ____________

Prerequisite Skills Inventory

Item	Grade 5 TEKS*	Common Error	Soar to Success Math
21	4.2.B	May not understand how to write whole numbers in expanded notation	2.26
22	4.2.H	May not understand how to identify a decimal location on a number line	26.36
23	4.8.C	May not understand how to solve problems involving intervals of time	51.16
24	4.2.G	May not understand how to relate decimals to fractions	26.36
25	4.7.C	May not understand how to determine the approximate measure of angles using a protractor	38.36
26	4.3.D	May not understand how to compare fractions with different numerators and different denominators	9.31, 9.38
27	4.6.C	May not understand how to use right angles to identify triangles	38.28
28	4.4.B	May not understand how to multiply by 100	18.27, 18.28
29	4.2.F	May not understand how to compare decimals to hundredths using models	8.40
30	4.9.B	May not understand how to solve 2-step problems involving data in fraction form in frequency tables	53.14
31	4.5.B	May not understand how to use an input-output table to determine values	33.20
32	4.4.E	May not understand how to find quotients using equations	13.30
33	4.2.A	May not understand how to use place value to find one tenth	2.27
34	4.3.B	May not understand how to add and subtract fractions	20.19
35	4.4.C	May not understand how to use area models to find squares of numbers	12.53
36	4.6.D	May not understand how to classify figures based on their sides and angles	38.27, 38.31
37	4.4.H	May not understand how to solve 2-step problems involving multiplication	71.03
38	4.5.D	May not understand how to find the perimeter of a rectangle	47.33
39	4.3.E	May not understand how to subtract fractions using models	20.27
40	4.4.H	May not understand how to solve 1-step problems involving division and interpreting remainders	13.40

***TEKS**—Texas Essential Knowledge and Skills; **RtI**—Response to Intervention

Student's Name ______________________ Date ____________

Beginning-of-Year Test

Item	Lesson	TEKS*	Common Error	Intervene with RtI* Tier 1 Lessons	Soar to Success Math
1	3.8	5.3.E	May have difficulty correctly placing the decimal point in the product of decimals	5.24	23.39
2	6.6	5.3.J	May have difficulty representing division of fractions with pictures	5.36	20.44
3	1.5	5.2.C	May not recall how to round numbers	5.4	25.23
4	14.1	5.8.A	May not understand how ordered pairs indicate movement on coordinate plane	5.73	37.16, 37.17
5	11.2	5.5.A	May not be able to sort triangles by attributes	5.60	38.35
6	16.5	5.9.B	May have difficulty representing data on a scatter plot	5.84	40.25
7	17.6	5.10.F	May have difficulty balancing a simple budget	5.19	57.04
8	13.7	5.7.A	May have difficulty converting metric units of capacity from larger to smaller units	5.72	46.37, 45.26, 44.36, 44.32
9	10.1	5.4.C	May have difficulty generating a number pattern	5.50	32.07
10	5.2	5.3.H	May have difficulty solving subtraction of fractions with pictorial models	5.29	20.31
11	1.2	5.2.A	May not understand the relationship between decimal place values	5.1	4.27
12	15.4	5.9.C	May have difficulty interpreting data to solve multi-step problems	5.81	53.12
13	9.4	5.4.H	May not recall the formula for area	5.58	47.34, 49.27, 49.30
14	12.2	5.6.B	May not understand how to use the volume of a rectangular prism to determine the number of layers	5.64	49.25, 49.28
15	1.8	5.3.K	May have difficulty following the standard algorithm for subtraction when working with decimal numbers	5.39	61.04
16	6.4	5.3.L	May have difficulty dividing unit fractions by whole numbers	5.34	20.44

***TEKS**—Texas Essential Knowledge and Skills; **RtI**—Response to Intervention

Student's Name ______________________ Date ____________

Beginning-of-Year Test (continued)

Item	Lesson	TEKS*	Common Error	Intervene with RtI* Tier 1 Lessons	Soar to Success Math
17	1.4	5.2.B	May have difficulty using place value to compare decimals	5.3	8.44
18	6.3	5.3.I	May have difficulty representing multiplication of fractions with area models	5.33	20.44
19	8.4	5.4.B	May have difficulty representing multi-step problems	5.48	14.57, 14.58
20	14.3	5.8.C	May have difficulty generating ordered pairs from real-world problems	5.75	33.17, 37.17
21	7.5	5.4.F	May have difficulty simplifying expressions	5.54	14.39, 14.41
22	2.1	5.3.A	May not understand how to estimate products using basic fact patterns	5.10	12.55, 12.59
23	10.2	5.4.D	May have difficulty recognizing an additive pattern	5.50	33.20
24	4.2	5.3.F	May have difficulty using models to divide decimals	5.25	24.32
25	6.5	5.3.L	May have difficulty dividing whole numbers by unit fractions	5.35	20.44
26	7.2	5.4.A	May have difficulty identifying prime numbers	5.46	31.29
27	2.3	5.3.C	May not understand how to model division of whole numbers	5.12	13.31
28	17.2	5.10.A	May not recall or understand the definition of property tax	5.19	57.04
29	5.5	5.3.K	May have difficulty adding fractions with different denominators	5.40	20.39
30	17.7	5.10.E	May have difficulty recognizing actions that result in a balanced budget	5.81	53.12
31	14.1	5.8.B	May not understand how to describe movements needed to graph an ordered pair	5.73	37.16, 37.17
32	9.1	5.4.H	May not recall the formula for perimeter	5.49	47.34, 49.27
33	1.5	5.2.C	May not recall how to round numbers	5.4	25.23

***TEKS**—Texas Essential Knowledge and Skills; **RtI**—Response to Intervention

Student's Name ______________________ Date ____________

Beginning-of-Year Test (continued)

Item	Lesson	TEKS*	Common Error	Intervene with RtI* Tier 1 Lessons	Soar to Success Math
34	4.1	5.3.G	May have difficulty recognizing and using patterns to divide decimals	5.27	12.49
35	2.4	5.3.C	May have difficulty dividing a 4-digit number by a 2-digit number	5.13	13.38
36	9.1	5.4.G	May have difficulty recognizing the formula for volume	5.49	47.34, 49.27
37	8.4	5.4.B	May have difficulty representing multi-step problems that include a variable	5.48	14.57, 14.58
38	1.4	5.2.B	May not understand the relationship between decimal place values	5.3	8.44
39	17.3	5.10.B	May not recall or understand the difference between net income and gross income	5.39	61.04
40	17.5	5.10.D	May have difficulty understanding or using a financial record system	5.39	61.04
41	5.1	5.3.H	May have difficulty adding fractions with unequal denominators	5.28	20.30
42	13.3	5.7.A	May have difficulty converting customary units of length from smaller to larger units	5.68	46.37
43	4.3	5.3.A	May not rename the dividend as tenths	5.8	19.25, 19.26
44	16.1	5.9.A	May have difficulty representing data on a dot plot	5.79	54.17
45	16.2	5.9.C	May have difficulty solving problems with data	5.82	54.17
46	7.3	5.4.E	May have difficulty matching an expression with parentheses to a word problem	5.53	14.39, 14.40
47	17.4	5.10.C	May have difficulty calculating the amount of money needed to purchase an item with a debit card	5.39	61.04
48	6.1	5.3.I	May have difficulty using models to multiply fractions	5.31	13.09
49	3.2	5.3.D	May have difficulty using an area model to multiply a whole number and a decimal	5.17	12.49
50	2.2	5.3.B	May not understand the steps in the standard algorithm for multiplication	5.11	12.52, 12.54, 12.58

***TEKS**—Texas Essential Knowledge and Skills; **RtI**—Response to Intervention

Student's Name ______________________ Date ____________

Middle-of-Year Test

Item	Lesson	TEKS*	Common Error	Intervene with RtI* Tier 1 Lessons	Soar to Success Math
1	3.7	5.3.E	May not recall how to use place value patterns to place a decimal in the product	5.23	23.39
2	6.4	5.3.J	May have difficulty using models to divide a whole number by a fraction	5.34	20.44
3	1.5	5.2.C	May not recall how to round numbers	5.4	25.23
4	14.1	5.8.A	May not understand how the *y*-coordinate indicates movement on the coordinate grid	5.73	37.16, 37.17
5	11.1	5.5.A	May not recognize properties necessary to sort polygons into sets	5.59	38.33
6	16.5	5.9.B	May have difficulty representing data on a scatter plot	5.84	40.25
7	17.6	5.10.F	May have difficulty balancing a simple budget	5.19	57.04
8	13.6	5.7.A	May have difficulty converting metric units of length from smaller to larger units	5.71	44.32, 45.26, 46.32
9	10.4	5.4.C	May have difficulty using a rule to generate and graph a coordinate pair	5.51	37.33
10	5.1	5.3.H	May have difficulty using models to add fractions	5.28	20.30
11	3.4	5.2.A	May have difficulty expressing decimals in expanded form	5.18	12.56
12	16.4	5.9.C	May have difficulty interpreting data from a stem-and-leaf plot to solve multi-step problems	5.83	2.17
13	9.4	5.4.H	May not recall the formula for the volume of a rectangular prism	5.58	47.34, 49.27, 49.30
14	12.2	5.6.B	May not understand how to use the volume of a rectangular prism to determine the number of layers	5.64	49.25, 49.28
15	1.7	5.3.K	May have difficulty adding positive rational numbers	5.38	21.37, 22.37
16	6.6	5.3.L	May have difficulty dividing a unit fraction by a whole number	5.36	20.44

***TEKS**—Texas Essential Knowledge and Skills; **RtI**—Response to Intervention

Student's Name ______________________ Date ____________

Middle-of-Year Test (continued)

Item	Lesson	TEKS*	Common Error	Intervene with RtI* Tier 1 Lessons	Soar to Success Math
17	1.4	5.2.B	May have difficulty using place value to order decimals	5.3	8.44
18	6.1	5.3.I	May have difficulty using models to multiply fractions	5.31	13.09
19	8.4	5.4.B	May have difficulty representing multi-step problems that include a variable	5.48	14.57, 14.58
20	14.3	5.8.C	May have difficulty graphing ordered pairs from an input/output table	5.75	33.17, 37.17
21	7.4	5.4.F	May have difficulty simplifying expressions	5.55	14.40
22	1.6	5.3.A	May have difficulty estimating with subtraction	5.6	21.36, 22.36
23	10.3	5.4.D	May have difficulty recognizing an additive pattern in a graph	5.52	33.19
24	4.4	5.3.F	May have difficulty using pictorial models to represent division of decimals	5.26	24.32
25	6.4	5.3.L	May have difficulty dividing whole numbers by unit fractions	5.34	20.44
26	7.2	5.4.A	May have difficulty identifying composite numbers	5.46	31.29
27	2.8	5.3.C	May not understand how to divide a 4-digit number by a 2-digit number	5.16	57.04
28	17.1	5.10.A	May not recall the definition of income tax	5.19	57.04
29	5.5	5.3.K	May have difficulty adding fractions with unequal denominators	5.40	20.39
30	17.7	5.10.E	May have difficulty recognizing actions that result in a balanced budget	5.81	53.12
31	14.1	5.8.B	May not understand how to describe movements needed to graph an ordered pair	5.73	37.16, 37.17
32	9.4	5.4.H	May not recall the formula for volume	5.58	47.34, 49.27, 49.30
33	1.5	5.2.C	May not recall how to round decimals to hundredths	5.4	25.23

***TEKS**—Texas Essential Knowledge and Skills; **RtI**—Response to Intervention

Student's Name ____________________ Date ____________

Middle-of-Year Test (continued)

Item	Lesson	TEKS*	Common Error	Intervene with RtI* Tier 1 Lessons	Soar to Success Math
34	4.5	5.3.G	May have difficulty dividing a decimal by a 2-digit number	5.26	24.39
35	2.4	5.3.C	May have difficulty dividing a 4-digit number by a 2-digit number	5.13	13.38
36	9.2	5.4.G	May have difficulty recognizing the formula for volume	5.56	49.28, 49.30
37	8.4	5.4.B	May have difficulty solving multi-step problems that include a variable	5.48	14.57, 14.58
38	1.4	5.2.B	May not understand the relationship between decimal place values	5.3	8.44
39	17.3	5.10.B	May not recall the difference between net income and gross income	5.39	61.04
40	17.5	5.10.D	May have difficulty understanding or using a financial record system	5.39	61.04
41	5.2	5.3.H	May have difficulty subtracting fractions	5.29	20.31
42	13.4	5.7.A	May have difficulty converting customary units of weight from smaller to larger units	5.69	45.30
43	5.3	5.3.A	May have difficulty estimating with fractions	5.9	20.34
44	15.1	5.9.A	May have difficulty representing data in a frequency table	5.77	53.08
45	15.2	5.9.C	May have difficulty solving problems with data from a frequency table	5.77	53.08
46	7.5	5.4.E	May have difficulty using brackets in numerical expressions	5.54	14.39, 14.41
47	17.4	5.10.C	May have difficulty calculating fees associated with electronic payments	5.39	61.04
48	6.3	5.3.I	May have difficulty multiplying fractions with models	5.33	20.44
49	3.2	5.3.D	May have difficulty using pictures to illustrate multiplying a whole number and a decimal	5.17	12.49
50	2.2	5.3.B	May have difficulty multiplying a 3-digit number by a 2-digit number	5.11	12.52, 12.54, 12.58

***TEKS**—Texas Essential Knowledge and Skills; **RtI**—Response to Intervention

Student's Name ________________________ Date ____________

End-of-Year Test

Item	Lesson	TEKS*	Common Error	Intervene with RtI* Tier 1 Lessons	Soar to Success Math
1	3.3	5.3.E	May have difficulty using the Distributive Property to find the product of a whole number and a decimal	5.22	12.59
2	6.4	5.3.J	May have difficulty modeling division with fractions	5.34	20.44
3	1.5	5.2.C	May not recall how to round numbers	5.4	25.23
4	14.1	5.8.A	May not recall the key attributes of the coordinate plane	5.73	37.16, 37.17
5	11.1	5.5.A	May not recognize properties necessary to sort polygons into sets	5.59	38.33
6	16.5	5.9.B	May have difficulty representing data on a scatter plot	5.84	40.25
7	17.6	5.10.F	May have difficulty balancing a simple budget	5.19	57.04
8	13.6	5.7.A	May have difficulty converting metric units of mass from smaller to larger units	5.71	44.32, 45.26, 46.32
9	10.1	5.4.C	May have difficulty generating a number pattern	5.50	32.07
10	5.2	5.3.H	May have difficulty representing subtraction of fractions with models	5.29	20.31
11	1.2	5.2.A	May not understand the relationship between decimal place values	5.1	4.27
12	16.4	5.9.C	May have difficulty interpreting data to solve multi-step problems	5.83	2.17
13	9.1	5.4.H	May not recall the formula for perimeter	5.49	47.34, 49.27
14	12.2	5.6.B	May not understand how to use the volume of a rectangular prism to determine the number of layers	5.64	49.25, 49.28
15	1.8	5.3.K	May have difficulty subtracting decimal numbers	5.39	61.04
16	6.4	5.3.L	May have difficulty dividing unit fractions by whole numbers	5.34	20.44

***TEKS**—Texas Essential Knowledge and Skills; **RtI**—Response to Intervention

Student's Name ______________________ Date ____________

End-of-Year Test (continued)

Item	Lesson	TEKS*	Common Error	Intervene with RtI* Tier 1 Lessons	Soar to Success Math
17	1.4	5.2.B	May have difficulty using place value to compare decimals	5.3	8.44
18	6.3	5.3.I	May have difficulty representing the multiplication of fractions with models	5.33	20.44
19	8.4	5.4.B	May have difficulty representing multi-step problems that include a variable	5.48	14.57, 14.58
20	14.3	5.8.C	May have difficulty graphing ordered pairs from an input/output table	5.75	33.17, 37.17
21	7.5	5.4.F	May have difficulty simplifying expressions	5.54	14.39, 14.41
22	3.7	5.3.A	May have difficulty estimating to subtract	5.23	23.39
23	10.3	5.4.D	May have difficulty recognizing a multiplicative pattern in a graph	5.52	33.19
24	4.2	5.3.F	May have difficulty using pictorial models to represent division of decimals	5.25	24.32
25	6.4	5.3.L	May have difficulty dividing whole numbers by unit fractions	5.34	20.44
26	7.2	5.4.A	May have difficulty identifying prime numbers	5.46	31.29
27	2.3	5.3.C	May not understand how to model division of a 3-digit number by a 2-digit number	5.12	13.31
28	17.1	5.10.A	May not recall the definition of sales tax	5.19	57.04
29	5.5	5.3.K	May have difficulty adding fractions with unequal denominators	5.40	20.39
30	17.7	5.10.E	May have difficulty recognizing actions that result in a balanced budget	5.81	53.12
31	14.1	5.8.B	May not understand how to describe movements needed to graph an ordered pair	5.73	37.16, 37.17
32	9.1	5.4.H	May not recall the formula for area	5.49	47.34, 49.27
33	1.5	5.2.C	May not recall how to round decimals to hundredths	5.4	25.23

***TEKS**—Texas Essential Knowledge and Skills; **RtI**—Response to Intervention

Student's Name ______________________ Date ______________

End-of-Year Test (continued)

Item	Lesson	TEKS*	Common Error	Intervene with RtI* Tier 1 Lessons	Soar to Success Math
34	4.1	5.3.G	May have difficulty dividing a decimal by a 2-digit number	5.27	12.49
35	2.4	5.3.C	May have difficulty dividing a 4-digit number by a 2-digit number	5.13	13.38
36	9.1	5.4.G	May have difficulty recognizing the formula for volume	5.49	47.34, 49.27
37	8.4	5.4.B	May have difficulty solving multi-step problems that include a variable	5.48	14.57, 14.58
38	1.4	5.2.B	May have difficulty ordering decimal numbers to the thousandths	5.3	8.44
39	17.3	5.10.B	May not understand the difference between net income and gross income	5.39	61.04
40	17.5	5.10.D	May have difficulty understanding how to use a financial record system	5.39	61.04
41	5.8	5.3.H	May have difficulty representing addition of fractions using properties	5.30	14.54
42	13.4	5.7.A	May have difficulty converting customary units of capacity from larger to smaller units	5.69	45.30
43	1.7	5.3.A	May have difficulty estimating to subtract	5.38	21.37, 22.37
44	16.3	5.9.A	May have difficulty representing data on a stem-and-leaf plot	5.80	2.17
45	16.4	5.9.C	May have difficulty solving problems with data	5.83	2.17
46	7.3	5.4.E	May have difficulty matching an expression with parentheses to a word problem	5.53	14.39, 14.40
47	17.4	5.10.C	May not understand advantages to different methods of payment	5.39	61.04
48	6.3	5.3.I	May have difficulty using models to multiply fractions	5.33	20.44
49	3.5	5.3.D	May not understand how to represent decimal multiplication with pictorial models	5.19	57.04
50	2.2	5.3.B	May have difficulty multiplying a 3-digit number by a 2-digit number	5.11	12.52, 12.54, 12.58

***TEKS**—Texas Essential Knowledge and Skills; **RtI**—Response to Intervention

Student's Name ____________________ Date ____________

Module 1 Test

Item	Lesson	TEKS*	Common Error	Intervene with RtI* Tier 1 Lessons	Soar to Success Math
1	1.4	5.2.B	May not understand the relationship between decimal place values	5.3	8.44
2	1.8	5.3.K	May have difficulty following the algorithm for subtraction when working with decimal numbers	5.39	61.04
3	1.5	5.2.C	May not identify place value position correctly when rounding	5.4	25.23
4	1.8	5.3.K	May have difficulty following the algorithm for subtraction when working with decimal numbers	5.39	61.04
5	1.5	5.2.C	May not recall how to round numbers	5.4	25.23
6	1.1	5.3.K	May not recognize or recall the Distributive Property	5.37	14.04, 14.19, 14.31, 14.32
7	1.4	5.2.B	May have difficulty comparing place value to order decimals	5.3	8.44
8	1.6	5.3.A	May not recall how to round numbers	5.6	21.36, 22.36
9	1.5	5.2.C	May not identify place value position correctly when rounding	5.4	25.23
10	1.7	5.3.K	May not recall how to round numbers	5.38	21.37, 22.37
11	1.2	5.2.A	May not understand the relationship between decimal place values	5.1	4.27
12	1.6	5.3.A	May not recall how to round numbers	5.6	21.36, 22.36
13	1.4	5.2.B	May have difficulty using place value to compare decimals	5.3	8.44
14	1.5	5.2.C	May not identify place value position correctly when rounding	5.4	25.23
15	1.3	5.2.A	May not understand how to represent the place value of digits in decimals	5.2	2.28, 4.28
16	1.1	5.3.K	May not recall the properties of addition	5.37	14.04, 14.19, 14.31, 14.32
17	1.3	5.2.A	May have difficulty representing decimals in expanded form	5.2	2.28, 4.28
18	1.6	5.3.A	May not recall how to round numbers	5.6	21.36, 22.36
19	1.7	5.3.K	May not recall the steps for adding decimals	5.38	21.37, 22.37
20	1.1	5.3.K	May not recognize or recall addition properties	5.37	14.04, 14.19, 14.31, 14.32

***TEKS**—Texas Essential Knowledge and Skills; **RtI**—Response to Intervention

Student's Name ______________________ Date ____________

Module 2 Test

Item	Lesson	TEKS*	Common Error	Intervene with RtI* Tier 1 Lessons	Soar to Success Math
1	2.6	5.3.C	May not recall the rules for dividing by 2-digit numbers	5.14	13.39
2	2.1	5.3.A	May not recall the steps for estimating when multiplying by a 1-digit number	5.10	12.55, 12.59
3	2.4	5.3.C	May not account for the remainder	5.13	13.38
4	2.1	5.3.B	May not understand the steps in the standard algorithm for multiplication	5.10	12.55, 12.59
5	2.3	5.3.C	May not understand how to model division of whole numbers	5.12	13.31
6	2.5	5.3.A	May not understand how to determine the more reasonable estimate	5.7	19.26
7	2.2	5.3.B	May not understand or recall rules for rounding when estimating	5.11	12.52, 12.54, 12.58
8	2.7	5.3.A	May not understand the rules for placing the first digit when estimating	5.15	13.37
9	2.6	5.3.C	May not understand rules for dividing by 2-digit divisors	5.14	13.39
10	2.2	5.3.A	May not understand how to estimate multiplication using basic fact patterns	5.11	12.52, 12.54, 12.58
11	2.1	5.3.B	May not understand the steps in the standard multiplication algorithm	5.10	12.55, 12.59
12	2.8	5.3.C	May not understand how to model division of whole numbers	5.16	57.04
13	2.4	5.3.C	May not understand how to use partial quotients to divide	5.13	13.38
14	2.6	5.3.C	May not understand how to determine how to use strategies to divide	5.14	13.39
15	2.5	5.3.A	May not understand how to determine the more reasonable estimate	5.7	19.26
16	2.2	5.3.A	May not understand the steps in the standard algorithm for multiplication	5.11	12.52, 12.54, 12.58
17	2.8	5.3.C	May not understand how to model division of whole numbers	5.16	57.04
18	2.1	5.3.A	May not understand how to estimate multiplication with basic fact patterns	5.10	12.55, 12.59
19	2.3	5.3.C	May not understand the steps in the standard algorithm for division	5.12	13.31
20	2.2	5.3.B	May not understand the steps in the standard algorithm for multiplication	5.11	12.52, 12.54, 12.58

***TEKS**—Texas Essential Knowledge and Skills; **RtI**—Response to Intervention

Student's Name ______________________ Date ______________

Module 3 Test

Item	Lesson	TEKS*	Common Error	Intervene with RtI* Tier 1 Lessons	Soar to Success Math
1	3.2	5.3.D	May have difficulty using an area model to multiply a whole number and a decimal	5.17	12.49
2	3.5	5.3.E	May not understand how to multiply a decimal by a whole number	5.19	57.04
3	3.1	5.3.E	May not understand how to use patterns when multiplying decimals	5.21	12.49
4	3.7	5.3.E	May have difficulty correctly placing the decimal point in the product	5.23	23.39
5	3.3	5.3.E	May not recall how to use the Distributive Property to find products of decimals	5.22	12.59
6	3.4	5.2.A	May have difficulty expressing decimals in expanded form	5.18	12.56
7	3.7	5.3.E	May not recall how to use place value patterns to place a decimal in the product	5.23	23.39
8	3.2	5.3.D	May have difficulty using an area model to multiply a whole number and a decimal	5.17	12.49
9	3.8	5.3.E	May have difficulty correctly placing the decimal point in the product	5.24	23.39
10	3.6	5.3.D	May have difficulty using an area model to multiply decimals	5.20	12.53
11	3.4	5.3.D	May not understand place value representation of decimals or whole numbers	5.18	12.56
12	3.3	5.3.A	May not understand how to round a decimal to a whole number to estimate	5.22	12.59
13	3.1	5.3.E	May not recall how to use place value patterns to multiply decimals	5.21	12.49
14	3.7	5.3.E	May not recall the steps in multiplying decimals	5.23	23.39
15	3.5	5.3.D	May not understand how to represent decimal multiplication with pictorial models	5.19	57.04
16	3.7	5.3.A	May not understand how to round decimals to whole numbers to estimate	5.23	23.39
17	3.8	5.3.E	May not multiply as with whole numbers and place the decimal point	5.24	23.39
18	3.1	5.3.E	May not recall how to use patterns to multiply decimals	5.21	12.49
19	3.3	5.3.E	May have difficulty finding the product of a whole number and a decimal	5.22	12.59
20	3.2	5.3.D	May not understand how to represent multiplication on a decimal model	5.17	12.49

***TEKS**—Texas Essential Knowledge and Skills; **RtI**—Response to Intervention

Student's Name ______________________ Date ____________

Module 4 Test

Item	Lesson	TEKS*	Common Error	Intervene with RtI* Tier 1 Lessons	Soar to Success Math
1	4.3	5.3.A	May not understand how to use a basic fact to estimate decimal quotients	5.8	19.25, 19.26
2	4.5	5.3.G	May have difficulty following the algorithm for division of decimals	5.26	24.39
3	4.4	5.3.G	May have difficulty following the algorithm for division of decimals	5.26	24.32
4	4.1	5.3.G	May have difficulty recognizing and using patterns to divide decimals	5.27	12.49
5	4.2	5.3.F	May have difficulty using area models to represent division of decimals	5.25	24.32
6	4.2	5.3.F	May have difficulty using objects to represent division of decimals	5.25	24.32
7	4.5	5.3.G	May have difficulty following the algorithm for division of decimals	5.26	24.39
8	4.3	5.3.A	May have difficulty estimating quotients	5.8	19.25, 19.26
9	4.1	5.3.G	May have difficulty recognizing and using patterns to divide decimals	5.27	12.49
10	4.4	5.3.F	May have difficulty representing division of decimals with pictorial models	5.26	24.32
11	4.4	5.3.G	May have difficulty following the algorithm for division of decimals	5.26	24.32
12	4.1	5.3.G	May have difficulty recognizing and using patterns to divide decimals	5.27	12.49
13	4.5	5.3.G	May have difficulty following the algorithm for division of decimals	5.26	24.39
14	4.2	5.3.F	May have difficulty using area models to represent division of decimals	5.25	24.32
15	4.3	5.3.A	May forget to rename the dividend as tenths when estimating	5.8	19.25, 19.26
16	4.5	5.3.G	May have difficulty following the algorithm for division of decimals	5.26	24.39
17	4.3	5.3.A	May have difficulty estimating quotients	5.8	19.25, 19.26
18	4.2	5.3.F	May have difficulty using objects to represent division of decimals	5.25	24.32
19	4.3	5.3.A	May have difficulty following the algorithm for division of decimals	5.8	19.25, 19.26
20	4.1	5.3.G	May have difficulty recognizing and using patterns to divide decimals	5.27	12.49

***TEKS**—Texas Essential Knowledge and Skills; **RtI**—Response to Intervention

Student's Name ______________________ Date ______________

Unit 1 Test

Item	Lesson	TEKS*	Common Error	Intervene with RtI* Tier 1 Lessons	Soar to Success Math
1	1.2	5.2.A	May not understand the relationship between decimal place values	5.1	4.27
2	4.3	5.3.A	May not understand how to estimate decimal quotients	5.8	19.25, 19.26
3	1.5	5.2.C	May not identify place value position correctly when rounding	5.4	25.23
4	3.7	5.3.E	May not recall how to use place value patterns to place a decimal in the product	5.23	23.39
5	2.3	5.3.C	May not understand how to model division of whole numbers	5.12	13.31
6	1.6	5.3.A	May not understand how to estimate decimal sums and differences	5.6	21.36, 22.36
7	4.2	5.3.F	May have difficulty using objects to represent division of decimals	5.25	24.32
8	3.3	5.3.E	May have difficulty finding the product of a whole number and a decimal	5.22	12.59
9	3.2	5.3.D	May not understand how to represent multiplication on a decimal model	5.17	12.49
10	2.5	5.3.A	May not understand how to determine the more reasonable estimate	5.7	19.26
11	1.4	5.2.B	May have difficulty using place value to compare decimals	5.3	8.44
12	2.2	5.3.B	May not understand the steps in the standard algorithm for multiplication	5.11	12.52, 12.54, 12.58
13	2.1	5.3.A	May not understand how to estimate multiplication with basic fact patterns	5.10	12.55, 12.59
14	3.2	5.3.D	May have difficulty using an area model to multiply a whole number and a decimal	5.17	12.49
15	1.5	5.2.C	May not recall rules for rounding	5.4	25.23
16	2.4	5.3.C	May not account for the remainder	5.13	13.38
17	4.1	5.3.G	May have difficulty recognizing and using patterns to divide decimals	5.27	12.49
18	1.4	5.2.B	May have difficulty comparing place value when ordering decimals	5.3	8.44
19	3.4	5.2.A	May have difficulty expressing decimals in expanded form	5.18	12.56
20	1.1	5.3.K	May not recognize or recall addition properties	5.37	14.04, 14.19, 14.31, 14.32

***TEKS**—Texas Essential Knowledge and Skills; **RtI**—Response to Intervention

Student's Name ______________________ Date __________

Unit 1 Test (continued)

Item	Lesson	TEKS*	Common Error	Intervene with RtI* Tier 1 Lessons	Soar to Success Math
21	3.5	5.3.E	May not understand how to multiply a decimal by a whole number	5.19	57.04
22	4.5	5.3.G	May have difficulty following the algorithm for division of decimals	5.26	24.39
23	1.8	5.3.K	May have difficulty following the algorithm for subtraction when working with decimal numbers	5.39	61.04
24	1.6	5.3.A	May not recall how to round decimals	5.6	21.36, 22.36
25	4.4	5.3.F	May have difficulty representing division of decimals with pictorial models	5.26	24.32
26	2.2	5.3.A	May not understand the steps in the standard algorithm for multiplication	5.11	12.52, 12.54, 12.58
27	1.6	5.3.A	May not recall how to round decimals	5.6	21.36, 22.36
28	1.4	5.2.B	May not understand the relationship between decimal place values	5.3	8.44
29	3.8	5.3.E	May have difficulty correctly placing the decimal point in the product	5.24	23.39
30	4.2	5.3.F	May have difficulty using area model to represent division of decimals	5.25	24.32

***TEKS**—Texas Essential Knowledge and Skills; **RtI**—Response to Intervention

Student's Name ______________________ Date ______________

Module 5 Test

Item	Lesson	TEKS*	Common Error	Intervene with RtI* Tier 1 Lessons	Soar to Success Math
1	5.2	5.3.H	May have difficulty subtracting fractions with unequal denominators	5.29	20.31
2	5.4	5.3	May have difficulty finding the least common denominator	5.5	20.37
3	5.1	5.3.H	May have difficulty adding fractions with unequal denominators	5.28	20.30
4	5.5	5.3.K	May have difficulty adding fractions with unequal denominators	5.40	20.39
5	5.2	5.3.H	May have difficulty subtracting fractions with unequal denominators	5.29	20.31
6	5.2	5.3.H	May have difficulty recognizing representations of subtraction of fractions	5.29	20.31
7	5.8	5.3.H	May have difficulty recognizing properties of addition	5.30	14.54
8	5.4	5.3	May have difficulty recognizing equivalent fractions	5.5	20.37
9	5.3	5.3.A	May have difficulty using benchmarks to estimate sums with fractions	5.9	20.34
10	5.1	5.3.H	May have difficulty recognizing representations of addition of fractions	5.28	20.30
11	5.5	5.3.K	May have difficulty subtracting fractions with unequal denominators	5.40	20.39
12	5.1	5.3.H	May have difficulty solving addition of fractions with pictorial models	5.28	20.30
13	5.6	5.3.K	May have difficulty subtracting mixed numbers	5.41	20.40
14	5.1	5.3.H	May have difficulty recognizing representations of addition of fractions	5.28	20.30
15	5.2	5.3.K	May have difficulty renaming fractions to subtract	5.29	20.31
16	5.8	5.3.H	May have difficulty recognizing properties of addition	5.30	14.54
17	5.7	5.3.K	May have difficulty renaming mixed numbers as fractions greater than 1	5.42	20.41
18	5.6	5.3.K	May have difficulty adding mixed numbers	5.41	20.40
19	5.1	5.3.K	May have difficulty renaming fractions to add	5.28	20.30
20	5.2	5.3.H	May have difficulty recognizing representations of subtraction of fractions	5.29	20.31

***TEKS**—Texas Essential Knowledge and Skills; **RtI**—Response to Intervention

Student's Name ______________________ Date ______________

Module 6 Test

Item	Lesson	TEKS*	Common Error	Intervene with RtI* Tier 1 Lessons	Soar to Success Math
1	6.1	5.3.I	May have difficulty representing the multiplication of fractions with objects	5.31	13.09
2	6.4	5.3.L	May have difficulty dividing whole numbers by unit fractions	5.34	20.44
3	6.6	5.3.J	May have difficulty interpreting pictures representing the division of fractions	5.36	20.44
4	6.1	5.3.I	May have difficulty finding the fractional part of a group	5.31	13.09
5	6.3	5.3.I	May have difficulty interpreting pictures representing the multiplication of fractions	5.33	20.44
6	6.2	5.3.I	May have difficulty multiplying a fraction by a whole number	5.32	20.44
7	6.6	5.3.J	May have difficulty dividing a unit fraction by a whole number	5.36	20.44
8	6.1	5.3.I	May have difficulty multiplying a whole number and a fraction	5.31	13.09
9	6.5	5.3.L	May have difficulty dividing whole numbers by unit fractions	5.35	20.44
10	6.1	5.3.I	May have difficulty identifying multiplication of fractions illustrated with pictures	5.31	13.09
11	6.4	5.3.L	May have difficulty dividing unit fractions by whole numbers	5.34	20.44
12	6.2	5.3.I	May have difficulty representing multiplication of fractions with objects	5.32	20.44
13	6.6	5.3.L	May have difficulty dividing whole numbers by unit fractions	5.36	20.44
14	6.4	5.3.J	May have difficulty representing division of fractions with objects	5.34	20.44
15	6.4	5.3.J	May have difficulty identifying division of fractions represented by objects	5.34	20.44
16	6.6	5.3.J	May have difficulty representing division of fractions using area models	5.36	20.44
17	6.3	5.3.I	May have difficulty solving multiplication of fractions using area models	5.33	20.44
18	6.2	5.3.I	May have difficulty multiplying a fraction by a whole number	5.32	20.44
19	6.2	5.3.I	May have difficulty interpreting pictures representing the multiplication of fractions	5.32	20.44
20	6.5	5.3.J	May have difficulty representing multiplication of fractions with diagrams	5.35	20.44

***TEKS**—Texas Essential Knowledge and Skills; **RtI**—Response to Intervention

Student's Name ______________________ Date ______________

Unit 2 Test

Item	Lesson	TEKS*	Common Error	Intervene with RtI* Tier 1 Lessons	Soar to Success Math
1	5.3	5.3.A	May have difficulty using benchmarks to estimate sums with fractions	5.9	20.34
2	6.1	5.3.I	May have difficulty multiplying a whole number and a fraction	5.31	13.09
3	5.8	5.3.H	May have difficulty recognizing properties of addition	5.30	14.54
4	5.2	5.3.H	May have difficulty subtracting fractions with unequal denominators	5.29	20.31
5	6.3	5.3.I	May have difficulty representing the multiplication of fractions with area models	5.33	20.44
6	5.1	5.3.H	May have difficulty adding fractions with unequal denominators	5.28	20.30
7	6.4	5.3.J	May have difficulty representing the division of fractions with objects	5.34	20.44
8	6.6	5.3.J	May have difficulty interpreting pictures representing the division of fractions	5.36	20.44
9	5.1	5.3.H	May have difficulty solving addition of fractions with pictorial models	5.28	20.30
10	5.8	5.3.H	May have difficulty recognizing properties of addition	5.30	14.54
11	5.5	5.3.K	May have difficulty subtracting fractions with unequal denominators	5.40	20.39
12	6.5	5.3.L	May have difficulty dividing whole numbers by unit fractions	5.35	20.44
13	6.6	5.3.J	May have difficulty representing the division of fractions with area models	5.36	20.44
14	5.1	5.3.H	May have difficulty recognizing representations of subtraction of fractions	5.28	20.30
15	5.7	5.3.K	May have difficulty renaming mixed numbers as fractions greater than 1	5.42	20.41
16	5.2	5.3.H	May have difficulty recognizing representations of subtraction of fractions	5.29	20.31
17	6.4	5.3.L	May have difficulty dividing unit fractions by whole numbers	5.34	20.44
18	5.4	5.3	May have difficulty finding the least common denominator	5.5	20.37
19	6.1	5.3.I	May have difficulty representing the multiplication of fractions with objects	5.31	13.09
20	6.2	5.3.I	May have difficulty representing the multiplication of fractions with pictures	5.32	20.44

***TEKS**—Texas Essential Knowledge and Skills; **RtI**—Response to Intervention

Student's Name ______________________ Date ____________

Unit 2 Test (continued)

Item	Lesson	TEKS*	Common Error	Intervene with RtI* Tier 1 Lessons	Soar to Success Math
21	6.2	5.3.I	May have difficulty multiplying a fraction by a whole number	5.32	20.44
22	5.2	5.3.H	May have difficulty subtracting fractions with unequal denominators	5.29	20.31
23	5.5	5.3.K	May have difficulty adding fractions with unequal denominators	5.40	20.39
24	6.4	5.3.J	May have difficulty representing the division of fractions with objects	5.34	20.44
25	5.1	5.3.H	May have difficulty recognizing representations of addition of fractions	5.28	20.30
26	6.5	5.3.J	May have difficulty representing the multiplication of fractions with diagrams	5.35	20.44
27	5.2	5.3.H	May have difficulty recognizing the representations of addition of fractions	5.29	20.31
28	6.6	5.3.J	May have difficulty dividing fractions with area models	5.36	20.44
29	5.6	5.3.K	May have difficulty adding mixed numbers	5.41	20.40
30	5.5	5.3.K	May have difficulty adding fractions with unequal denominators	5.40	20.39

***TEKS**—Texas Essential Knowledge and Skills; **RtI**—Response to Intervention

Student's Name ______________________ Date ______________

Module 7 Test

Item	Lesson	TEKS*	Common Error	Intervene with RtI* Tier 1 Lessons	Soar to Success Math
1	7.2	5.4.A	May have difficulty identifying a composite number	5.46	31.29
2	7.3	5.4.E	May have difficulty matching an expression with parentheses to a word problem	5.53	14.39, 14.40
3	7.4	5.4.F	May have difficulty simplifying expressions	5.55	14.4
4	7.4	5.4.F	May have difficulty simplifying expressions	5.55	14.4
5	7.5	5.4.E	May have difficulty matching an expression with parentheses to a word problem	5.54	14.39, 14.41
6	7.3	5.4.E	May have difficulty matching an expression with parentheses to a word problem	5.53	14.39, 14.40
7	7.2	5.4.A	May have difficulty identifying a prime number	5.46	31.29
8	7.5	5.4.E	May have difficulty simplifying a numerical expression that contains brackets	5.54	14.39, 14.41
9	7.5	5.4.F	May have difficulty simplifying expressions with two levels of grouping symbols	5.54	14.39, 14.41
10	7.1	5.4.A	May have difficulty identifying factors of a number	5.45	31.3
11	7.3	5.4.E	May have difficulty matching an expression with parentheses to a word problem	5.53	14.39, 14.40
12	7.2	5.4.A	May have difficulty identifying a prime number	5.46	31.29
13	7.4	5.4.F	May have difficulty simplifying expressions	5.55	14.4
14	7.1	5.4.A	May have difficulty identifying factors of a number	5.45	31.3
15	7.5	5.4.F	May have difficulty simplifying expressions with two levels of grouping symbols	5.54	14.39, 14.41
16	7.3	5.4.E	May have difficulty matching an expression with parentheses to a word problem	5.53	14.39, 14.40
17	7.5	5.4.E	May have difficulty simplifying a numerical expression that contains brackets	5.54	14.39, 14.41
18	7.5	5.4.F	May have difficulty simplifying expressions with two levels of grouping symbols	5.54	14.39, 14.41
19	7.2	5.4.A	May have difficulty identifying a composite number	5.46	31.29
20	7.5	5.4.E	May have difficulty matching an expression with parentheses to a word problem	5.54	14.39, 14.41

***TEKS**—Texas Essential Knowledge and Skills; **RtI**—Response to Intervention

Student's Name ____________________ Date ____________

Module 8 Test

Item	Lesson	TEKS*	Common Error	Intervene with RtI* Tier 1 Lessons	Soar to Success Math
1, 20	8.3	5.4.B	May have difficulty solving multi-step problems involving multiplication	5.47	14.51, 14.52
2, 15	8.2	5.4	May not understand the concepts of equations and expressions	5.44	14.48, 14.49
3	8.4	5.4.B	May have difficulty representing multi-step problems involving multiplication	5.48	14.57, 14.58
4, 10	8.4	5.4.B	May have difficulty solving multi-step problems involving division	5.48	14.57, 14.58
5	8.1	5.4.B	May have difficulty solving multi-step problems involving addition	5.43	14.56
6	8.3	5.4.B	May have difficulty representing multi-step problems involving division	5.47	14.51, 14.52
7	8.4	5.4.B	May have difficulty solving multi-step problems involving subtraction	5.48	14.57, 14.58
8	8.1	5.4.B	May have difficulty solving multi-step problems involving multiplication	5.43	14.56
9	8.3	5.4.B	May have difficulty solving multi-step problems involving division	5.47	14.51, 14.52
11	8.1	5.4.B	May have difficulty solving multi-step problems involving addition	5.43	14.56
12	8.3	5.4.B	May have difficulty identifying operations to solve for an unknown	5.47	14.51, 14.52
13	8.4	5.4.B	May have difficulty representing multi-step problems involving addition	5.48	14.57, 14.58
14	8.4	5.4.B	May have difficulty solving multi-step problems involving multiplication	5.48	14.57, 14.58
16, 17	8.4	5.4.B	May have difficulty representing multi-step problems involving subtraction	5.48	14.57, 14.58
18	8.3	5.4.B	May have difficulty identifying operations to solve for an unknown	5.47	14.51, 14.52
19	8.4	5.4.B	May have difficulty solving multi-step problems involving addition	5.48	14.57, 14.58

***TEKS**—Texas Essential Knowledge and Skills; **RtI**—Response to Intervention

Student's Name ______________________ Date ______________

Module 9 Test

Item	Lesson	TEKS*	Common Error	Intervene with RtI* Tier 1 Lessons	Soar to Success Math
1	9.3	5.4.G	May have difficulty recognizing the formula for the volume of a cube	5.57	49.29
2	9.1	5.4.B	May have difficulty recognizing the formula for perimeter	4.49	47.34, 49.27
3	9.4	5.4.H	May have difficulty representing problems related to area and perimeter	5.58	47.34, 49.27, 49.30
4	9.2	5.4.G	May have difficulty using pictorial models to develop the formula for the volume of a rectangular prism	5.56	49.28, 49.30
5, 14	9.1	5.4.B	May have difficulty solving problems involving addition	4.49	47.34, 49.27
6	9.4	5.4.H	May have difficulty solving for the volume of a rectangular prism	5.58	47.34, 49.27, 49.30
7	9.3	5.4.G	May have difficulty using pictorial models to develop the formula for the volume of a cube	5.57	49.29
8	9.1	5.4.H	May have difficulty solving problems related to area	4.49	47.34, 49.27
9	9.2	5.4.G	May have difficulty using concrete objects to develop the formula for the volume of a rectangular prism	5.56	49.28, 49.30
10, 11	9.1	5.4.H	May confuse formulas for area and perimeter	4.49	47.34, 49.27
12	9.2	5.4.G	May have difficulty recognizing the formula for volume	5.56	49.28, 49.30
13	9.1	5.4.H	May have difficulty representing and solving problems related to area	4.49	47.34, 49.27
15	9.4	5.4.H	May have difficulty representing and solving problems related to area	5.58	47.34, 49.27, 49.30
16	9.3	5.4.G	May have difficulty using pictorial models to develop the formula for the volume of a cube	5.57	49.29
17	9.3	5.4.G	May have difficulty recognizing the formula for the volume of a cube	5.57	49.29
18	9.1	5.4.H	May not recall the formula for perimeter	4.49	47.34, 49.27
19	9.1	5.4.B	May have difficulty solving problems involving multiplication	5.56	49.28, 49.30
20	9.2	5.4.G	May have difficulty recognizing the formula for volume	5.56	49.28, 49.30

***TEKS**—Texas Essential Knowledge and Skills; **RtI**—Response to Intervention

Student's Name ______________________ Date ____________

Module 10 Test

Item	Lesson	TEKS*	Common Error	Intervene with RtI* Tier 1 Lessons	Soar to Success Math
1	10.4	5.4.C	May have difficulty generating a numerical pattern when given a rule	5.51	37.33
2	10.3	5.4.D	May have difficulty recognizing an additive pattern	5.52	33.19
3	10.4	5.4.C	May have difficulty graphing a numerical pattern when given a rule	5.51	37.33
4	10.3	5.8.B	May have difficulty graphing ordered pairs of numbers in a coordinate plane	5.52	33.19
5	10.1	5.4.C	May have difficulty generating a number pattern	5.50	32.07
6	10.2	5.4.D	May have difficulty recognizing an multiplicative pattern	5.50	33.2
7, 8	10.4	5.4.C	May have difficulty generating a numerical pattern when given a rule	5.51	37.33
9	10.4	5.8.C	May have difficulty graphing ordered pairs of numbers in a coordinate plane	5.51	37.33
10	10.1	5.4.C	May have difficulty generating a numerical pattern when given a rule	5.50	32.07
11	10.2	5.4.D	May have difficulty recognizing an additive pattern	5.50	33.2
12	10.1	5.4.C	May have difficulty generating a numerical pattern when given a rule	5.50	32.07
13	10.1	5.4.C	May have difficulty generating a numerical pattern when given a rule	5.50	32.07
14	10.4	5.4.C	May have difficulty graphing a numerical pattern	5.51	37.33
15	10.4	5.4.C	May have difficulty generating a numerical pattern when given a rule	5.51	37.33
16	10.3	5.4.D	May have difficulty recognizing the difference between an additive and a multiplicative pattern	5.52	33.19
17	10.4	5.4.C	May have difficulty graphing a numerical pattern when given a rule	5.51	37.33
18	10.4	5.4.C	May have difficulty generating a numerical pattern when given a rule	5.51	37.33
19	10.1	5.4.C	May have difficulty generating a numerical pattern when given a rule	5.50	32.07
20	10.4	5.4.C	May have difficulty graphing a numerical pattern when given a rule	5.51	37.33

***TEKS**—Texas Essential Knowledge and Skills; **RtI**—Response to Intervention

Student's Name ______________________ Date ______________

Unit 3 Test

Item	Lesson	TEKS*	Common Error	Intervene with RtI* Tier 1 Lessons	Soar to Success Math
1	7.4	5.4.F	May have difficulty simplifying expressions	5.55	14.4
2	9.3	5.4.G.	May have difficulty recognizing the formula for the volume of a cube	5.57	49.29
3	8.4	5.4.B	May have difficulty solving multi-step problems with variables	5.48	14.57, 14.58
4	9.3	5.4.G	May not recall the formula for the volume of a cube	5.57	49.29
5	8.3	5.4.B	May have difficulty representing multi-step problems	5.47	14.51, 14.52
6	10.3	5.4.D	May have difficulty recognizing an additive pattern	5.52	33.19
7	10.4	5.4.C	May have difficulty graphing a number pattern	5.51	37.33
8	7.2	5.4.A	May have difficulty identifying a prime number	5.46	31.29
9	9.1	5.4.B	May not recall the formula for perimeter	4.49	47.34, 49.27
10	8.3	5.4.B	May have difficulty solving multi-step problems with variables	5.47	14.51, 14.52
11	8.4	5.4.B	May have difficulty representing multi-step problems	5.48	14.57, 14.58
12	7.5	5.4.F	May have difficulty simplifying expressions	5.54	14.39, 14.41
13	9.2	5.4.G	May have difficulty recognizing the formula for the volume of a rectangular prism	5.56	49.28, 49.30
14	10.2	5.4.D	May have difficulty recognizing an additive pattern	5.50	33.2
15	9.1	5.4.B	May have difficulty recognizing the formula for perimeter	4.49	47.34, 49.27

***TEKS**—Texas Essential Knowledge and Skills; **RtI**—Response to Intervention

Student's Name ______________________ Date __________

Unit 3 Test (continued)

Item	Lesson	TEKS*	Common Error	Intervene with RtI* Tier 1 Lessons	Soar to Success Math
16	8.1	5.4.B	May have difficulty solving multi-step problems involving addition	5.43	14.56
17	10.1	5.4.C	May have difficulty generating a numerical pattern when given a rule	5.50	32.07
18	10.4	5.4.C	May have difficulty using a rule to generate a number pair	5.51	37.33
19	7.5	5.4.E	May have difficulty simplifying a numerical expression that contain brackets	5.54	14.39, 14.41
20	7.1	5.4.A	May have difficulty identifying factors of a number	5.45	31.3
21	8.1	5.4.B	May have difficulty solving multi-step problems involving multiplication	5.43	14.56
22	8.4	5.4.B	May have difficulty representing multi-step problems involving addition	5.48	14.57, 14.58
23	9.2	5.4.B	May have difficulty recognizing the formula for volume	5.56	49.28, 49.30
24	9.2	5.4.G	May have difficulty using concrete objects to develop the formula for the volume of a rectangular prism	5.56	49.28, 49.30
25	9.4	5.4.H	May have difficulty solving for the volume of a rectangular prism	5.58	47.34, 49.27, 49.30
26	7.3	5.4.E	May have difficulty matching an expression with parentheses to a word problem	5.53	14.39, 14.40
27	9.1	5.4.H	May not recall the formula for perimeter	4.49	47.34, 49.27
28	8.1	5.4.B	May have difficulty solving multi-step problems involving addition	5.43	14.56
29	10.4	5.4.C	May have difficulty generating a numerical pattern when given a rule	5.51	37.33
30	9.4	5.4.H	May not recall the formula for area	5.58	47.34, 49.27, 49.30

***TEKS**—Texas Essential Knowledge and Skills; **RtI**—Response to Intervention

Student's Name ______________________ Date ____________

Module 11 Test

Item	Lesson	TEKS*	Common Error	Intervene with RtI* Tier 1 Lessons	Soar to Success Math
1	11.3	5.5	May not recall the attributes of different types of quadrilaterals	5.61	38.31, 38.34
2	11.2	5.5	May not recall how to classify triangles	5.60	38.35
3	11.3	5.5	May not understand how to sort quadrilaterals by attributes	5.61	38.31, 38.34
4	11.3	5.5	May not recall the attributes of different types of quadrilaterals	5.61	38.31, 38.34
5	11.1	5.5	May not recall polygons by name	5.59	38.33
6	11.3	5.5	May not recall the attributes of different types of quadrilaterals	5.61	38.31, 38.34
7	11.1	5.5	May not recognize the description of a polygon	5.59	38.33
8	11.1	5.5	May not recall polygons by name	5.59	38.33
9	11.1	5.5	May not recall the attributes of polygons	5.59	38.33
10	11.3	5.5	May not recognzie attributes of polygons	5.61	38.31, 38.34
11	11.2	5.5	May not recall how to classify triangles	5.60	38.35
12	11.1	5.5	May not recognize the description of a polygon	5.59	38.33
13	11.2	5.5	May not recall the attributes of triangles	5.60	38.35
14	11.4	5.5	May not recall how to classify triangles based on properties	5.62	38.12, 38.13
15	11.2	5.5	May not recall how to classify triangles	5.60	38.35
16	11.2	5.5	May not know the attributes of right triangles	5.60	38.35
17	11.2	5.5	May not know the attributes of triangles	5.60	38.35
18	11.3	5.5	May not recall the attributes of different types of quadrilaterals	5.61	38.31, 38.34
19	11.1	5.5	May not recall the differences between regular and irregular polygons	5.59	38.33
20	11.4	5.5	May not recall the attributes of a triangle	5.62	38.12, 38.13

*TEKS—Texas Essential Knowledge and Skills; **RtI**—Response to Intervention

Student's Name ______________________ Date ____________

Module 12 Test

Item	Lesson	TEKS*	Common Error	Intervene with RtI* Tier 1 Lessons	Soar to Success Math
1	12.2	5.6.B	May not understand how to determine the number of unit cubes in one layer of a prism	5.64	49.25, 49.28
2, 3	12.3	5.6.B	May not understand the relationship between the base, the number of layers, and the volume of a prism	5.56	49.25, 49.28
4	12.4	5.6.B	May not recall the formula $V = l \times w \times h$	5.57	49.30
5, 10	12.1	5.6.A	May not recall how to count unit cubes making up a solid figure	5.63	49.24
6	12.2	5.6.A	May not recall the formula $V = l \times w \times h$	5.64	49.25, 49.28
7	12.4	5.6.B	May not understand the relationship between the base, the number of layers, and the volume of a prism	5.57	49.30
8	12.5	5.6.B	May not understand the relationship between the base, the number of layers, and the volume of a prism	5.65	49.29
9	12.3	5.4.G	May not recall the formula $V = l \times w \times h$	5.56	49.25, 49.28
11	12.4	5.4.H	May not recall how to determine volume	5.57	49.30
12	12.1	5.6.A	May not understand how to count unit cubes making up a solid figure	5.63	49.24
13	12.2	5.6.A	May not recall how to determine volume	5.64	49.25, 49.28
14	12.5	5.6.B	May not understand the relationship between the base, the number of layers, and the volume of a prism	5.65	49.29
15	12.4	5.4.H	May not recall the formula $V = l \times w \times h$	5.57	49.30
16	12.5	5.6.B	May not understand how to compare different prisms with the same volume	5.65	49.29
17	12.4	5.6.B	May not recall the formula $V = B \times h$	5.57	49.30
18	12.2	5.6.A	May not understand how the area of the base relates to volume	5.64	49.25, 49.28
19	12.2	5.6.B	May not understand how the area of the base relates to volume	5.64	49.25, 49.28
20	12.3	5.4.G	May not recall the formula $V = B \times h$	5.56	49.25, 49.28

***TEKS**—Texas Essential Knowledge and Skills; **RtI**—Response to Intervention

Student's Name ________________________ Date ____________

Module 13 Test

Item	Lesson	TEKS*	Common Error	Intervene with RtI* Tier 1 Lessons	Soar to Success Math
1	13.4	5.7	May have difficulty converting customary units of weight from larger to smaller units	5.69	45.30
2	13.6	5.7	May have difficulty converting metric units of length from larger to smaller units	5.71	44.32, 45.26, 46.32
3, 12	13.1	5.7	May have difficulty choosing appropriate units of measure	5.66	41.16, 41.17, 42.09, 42.10, 43.11, 43.12
4	13.3	5.7	May have difficulty comparing customary units of capacity	5.68	46.37
5	13.5	5.7	May have difficulty converting customary units of length to smaller units	5.70	44.36, 46.37, 45.30
6	13.6	5.7	May have difficulty solving problems involving units of metric measurement	5.71	44.32, 45.26, 46.32
7	13.2	5.7	May have difficulty converting customary units of length from larger to smaller units	5.67	44.36
8	13.4	5.7	May have difficulty solving problems involving customary units of weight	5.69	45.30
9, 18	13.1	5.7	May have difficulty choosing appropriate measuring tools	5.66	41.16, 41.17, 42.09, 42.10, 43.11, 43.12
10	13.7	5.7	May have difficulty solving problems involving units of metric measurement	5.72	46.37, 45.26, 44.36, 44.32
11	13.5	5.7	May have difficulty solving problems involving customary units of weight	5.70	44.36, 46.37, 45.30
13	13.5	5.7	May have difficulty solving problems involving customary units of length	5.70	44.36, 46.37, 45.30
14	13.3	5.7	May have difficulty converting customary units of capacity from larger to smaller units	5.68	46.37
15	13.4	5.7	May have difficulty converting customary units of weight from smaller to larger units	5.69	45.30
16	13.7	5.7	May have difficulty converting metric units of capacity from smaller to larger units	5.72	46.37, 45.26, 44.36, 44.32
17	13.2	5.7	May have difficulty comparing customary units of length	5.67	44.36
19	13.6	5.7	May have difficulty solving problems involving metric units of capacity	5.71	44.32, 45.26, 46.32
20	13.7	5.7	May have difficulty solving problems involving metric units of weight	5.72	46.37, 45.26, 44.36, 44.32

***TEKS**—Texas Essential Knowledge and Skills; **RtI**—Response to Intervention

Student's Name ______________________ Date ____________

Module 14 Test

Item	Lesson	TEKS*	Common Error	Intervene with RtI* Tier 1 Lessons	Soar to Success Math
1, 12	14.2	5.8.C	May not be able to determine ordered pairs on a coordinate plane from numbers found in an input/output table	5.74	37.16, 37.17
2, 17	14.3	5.4.C	May not understand how to graph a numerical pattern	5.75	33.17, 37.17
3	14.1	5.8.A	May not understand how ordered pairs indicate location on a coordinate plane	5.73	37.16, 37.17
4	14.4	5.8.C	May not be able to determine ordered pairs on a coordinate plane from numbers found in an input/output table	5.76	33.19, 37.17
5	14.4	5.8.C	May not be able to determine ordered pairs on a coordinate plane from numbers found in real-world problems	5.76	33.19, 37.17
6	14.3	5.4.C	May not be able to graph on a coordinate plane ordered pairs of numbers	5.75	33.17, 37.17
7	14.3	5.8.C	May not understand how to generate a number pattern when given a rule in the form $y = x + a$	5.75	33.17, 37.17
8, 10	14.1	5.8.A	May not understand how ordered pairs indicate location on a coordinate plane	5.73	37.16, 37.17
9	14.1	5.8.B	May not understand the process for graphing ordered pairs of numbers	5.73	37.16, 37.17
11, 15	14.3	5.8.C	May not be able to determine ordered pairs on a coordinate plane from numbers generated by number patterns	5.75	33.17, 37.17
13	14.3	5.8.C	May not be able to determine ordered pairs on a coordinate plane from numbers found in real-world problems	5.75	33.17, 37.17
14	14.3	5.4.C	May not understand how to generate a numerical pattern when given a rule in the form $y = ax$	5.75	33.17, 37.17
16	14.1	5.8.B	May not understand the process for graphing ordered pairs of numbers	5.73	37.16, 37.17
18	14.4	5.8.C	May not be able to determine ordered pairs on a coordinate plane from numbers found in an input/output table	5.76	33.19, 37.17
19	14.4	5.8.C	May not be able to determine ordered pairs on a coordinate plane from numbers generated by number patterns	5.76	33.19, 37.17

***TEKS**—Texas Essential Knowledge and Skills; **RtI**—Response to Intervention

Student's Name ______________________ Date ____________

Unit 4 Test

Item	Lesson	TEKS*	Common Error	Intervene with RtI* Tier 1 Lessons	Soar to Success Math
1	11.3	5.5	May not recall the attributes of quadrilaterals	5.61	38.31, 38.34
2	12.3	5.4.G	May not recall the formula $V = l \times w \times h$	5.56	49.25, 49.28
3	13.1	5.7	May have difficulty choosing appropriate measuring tools	5.66	41.16, 41.17, 42.09, 42.10, 43.11, 43.12
4	14.1	5.8.B	May not understand how to name the location of a named point on a coordinate grid as an ordered pair	5.73	37.16, 37.17
5	14.1	5.8.A	May not understand how ordered pairs indicate movement on a coordinate grid	5.73	37.16, 37.17
6	12.4	5.4.H	May not be able to solve problems related to volume	5.57	49.30
7	14.3	5.4.C	May have difficulty using a rule to generate a pattern	5.75	33.17, 37.17
8	14.3	5.8.C	May not be able to determine ordered pairs on a coordinate plane from numbers generated by number patterns	5.75	33.17, 37.17
9	13.4	5.7	May have difficulty solving problems involving customary units of measurement	5.69	45.30
10	11.2	5.5	May have difficulty sorting triangles by attributes	5.60	38.35
11	13.6	5.7	May have difficulty solving problems involving metric units of measurement	5.71	44.32, 45.26, 46.32
12	12.5	5.6.B	May not understand how to compare different prisms with the same volume	5.65	49.29
13	11.1	5.5	May have difficulty classifying polygons by attributes and properties	5.59	38.33
14	13.1	5.7	May have difficulty choosing appropriate units to solve problems involving measurement	5.66	41.16, 41.17, 42.09, 42.10, 43.11, 43.12
15	14.3	5.8.C	May not be able to determine ordered pairs on a coordinate plane from numbers found in real-world problems	5.75	33.17, 37.17
16	14.3	5.4.C	May have difficulty using a rule to generate a pattern	5.75	33.17, 37.17

***TEKS**—Texas Essential Knowledge and Skills; **RtI**—Response to Intervention

Student's Name ______________________ Date ____________

Unit 4 Test (continued)

Item	Lesson	TEKS*	Common Error	Intervene with RtI* Tier 1 Lessons	Soar to Success Math
17	13.3	5.7	May have difficulty converting customary units of capacity from a smaller to larger unit	5.68	46.37
18	12.3	5.4.G	May not recall the formula $V = Bh$	5.56	49.25, 49.28
19	11.2	5.5.1	May not be able to classify triangles based on their attributes	5.60	38.35
20	14.2	5.8.C	May not be able to determine ordered pairs on a coordinate plane from numbers found in an input/output table	5.74	37.16, 37.17
21	13.2	5.7	May have difficulty solving problems involving customary units of measurement	5.67	44.36
22	13.7	5.7	May have difficulty converting metric units of capacity from larger to smaller units	5.72	46.37, 45.26, 44.36, 44.32
23	11.4	5.5	May not recall how to classify triangles	5.62	38.12, 38.13
24	12.1	5.6.A	May not understand how to count unit cubes making up a solid figure	5.63	49.24
25	14.4	5.8.C	May not be able to graph on a coordinate plane ordered pairs of numbers arising from real-world problems	5.76	33.19, 37.17
26	14.4	5.8.C	May not be able to graph on a coordinate plane ordered pairs of numbers found in an input/output table	5.76	33.19, 37.17
27	12.2	5.6.A	May have difficulty recognizing the volume of a three-dimensional figure as the number of unit cubes needed to fill it	5.64	49.25, 49.28
28	13.5	5.7	May have difficulty solving problems involving measurement	5.70	44.36, 46.37, 45.30
29	11.1	5.5	May have difficulty recognizing the attributes necessary to sort polygons into sets	5.59	38.33
30	11.3	5.5	May have difficulty recognizing the attributes necessary to sort polygons into sets	5.61	38.31, 38.34

***TEKS**—Texas Essential Knowledge and Skills; **RtI**—Response to Intervention

Student's Name ______________________ Date ____________

Module 15 Test

Item	Lesson	TEKS*	Common Error	Intervene with RtI* Tier 1 Lessons	Soar to Success Math
1	15.1	5.9.A	May have difficulty representing data in a frequency table	5.77	53.08
2	15.2	5.9.C	May have difficulty using data from a frequency table to solve two-step problems	5.77	53.08
3, 10	15.2	5.9.C	May have difficulty using data in a frequency table to solve one-step problems	5.77	53.08
4	15.2	5.9.C	May have difficulty using data from a frequency table to solve multi-step problems	5.77	53.08
5	15.3	5.9.A	May have difficulty representing data in a bar graph	5.78	53.12
6	15.4	5.9.C	May have difficulty using data in a bar graph to solve two-step problems	5.81	53.12
7	15.4	5.9.C	May have difficulty using data in a bar graph to solve one-step problems	5.81	53.12
8	15.3	5.9.A	May have difficulty representing data in a bar graph	5.78	53.12
9	15.1	5.9.A	May have difficulty representing data in a frequency table	5.77	53.08
11	15.1	5.9.A	May have difficulty representing data in a frequency table	5.77	53.08
12	15.4	5.9.C	May have difficulty using data from a bar graph to solve one-step problems	5.81	53.12
13	15.4	5.9.C	May have difficulty using data from a bar graph to solve two-step problems	5.81	53.12
14	15.3	5.9.A	May have difficulty representing data in a bar graph	5.78	53.12
15	15.1	5.9.A	May have difficulty representing data in a frequency table	5.77	53.08
16	15.2	5.9.C	May have difficulty using data in a frequency table to solve two-step problems	5.77	53.08
17	15.4	5.9.C	May have difficulty using data from a bar graph to solve one-step problems	5.81	53.12
18	15.4	5.9.C	May have difficulty using data from a bar graph to solve multi-step problems	5.81	53.12

***TEKS**—Texas Essential Knowledge and Skills; **RtI**—Response to Intervention

Student's Name ______________________ Date ____________

Module 16 Test

Item	Lesson	TEKS*	Common Error	Intervene with RtI* Tier 1 Lessons	Soar to Success Math
1	16.3	5.9.A	May have difficulty representing data on a stem-and-leaf plot	5.80	2.17
2	16.4	5.9.C	May have difficulty solving one-step problems using data from a stem-and-leaf plot	5.83	2.17
3, 4	16.5	5.9.B	May have difficulty representing data on a scatter plot	5.84	40.25
5	16.1	5.9.A	May have difficulty representing data sets of measurements in fractions on a dot plot	5.79	54.17
6	16.2	5.9.C	May have difficulty solving one-step problems using data on a dot plot	5.82	54.17
7, 15	16.2	5.9.C	May have difficulty solving two-step problems using data on a dot plot	5.82	54.17
8	16.6	5.9.C	May have difficulty solving one-step problems using data on a scatter plot	5.84	40.25
9	16.6	5.9.C	May have difficulty solving problems using data on a scatter plot	5.84	40.25
10	16.5	5.9.B	May have difficulty representing data on a scatter plot	5.84	40.25
11	16.1	5.9.A	May have difficulty representing data on a dot plot	5.79	54.17
12	16.2	5.9.C	May have difficulty solving one-step problems using data on a dot plot	5.82	54.17
13	16.3	5.9.A	May have difficulty representing data on a stem-and-leaf plot	5.80	2.17
14	16.4	5.9.C	May have difficulty solving problems using data on a stem-and-leaf plot	5.83	2.17
16	16.4	5.9.C	May have difficulty solving one-step problems using data on a stem-and-leaf plot	5.83	2.17
17	16.4	5.9.C	May have difficulty solving two-step problems using data on a stem-and-leaf plot	5.83	2.17
18	16.1	5.9.A	May have difficulty representing data on a dot plot	5.79	54.17
19	16.5	5.9.B	May have difficulty representing data on a scatter plot	5.84	40.25

***TEKS**—Texas Essential Knowledge and Skills; **RtI**—Response to Intervention

Student's Name ______________________ Date __________

Unit 5 Test

Item	Lesson	TEKS*	Common Error	Intervene with RtI* Tier 1 Lessons	Soar to Success Math
1	15.4	5.9.C	May have difficulty solving one-step problems using data from a bar graph	5.81	53.12
2	15.4	5.9.C	May have difficulty solving two-step problems using data from a bar graph	5.81	53.12
3	16.5	5.9.B	May have difficulty representing data on a scatter plot	5.84	40.25
4	16.6	5.9.C	May have difficulty solving problems using data from a scatter plot	5.84	40.25
5	15.1	5.9.A	May have difficulty representing data in a frequency table	5.77	53.08
6	15.2	5.9.C	May have difficulty solving one-step problems using data from a frequency table	5.77	53.08
7	15.2	5.9.C	May have difficulty solving two-step problems using data from a frequency table	5.77	53.08
8	16.5	5.9.B	May have difficulty representing data on a scatter plot	5.84	40.25
9	16.5	5.9.B	May have difficulty representing data on a scatter plot	5.84	40.25
10	15.4	5.9.C	May have difficulty solving one-step problems using data from a bar graph	5.81	53.12
11	15.4	5.9.C	May have difficulty solving two-step problems using data from a bar graph	5.81	53.12
12	16.1	5.9.A	May have difficulty representing data on a dot plot	5.79	54.17
13	16.2	5.9.C	May have difficulty solving one-step problems using data from a dot plot	5.82	54.17
14	15.1	5.9.A	May have difficulty representing data in a frequency table	5.77	53.08

*TEKS—Texas Essential Knowledge and Skills; RtI—Response to Intervention

Student's Name ______________________________ Date ______________

Unit 5 Test (continued)

Item	Lesson	TEKS*	Common Error	Intervene with RtI* Tier 1 Lessons	Soar to Success Math
15	15.2	5.9.C	May have difficulty solving one-step problems using data from a frequency table	5.77	53.08
16	15.2	5.9.C	May have difficulty solving two-step problems using data from a frequency table	5.77	53.08
17	16.3	5.9.A	May have difficulty representing data on a stem-and-leaf plot	5.80	2.17
18	16.4	5.9.C	May have difficulty solving one-step problems using data from a stem-and-leaf plot	5.83	2.17
19	15.2	5.9.C	May have difficulty solving one-step problems using data from a frequency table	5.77	53.08
20	16.4	5.9.C	May have difficulty solving one-step problems using data from a stem-and-leaf plot	5.83	2.17
21	16.4	5.9.C	May have difficulty solving two-step problems using data from a stem-and-leaf plot	5.83	2.17
22	15.1	5.9.A	May have difficulty representing data in a frequency table	5.77	53.08
23	15.2	5.9.C	May have difficulty solving one-step problems using data from a frequency table	5.77	53.08
24	16.2	5.9.C	May have difficulty solving two-step problems using data from a dot plot	5.82	54.17
25	16.1	5.9.A	May have difficulty representing data sets of measurements in decimals on a dot plot	5.79	54.17
26	15.4	5.9.C	May have difficulty solving two-step problems using data from a bar graph	5.81	53.12

***TEKS**—Texas Essential Knowledge and Skills; **RtI**—Response to Intervention

Student's Name ________________________ Date ____________

Unit 6 Test

Item	Lesson	TEKS*	Common Error	Intervene with RtI* Tier 1 Lessons	Soar to Success Math
1	17.3	5.10.B	May not recall the difference between net income and gross income	5.39	61.04
2	17.6	5.10.F	May have difficulty balancing a simple budget	5.19	57.04
3	17.1	5.3.K	May have difficulty adding rational numbers	5.19	57.04
4	17.2	5.3.E	May not recall how to multiply decimal money amounts	5.19	57.04
5	17.4	5.10.C	May not understand advantages of different methods of payment	5.39	61.04
6	17.6	5.10.F	May have difficulty balancing a simple budget	5.19	57.04
7	17.1	5.10.A	May not recall the definition of income tax	5.19	57.04
8	17.5	5.10.D	May have difficulty using a financial record system	5.39	61.04
9	17.5	5.10.D	May have difficulty using a financial record system	5.39	61.04
10	17.4	5.10.C	May not understand the advantages of different methods of payment	5.39	61.04
11	17.7	5.10.E	May not understand how to balance a budget	5.81	53.12
12	17.2	5.10.A	May not recall the definition of property tax	5.19	57.04
13	17.4	5.4.B	May have difficulty representing total cost as an equation	5.39	61.04
14	17.3	5.3.K, 5.10.B	May not understand the difference between net income and gross income	5.39	61.04
15	17.6	5.10.F	May have difficulty balancing a simple budget	5.19	57.04

*TEKS—Texas Essential Knowledge and Skills; RtI—Response to Intervention

Student's Name ______________________ Date ______________

Unit 6 Test (continued)

Item	Lesson	TEKS*	Common Error	Intervene with RtI* Tier 1 Lessons	Soar to Success Math
16	17.2,	5.3.K, 5.10.A	May not understand how to apply sales tax to item price	5.77	53.08
17	17.7	5.10.E	May have difficulty identifying changes that result in a balanced budget	5.81	53.12
18	17.4	5.10.C	May not understand the advantages of different methods of payment	5.39	61.04
19	17.1	5.10.A	May not recall the definition of payroll tax	5.19	57.04
20	17.6	5.10.F	May have difficulty balancing a simple budget	5.19	57.04
21	17.7	5.10.E	May have difficulty recognizing changes that result in a balanced budget	5.81	53.12
22	17.7	5.10.E	May have difficulty recognizing changes that result in a balanced budget	5.81	53.12
23	17.1	5.3.E	May not recall how to multiply decimal money amounts	5.19	57.04
24	17.3	5.10.B	May not recall the difference between net income and gross income	5.39	61.04
25	17.4	5.4.F	May have difficulty finding the total cost of an item	5.39	61.04
26	17.4	5.10.C	May not understand the disadvantages of different methods of payment	5.39	61.04
27	17.3	5.3.K, 5.10.B	May not recall or understand the difference between net income and gross income	5.39	61.04
28	17.2	5.10.A	May not recall the definition of sales tax	5.19	57.04
29	17.5	5.10.D	May have difficulty using a financial record system	5.39	61.04
30	17.5	5.10.D	May have difficulty using a financial record system	5.39	61.04

*TEKS—Texas Essential Knowledge and Skills; RtI—Response to Intervention

Correlations

Texas Essential Knowledge and Skills for Mathematics		Test: Item Numbers
5.2	**Number and operations.** The student applies mathematical process standards to represent, compare, and order positive rational numbers and understand relationships as related to place value. The student is expected to:	
5.2.A	represent the value of the digit in decimals through the thousandths using expanded notation and numerals;	Module 1 Test: 11, 15, 17 Module 3 Test: 6 Unit 1 Test: 1, 19 Beginning-/Middle-/End-of-Year Tests: 11
5.2.B	compare and order two decimals to thousandths and represent comparisons using the symbols $>$, $<$, or $=$; and	Module 1 Test: 1, 7, 13 Unit 1 Test: 11, 18, 28 Beginning-/Middle-/End-of-Year Tests: 17, 38
5.2.C	round decimals to tenths or hundredths.	Module 1 Test: 3, 5, 9, 14 Unit 1 Test: 3, 15 Beginning-/Middle-/End-of-Year Tests: 3, 33
5.3	**Number and operations.** The student applies mathematical process standards to develop and use strategies and methods for positive rational number computations in order to solve problems with efficiency and accuracy. The student is expected to:	Module 5 Test: 2, 8 Unit 2 Test: 18
5.3.A	estimate to determine solutions to mathematical and real-world problems involving addition, subtraction, multiplication, or division;	Module 1 Test: 8, 12, 18 Module 2 Test: 2, 6, 8, 10, 15, 16, 18 Module 3 Test: 12, 16 Module 4 Test: 1, 8, 15, 17, 19 Unit 1 Test: 2, 6, 10, 13, 24, 26, 27 Module 5 Test: 9 Unit 2 Test: 1 Beginning-/Middle-/End-of-Year Tests: 22, 43
5.3.B	multiply with fluency a three-digit number by a two-digit number using the standard algorithm;	Module 2 Test: 4, 7, 11, 20 Unit 1 Test: 12 Beginning-/Middle-/End-of-Year Tests: 50
5.3.C	solve with proficiency for quotients of up to a four-digit dividend by a two-digit divisor using strategies and the standard algorithm;	Module 2 Test: 1, 3, 5, 9, 12, 13, 14, 17, 19 Unit 1 Test: 5, 16 Beginning-/Middle-/End-of-Year Tests: 27, 35
5.3.D	represent multiplication of decimals with products to the hundredths using objects and pictorial models, including area models;	Module 3 Test: 1, 8, 10, 11, 15, 20 Unit 1 Test: 9, 14 Beginning-/Middle-/End-of-Year Tests: 49
5.3.E	solve for products of decimals to the hundredths, including situations involving money, using strategies based on place-value understandings, properties of operations, and the relationship to the multiplication of whole numbers;	Module 3 Test: 2, 3, 4, 5, 7, 9, 13, 14, 17, 18, 19 Unit 1 Test: 4, 8, 21, 29 Unit 6 Test: 4, 23 Beginning-/Middle-/End-of-Year Tests: 1
5.3.F	represent quotients of decimals to the hundredths, up to four-digit dividends and two-digit whole number divisors, using objects and pictorial models, including area models;	Module 4 Test: 5, 6, 10, 14, 18 Unit 1 Test: 7, 25, 30 Beginning-/Middle-/End-of-Year Tests: 24

Correlations

Texas Essential Knowledge and Skills for Mathematics		Test: Item Numbers
5.3.G	solve for quotients of decimals to the hundredths, up to four-digit dividends and two-digit whole number divisors, using strategies and algorithms, including the standard algorithm;	Module 4 Test: 2, 3, 4, 7, 9, 11, 12, 13, 16, 20 Unit 1 Test: 17, 22 Beginning-/Middle-/End-of-Year Tests: 34
5.3.H	represent and solve addition and subtraction of fractions with unequal denominators referring to the same whole using objects and pictorial models and properties of operations;	Module 5 Test: 1, 3, 5, 6, 7, 10, 12, 14, 16, 20 Unit 2 Test: 3, 4, 6, 9, 10, 14, 16, 22, 25, 27 Beginning-/Middle-/End-of-Year Tests: 10, 41
5.3.I	represent and solve multiplication of a whole number and a fraction that refers to the same whole using objects and pictorial models, including area models;	Module 6 Test: 1, 4, 5, 6, 8, 10, 12, 17, 18, 19 Unit 2 Test: 2, 5, 19, 20, 21 Beginning-/Middle-/End-of-Year Tests: 18, 48
5.3.J	represent division of a unit fraction by a whole number and the division of a whole number by a unit fraction such as $1/3 \div 7$ and $7 \div 1/3$ using objects and pictorial models, including area models;	Module 6 Test: 3, 7, 14, 15, 16, 20 Unit 2 Test: 7, 8, 13, 24, 26, 28 Beginning-/Middle-/End-of-Year Tests: 2
5.3.K	add and subtract positive rational numbers fluently; and	Module 1 Test: 2, 4, 6, 10, 16, 19, 20 Unit 1 Test: 20, 23 Module 5 Test: 4, 11, 13, 15, 17, 18, 19 Unit 2 Test: 11, 15, 23, 29, 30 Unit 6 Test: 3, 14, 16, 27 Beginning-/Middle-/End-of-Year Tests: 15, 29
5.3.L	divide whole numbers by unit fractions and unit fractions by whole numbers.	Module 6 Test: 2, 9, 11, 13 Unit 2 Test: 12, 17 Beginning-/Middle-/End-of-Year Tests: 16, 25
5.4	**Algebraic reasoning.** The student applies mathematical process standards to develop concepts of expressions and equations. The student is expected to:	Module 8 Test: 2, 15
5.4.A	identify prime and composite numbers;	Module 7 Test: 1, 7, 10, 12, 14, 19 Unit 3 Test: 8, 20 Beginning-/Middle-/End-of-Year Tests: 26
5.4.B	represent and solve multi-step problems involving the four operations with whole numbers using equations with a letter standing for the unknown quantity;	Module 8 Test: 1, 3, 4, 5, 6, 7, 8, 9, 10, 11, 12, 13, 14, 16, 17, 18, 19, 20 Module 9 Test: 2, 5, 14, 19 Unit 3 Test: 3, 5, 9, 10, 11, 15, 16, 21, 22, 23, 28 Unit 6 Test: 13 Beginning-/Middle-/End-of-Year Tests: 19, 37
5.4.C	generate a numerical pattern when given a rule in the form $y = ax$ or $y = x + a$ and graph;	Module 10 Test: 1, 3, 5, 7, 8, 10, 12, 13, 14, 15, 17, 18, 19, 20 Unit 3 Test: 7, 17, 18, 29 Module 14 Test: 2, 6, 14, 17 Unit 4 Test: 7, 16 Beginning-/Middle-/End-of-Year Tests: 9
5.4.D	recognize the difference between additive and multiplicative numerical patterns given in a table or graph;	Module 10 Test: 2, 6, 11, 16 Unit 3 Test: 6, 14 Beginning-/Middle-/End-of-Year Tests: 23

Correlations

Texas Essential Knowledge and Skills for Mathematics		Test: Item Numbers
5.4.E	describe the meaning of parentheses and brackets in a numeric expression;	Module 7 Test: 2, 5, 6, 8, 11, 16, 17, 20 Unit 3 Test: 19, 26 Beginning-/Middle-/End-of-Year Tests: 46
5.4.F	simplify numerical expressions that do not involve exponents, including up to two levels of grouping;	Module 7 Test: 3, 4, 9, 13, 15, 18 Unit 3 Test: 1, 12 Unit 6 Test: 25 Beginning-/Middle-/End-of-Year Tests: 21
5.4.G	use concrete objects and pictorial models to develop the formulas for the volume of a rectangular prism, including the special form for a cube ($V = l \times w \times h$, $V = s \times s \times s$, and $V = Bh$); and	Module 9 Test: 1, 4, 7, 9, 12, 16, 17, 20 Unit 3 Test: 2, 4, 13, 24 Module 12 Test: 9, 20 Unit 4 Test: 2, 18 Beginning-/Middle-/End-of-Year Tests: 36
5.4.H	represent and solve problems related to perimeter and/or area and related to volume.	Module 9 Test: 3, 6, 8, 10, 11, 13, 15, 18 Unit 3 Test: 25, 27, 30 Module 12 Test: 11, 15 Unit 4 Test: 6 Beginning-/Middle-/End-of-Year Tests: 13, 32
5.5	**Geometry and measurement.** The student applies mathematical process standards to classify two-dimensional figures by attributes and properties. The student is expected to:	Module 11 Test: 1–20 Unit 4 Test: 1, 10, 13, 19, 23, 29, 30
5.5.A	classify two-dimensional figures in a hierarchy of sets and subsets using graphic organizers based on their attributes and properties.	Beginning-/Middle-/End-of-Year Tests: 5
5.6	**Geometry and measurement.** The student applies mathematical process standards to understand, recognize, and quantify volume. The student is expected to:	
5.6.A	recognize a cube with side length of one unit as a unit cube having one cubic unit of volume and the volume of a three-dimensional figure as the number of unit cubes (*n* cubic units) needed to fill it with no gaps or overlaps if possible; and	Module 12 Test: 5, 6, 10, 12, 13, 18 Unit 4 Test: 24, 27
5.6.B	determine the volume of a rectangular prism with whole number side lengths in problems related to the number of layers times the number of unit cubes in the area of the base.	Module 12 Test: 1, 2, 3, 4, 7, 8, 14, 16, 17, 19 Unit 4 Test: 12 Beginning-/Middle-/End-of-Year Tests: 14
5.7	**Geometry and measurement.** The student applies mathematical process standards to select appropriate units, strategies, and tools to solve problems involving measurement. The student is expected to:	Module 13 Test: 1–20 Unit 4 Test: 3, 9, 11, 14, 17, 21, 22, 28
5.7.A	solve problems by calculating conversions within a measurement system, customary or metric.	Beginning-/Middle-/End-of-Year Tests: 8, 42
5.8	**Geometry and measurement.** The student applies mathematical process standards to identify locations on a coordinate plane. The student is expected to:	

Correlations

Texas Essential Knowledge and Skills for Mathematics		Test: Item Numbers
5.8.A	describe the key attributes of the coordinate plane, including perpendicular number lines (axes) where the intersection (origin) of the two lines coincides with zero on each number line and the given point (0, 0); the *x*-coordinate, the first number in an ordered pair, indicates movement parallel to the *x*-axis starting at the origin; and the *y*-coordinate, the second number, indicates movement parallel to the *y*-axis starting at the origin;	Module 14 Test: 3, 8, 10 Unit 4 Test: 5 Beginning-/Middle-/End-of-Year Tests: 4
5.8.B	describe the process for graphing ordered pairs of numbers in the first quadrant of the coordinate plane; and	Module 10 Test: 4 Module 14 Test: 9, 16 Unit 4 Test: 4 Beginning-/Middle-/End-of-Year Tests: 31
5.8.C	graph in the first quadrant of the coordinate plane ordered pairs of numbers arising from mathematical and real-world problems, including those generated by number patterns or found in an input-output table.	Module 10 Test: 9 Module 14 Test: 1, 4, 5, 7, 11, 12, 13, 15, 18, 19 Unit 4 Test: 8, 15, 20, 25, 26 Beginning-/Middle-/End-of-Year Tests: 20
5.9	**Data analysis.** The student applies mathematical process standards to solve problems by collecting, organizing, displaying, and interpreting data. The student is expected to:	
5.9.A	represent categorical data with bar graphs or frequency tables and numerical data, including data sets of measurements in fractions or decimals, with dot plots or stem-and-leaf plots;	Module 15 Test: 1, 5, 8, 9, 11, 12, 14, 15 Module 16 Test: 1, 5, 11, 13, 18 Unit 5 Test: 5, 12, 14, 17, 22, 25 Beginning-/Middle-/End-of-Year Tests: 44
5.9.B	represent discrete paired data on a scatterplot; and	Module 16 Test: 3, 4, 10, 19 Unit 5 Test: 3, 8, 9 Beginning-/Middle-/End-of-Year Tests: 6
5.9.C	solve one- and two-step problems using data from a frequency table, dot plot, bar graph, stem-and-leaf plot, or scatterplot.	Module 15 Test: 2, 3, 4, 6, 7, 10, 12, 13, 16, 18 Module 16 Test: 2, 6, 7, 8, 9, 12, 14, 15, 16, 17, 18 Unit 5 Test: 1, 2, 4, 6, 7, 10, 11, 13, 15, 16, 18, 19, 20, 21, 23, 24, 26 Beginning-/Middle-/End-of-Year Tests: 12, 45
5.10	**Personal financial literacy.** The student applies mathematical process standards to manage one's financial resources effectively for lifetime financial security. The student is expected to:	
5.10.A	define income tax, payroll tax, sales tax, and property tax;	Unit 6 Test: 7, 12, 16, 19, 28 Beginning-/Middle-/End-of-Year Tests: 28
5.10.B	explain the difference between gross income and net income;	Unit 6 Test: 1, 14, 24, 27 Beginning-/Middle-/End-of-Year Tests: 39
5.10.C	identify the advantages and disadvantages of different methods of payment, including check, credit card, debit card, and electronic payments;	Unit 6 Test: 5, 10, 18, 26 Beginning-/Middle-/End-of-Year Tests: 47
5.10.D	develop a system for keeping and using financial records;	Unit 6 Test: 8, 9, 29, 30 Beginning-/Middle-/End-of-Year Tests: 40

Correlations

Texas Essential Knowledge and Skills for Mathematics		Test: Item Numbers
5.10.E	describe actions that might be taken to balance a budget when expenses exceed income; and	Unit 6 Test: 11, 17, 21, 22 Beginning-/Middle-/End-of-Year Tests: 30
5.10.F	balance a simple budget.	Unit 6 Test: 2, 6, 15, 20 Beginning-/Middle-/End-of-Year Tests: 7